Sing Out, Louise!

SING OUT, LOUISE!

150 Broadway
Musical Stars
Remember 50 Years

DENNIS McGOVERN

DEBORAH GRACE WINER

FORWARD BY JERRY ORBACH

SCHIRMER BOOKS
AN IMPRINT OF SIMON & SCHUSTER MACMILLAN
NEW YORK

PRENTICE HALL INTERNATIONAL
LONDON · MEXICO CITY · NEW DELHI · SINGAPORE · SYDNEY · TORONTO

Schirmer Books
An Imprint of Simon & Schuster Macmillan
1633 Broadway
New York, NY 10019

Library of Congress Catalog Card Number: 92-33312

Printed in the Untied States of America

printing number
1 2 3 4 5 6 7 8 9 10

Library of Congress Cataloging-in-Publication Data

McGovern, Dennis.
     Sing out, Louise! : 150 Broadway musical stars remember 50 years / Dennis
McGovern and Deborah Grace Winer.
          p.   cm.
     Includes index.
     ISBN 0-02-871394-X (hc)
     ISBN 0-02-864618-5 (pb)
     1. Musical theater—New York (N.Y.)—History. 2. Actors—New York
(N.Y.)—Interviews. I. Winer, Deborah Grace. II. Title.
ML1711.8.N3M265 1993
782.1'4'097471—dc20   92-333132
                                                       CIP
                                                       MN

This paper meets the requirements of ANSI/NISO Z.39.48. 1992 (Permanence of Paper).

WE DEDICATE THIS WORK TO
AGNES MALIA AND THOMAS F. WALL,
TOBA BRILL WINER, AND ITA PASZTOR,
FOR THEIR LOVE AND ENCOURAGEMENT

Contents

Illustrations

These illustrations follow page 78.

Foreword

I was born in New York. Broadway was there for me. Then I was in college—facing my senior year at Northwestern. That was going to cost a fortune, and I needed a couple of science and math credits to get a degree. By that time, I already had three seasons of professional stock and my Equity card. So I decided to strike out and head back to New York.

I had some friends who were in the business, and one of them, Tom Poston, introduced me to Peyton Price, who was doing a season at the Grist Mill Playhouse, and I got hired there for the summer season.

The Threepenny Opera off-Broadway was the next thing for me, and I got that through a friend, too. You know, this business is like one big network of friends. Jo Wilder was playing Polly at the time and she got me the job. I first went into *Threepenny* as the Streetsinger's understudy. Then I went on in that role and played a lot of smaller roles. Eventually, I got to understudy Mack. I actually got to go on in that role. Interesting to have a twenty-year-old playing opposite Lotte Lenya!

Then there was *The Fantasticks*. I met Word Baker [the director] along with a few friends of his from Texas when I was at Grist Mill. At that point, I was kind of down and out and looking for something to do. I ran into Word and he said he had a "little" show he thought I'd be perfect for. At the same time I got an offer to do a Broadway show, *Lock Up Your Daughters*, which would have paid me the fabulous sum of $250 a week. *Fantasticks* was going to pay $45 a week, but once I heard that score and read the script, I knew that was it.

That show really gave me the opportunity to go on. *Carnival* was next and then *Scuba Duba*. That was the show that got me *Promises, Promises*. Either Neil Simon or David Merrick came to see that show and realized I could be funny, and then convinced the other one that I was right for the role. I still don't know which one to blame or thank. I was always lucky to be able to do straight plays, too, and then I had those long runs in *Promises*, *Chicago*, and *42nd Street*.

The big difference between doing a straight play and a musical is that they involve different levels of emotion. When I was doing the TV version of *Broadway Bound*, Anne Bancroft and I had a lot of really big scenes. One morning I came in and said, "Well, the overture is going to start in ten minutes." And she said, "Oh God, wouldn't it be great if we had an overture!" It's true. In a musical, when you hear that orchestra, it gets your heart pumping. It gets you to an emotional level that is different from doing a naturalistic play or Shakespeare. The music just raises you to that level to that point where you can burst into song.

If it's all done right in a musical, the audience should feel that whatever you're saying could only be said if you burst into song. The dialogue is just a springboard, and then you have to do it bigger and bigger!

When I would leave *42nd Street* and be out for a few months to do a movie and then come back to the show, I used to think that everybody on the stage was crazy. I thought they were all screaming their heads off. I was insane! Then I'd reach a point in a scene and I'd realize I was too low. I was too down and I had no reason to break into song.

I've been lucky to be in some huge hits. A lot of performers just aren't comfortable with long runs. They get bored or something, but I've never had that problem. For me, they're great. I can walk to work and still be home in time for the eleven o'clock news.

When people ask how I do it, I just say, "Well, there's a new audience there every night." It's like telling the same joke to a new group of people. But in reality it *isn't* the same thing every night. There are always slight differences. Sometimes you go on automatic pilot and you might not really be there. Usually I go on and I'm just trying to perfect something.

This really came home to me near the end of the road tour of *Chicago*. I think we were in our last week in San Francisco, and I'd been doing the show for three and a half years. I came offstage and I said to Gwen Verdon, "Tonight I did it perfect," and she said, "You mean in three years you never had a night when you thought it was perfect?" And I had to say to her, "No—maybe ninety-nine-point-nine percent, but tonight I got it right." For those three years I had been looking and changing and trying things to make it perfect.

That's when I realized that long runs never fazed me. I was always fine-tuning and trying to focus the audience's attention. I was just trying to get it right. You become like your own director. While you don't change anything, it's your job to go out there and refine the work and make it as perfect as you can.

On *42nd Street*, a stage manager came to me on a Saturday night and said, "The show ran four minutes long tonight." Well, I said to him, "Do you realize how stupid that is? What you just said? What is this—a Saturday night as opposed to a Tuesday night? Go look it up. This show can vary by eight or ten minutes. We have to slow down to let them get the jokes and hopefully to let them laugh." The Lunts used to vary up to fifteen minutes in a show because they were playing to what the audience gave them. It's always going to vary, and I know everyone says this, but it's true: Every audience is different.

That's what makes this fun. Also, when you have cast changes the show is going to be different. It has to be. We were all pals when we did *Chicago*. Then Gwen was out for a few weeks and Liza Minnelli came in. Now Liza's a great girl, but Gwen and I had this really special adversarial relationship onstage. Then there was Liza with all that vulnerability. If I had given her the same kind of crap I was giving Gwen, the audience would have booed me off the stage. The whole relationship changed and it became more of a father–daughter thing. It wouldn't have worked if we had played it the way it was originally.

I honestly enjoy my work and the people I've worked with. For some reason I don't seem to have problems with people that a lot of others do. Other performers or people in the business would say, "Oh, you're working with so and so. He or she is a real prima donna!" But I've never had problems like that. I'm sort of like the doctor in a psycho ward. I just come in and everyone seems to quiet down. Maybe people are afraid of me—in a good way. I don't really think so, but I don't know.

Also I've never been in awe of the people I was working with—even Ethel Merman. We're all in the same business and that's what it is, a business that just happens to also be a lot of fun. The theatre is by its nature an ephemeral thing. It's a thing of shadows and memories. There's no solid record of what we've done the way there is in the movies.

It's important that we remember things and put them down on paper. That's what makes this book important. It's our lives.

—Jerry Orbach

Preface

WHEN we decided to do a book on musical comedy, we wanted it to be a living account of what day-to-day life is like as a performer in the American musical theatre. Though books have been written about composers, lyricists, and directors, we wanted *Sing Out, Louise!* to be a place where the performers of musical comedy could have their say.

It would have been nice if we could have included every performer who made a mark on the musical theatre; unfortunately, that would be impossible.

Life in the theatre is not about the glamour of an opening night frozen in time, but about the day-to-day: getting out there and doing the work—consistently, again and again, sometimes for years—making it fresh for each new audience. But as Carol Lawrence says, "You can't get bored if you're doing something that sets your heart on fire."

For their help in putting together *Sing Out, Louise!*, our thanks go out first to Deborah Savadge Peterson, Timothy Jenkins, and Michael Rubino of AGMA.

A special thanks to Peter Weed, who believed in the project from the first, and Jeff Hochhauser and Michael Shectman, for their encyclopedic knowledge of musical comedy; and to Bert Fink of the Rodgers and Hammerstein office.

We are also grateful to Toba Brill Winer, Jessica Daryl Winer, Edith Cooper, Elizabeth Lascautx, Gerard Allesandrini, Jay Black, Arthur Pober, John Tagler, Jennifer Lyons of Writers House, our editors, Robert Axelrod and Jonathan Wiener, and our friend Elaine Stritch.

Also, special thanks to Laurie Franks, Zoya Leporska, Rose Ingram, Ellen Hanley, Sheila Smith, Dolores Wilson, June Havoc, Terpsie Toon, Susan Marchand, and Michael Kermoyan, who dug into their photo files to help us.

We're happy that Arthur Laurents was gracious enough to allow us to use for our title Ethel Merman's first line from *Gypsy*; and our gratitude also to Jerry Orbach for his foreword.

Although many people don't realize it, performers frequently are shy, and don't really want to talk about their careers in the past, especially when they are always looking toward the future. Fortunately, their agents and managers were very helpful. A special thanks to Lee Mimms, who did his best to get us an interview with Larry Kert (Tony of *West Side Story*, Bobby in *Company*). Although Larry was willing to talk and would have been an asset to the book, we started this project too late for him. As with so many of his colleagues in the theatre, he died of complications resulting from AIDS, in 1991.

Our deepest thanks go to the artists who gave us their time. More importantly, over the years they have given their lives to entertaining us.

Dennis McGovern
Deborah Grace Winer

Sing Out, Louise!

1

"Sing Out, Louise!"

T HE Winter Garden Theatre: Sunday afternoon. Theatrical history is about to be made. There's nothing but a bare stage—no scenery, no lighting, no costumes. In a time-honored theatrical tradition, the cast of *Gypsy* is about to do a run-through of the show for the casts of other current Broadway shows.

"We were doing *First Impressions*, and we were invited to the rehearsal, and everybody was there—Joshua Logan, Mary Martin, everybody," remembers Farley Granger. "There were no costumes and no set. Just a bare stage and a piano." Granger was already a star—in Alfred Hitchcock's *Strangers on a Train* and *Rope*—and was about to make his Broadway musical comedy debut. The impact of that afternoon is still with him.

Gypsy was the first big Broadway musical for Peg Murray, who went on to win a Tony for her performance in *Cabaret*. "What a day! I'd had a scene with Uncle Jocko and the children before Ethel entered, but the scene was cut on the road; we were running way too long. But from the moment she yelled out, 'Sing out, Louise!' from the back of the house, you knew this was something special."

"That show was magic," recalls Leila Martin. "I was hired to understudy Louise/Gypsy the day before that historic run-through. That rehearsal was so

1

thrilling—a story was being told in the atmosphere it really belonged in, with no sets, a bare stage, and no costumes. I think it was the best performance Merman ever gave."

Director/choreographer/dancer Gene Foote remembers Merman entering from the back of the house in a simple but elegant beige suit, while the other performers all wore standard rehearsal clothes. "I was nineteen years old and new to New York. My first job was working backstage at the Cherry Lane Theatre. I would sweep the stage, iron the costumes, make sure that the leading man, who was a little senile, was onstage for all his entrances—everything. The stage manager at the Cherry Lane took me to the 'gypsy run-through' of *Gypsy*—and it was unbelievable.

"I was just sitting there, not really expecting much, and then, from the back of the theatre, you heard, 'Sing out, Louise!'—and the entire audience stood up. Nobody said anything. You didn't dare. She got this ovation, and I think she said, 'Thanks,' and then just went on with the show. It was one of the most incredible things I've ever seen in my life. Nobody applauded. The ovation was just everybody standing. You heard this voice, and everybody just came to attention. I remember walking out of the theatre and remembering that score—one hit after another—and that day they were just played by a piano. Incredible."

GRANGER: "It was one of the most exciting things I've ever seen in my life, and no matter how many times I see the show, seeing it that way will always be the most exciting."

In *Gypsy*, Merman played the overbearing mother of June Havoc and Gypsy Rose Lee, and her words to the young Gypsy (Louise) became a catch-phrase in the theatre for doing it loud and doing it right, for just doing it and loving it.

The dream of having an afternoon like that, of sharing in a performance like that run-through, has inspired thousands of performers. Carol Lawrence, the original Maria in *West Side Story*, recalls, "I dreamed of working on Broadway from the time I could walk and talk. In fact, they said I came out singing—so that was always my dream."

Iggie Wolfington, *The Music Man*'s original Marcellus, got the call later in life. "I knew I wanted this when I was in a foxhole with shells going off around me. I said a little prayer to God that I would get through it, and then decided that if I got out alive, I was going to make myself happy. Being an actor was the thing I knew would make me happy."

"I went into the theatre because it was really the first thing I ever did that I got praise for," says David Holliday, who starred in *Coco* and *Man of La Mancha*. "My father was a Lutheran minister, and that's what I was going to be. I went to a small Lutheran college, and got into theatre, and people really liked me."

Getting the big break and making it to Broadway sometimes comes in strange and mysterious ways.

KATHI MOSS: "When I moved to New York, I was working in an agent's office because I didn't really feel I was ready to go out there and do it. One day a friend of mine came into the office and told me about a show that was auditioning, and he thought there was a part in it that was right for me. So we both went, and my friend got a callback and I didn't. I was very upset, and went home to New Orleans. Then I was in the French Quarter, and I called my agent, and he told me I had a callback. So I flew back to New York, auditioned, flew back to New Orleans for a party on New Year's Eve, and got a call that I had the job on New Year's Day. Happy New Year!" Moss went on to play that part—Cha-Cha, in *Grease*—for most of its marathon run on Broadway, before going on to *Nine* and *Grand Hotel*.

Carole Schweid's debut was in *Minnie's Boys*. "I was a dance major in Juilliard, and Patty Birch was my modern dance teacher. She was looking for girls who could dance like boys. You know, a lot of chorus jobs require long legs and high heels, and I was never really good at that. So I auditioned and got the job. It was at the Imperial Theatre, where I'd seen my first Broadway show, *Wish You Were Here*, the show with the swimming pool—and there I was, out on that stage!"

The star of Schweid's first Broadway show, Patricia Marand, was then a beginner herself: "I was one of the nurses in *South Pacific* before I got the part of Teddy in *Wish You Were Here*. Martha Wright was playing Nellie then. I remember we had to stand in the wings to wait for an entrance, and Martha came over to me one night and said, 'Isn't it good to get back to work again?' and the 'again' really got to me. She actually thought I had worked before. I was thrilled. She made me feel like such a pro!

"I started when I was really young. In fact, I hadn't even finished school, and my parents got me a tutor. I auditioned as a lark, really, for Rodgers and Hammerstein, and got the job in *South Pacific*. From then on, Dick Rodgers was my agent. I have a picture from him inscribed, 'From your proud agent.'"

Zina Bethune, Allan Weeks, Nita Novy, Colin Duffy, and Neva Small were all still children when they made their debuts in Broadway musicals.

ZINA BETHUNE (*The Most Happy Fella*): "It was very exciting for me, and I loved doing the show. I was only in the first act, so I got to go home early. On matinee days, I would get to go to a movie in between shows. I think I only had something like twelve lines, maybe a few more, but even then I

The Downside of the "Biz"

O NE of the biggest troubles performers encounter on the road is the loneliness that comes with being separated from friends and loved ones while involved in uncertain projects.

Set to make her Broadway debut in *Street Scene*, Anne Jeffreys suffered the agonies of being alone in a strange town.

"After rehearsing in New York, we opened in Philadelphia. It was Christmas, and it was the first one I had spent away from my mother and family, and everyone in the company had come down with the flu. It was a depressing show to do, and with all the crying during the performances, it just fed into my homesickness. I also remember the bellboy had brought a wreath to put on my door because he knew how lonely I was.

"Usually, after a matinee, I would go back to my room and eat there, but that was lonely, too. So since it was Christmas, I decided to go down to the dining room.

"Norman Cordon was in the cast, and he was from North Carolina like I was. So we had a bond right there, but he was also staying in the same hotel. Well, I walked into the dining room and Norman was sitting there eating all alone, and he looked at me and said, 'Are you alone?' and I nodded 'Yes,' and he said he was too and why didn't we have Christmas dinner together? So we did. Then we went back to the theatre, where so many people were sick, and it was so depressing—but the dinner was wonderful."

---

knew it was something special. I knew it was different, a classic—as young as I was, I knew that. And I loved hearing Jo Sullivan sing 'Somebody, Somewhere' every night."

ALLAN WEEKS (*The Body Beautiful*): "That was Bock and Harnick's first show, and Herb Ross was the choreographer. God, what a great experience that was as a kid. I had seen *Mr. Wonderful* in the same theatre, the Broadway, the year before. I was ten years old, and it was my first show. I told my mother I wanted to be up there onstage like that, and a year later I was."

NITA NOVY (*Gypsy*): "I was seven, and I'd done one local commercial, and an agent saw me and I finally got an audition for the show. I was hired as the Balloon Girl in the first act and had to stand by for Baby June. It was

August, and I was offered a two-week contract—and to show you how naïve my mother and I were, we didn't realize that either side could break the contract after two weeks. We thought I'd just be doing it for two weeks. But I stayed with the show until I left to do *The Sound of Music*. Everyone was really protective of me backstage. I wasn't really cognizant of the fact that I was going into this monumental and legendary production. I was mesmerized by the mechanics of it all. I don't think that I even knew what the show was really about."

COLIN DUFFY (*The Grass Harp*): "It was lot of fun, but a lot of hard work, too. We rehearsed for twelve hours a day for the two weeks before we opened. We worked at the New Amsterdam theatre, and even then the place was falling down and the halls were filled with heroin addicts. It was really disgusting. But opening night, the audience went absolutely bonkers after every number. Of course, they could have been everyone's friends and backers and all, but still, I was surprised when we didn't do better with the critics and we didn't run longer. That would have been nice."

NEVA SMALL (*Henry, Sweet Henry*): "That show was really Broadway the way it used to be. Here I was, this teenager, and I was a real observer. I remember watching and listening and learning. I had worked really hard on developing a relationship with the girl who played opposite me [Robin Wilson], and on opening night she was scared; we both were. At one point she stopped singing—and I went, 'Uh oh,' and started singing her part. I guess that's just what a kid in that situation would do."

With the exception of Duffy, who retired from the theatre at an early age, the others went on to sing out on Broadway as adults: Bethune in *Grand Hotel*, Weeks in *The Wiz* and *The Tap Dance Kid*, Novy in *Grease*, and Small in *Something's Afoot*.

Some children are naturally musical. Glynis Johns was "a dancer and singer as a youngster. A *Little Night Music* was not altogether my first musical, but it was my first on Broadway, and my first really big musical."

Other children are not. As a child in school and at camp, Barbara Colton was always told to "'mouth the words.' I couldn't sing. I just wasn't musical. That was a given. When I started getting cast in musicals like *Fiddler* and *Milk and Honey*, it was hysterical to me. I always felt that someone was going to find me out."

Working in the theatre is often a family affair. Mary Ann O'Reilly met her future husband, Andy Bew, when they were both in the chorus of *The Happy Time*. "Andy and I have always been able to work very well together. No bullshit." They toured with their growing family in *A Chorus Line* and later in *Sugar*. "We took all five kids to LA when we went to do *Sugar* with

Joe Namath, and I found out after we were there that I was pregnant. Finally I had to leave the show before the end of the run—not because of the pregnancy, but because Joe and my dance partner nearly cracked my ribs. The guy dancing with me got so paranoid about dropping me that he overcompensated and cracked my ribs. And every time Joe would hug me, it was like he was tackling me.

"Andy and I have been married twenty years, with seven kids, and the 'happy time' is still going on. We're happier than ever."

The same could be said for Maria Karnilova and George S. Irving, who met when they both appeared in *Call Me Mister* and went on to appear together in *Bravo, Giovanni!*

IRVING: "She was wonderful in that show."

KARNILOVA: "So were you."

IRVING: "We didn't have any scenes together. She had a very long dance number, fifteen minutes, and then a quick change, and then she had to do a scene. They got her a tank of oxygen backstage."

KARNILOVA: "I only used that opening night. Actually, the doctor told me it would be bad for me. But this man! I go to pieces every time I watch him on the stage."

IRVING: "I got my Equity card in 1941."

KARNILOVA: "I beat you. I got mine in 1938."

Many people feel that the whole theatre community was once a family. According to Chita Rivera, that was the case when she started in the business. "It *was* a family. And all the dancers were excellent, and many of them from those days have gone on to careers as choreographers or principal dancers. I was very young. So the girls taught me a lot. I was like the little innocent one in the dressing room that they led around and put makeup on."

The same was true for Patti Karr, who went on to star in such shows as *Pippin* and *Seesaw*. "We were all going up for the same jobs in those days— me, and Chita and Skipper [Cathryn] Damon. One of us would get the job and the others wouldn't, but there was never any backstabbing or anything. We were all friends."

"There was a real sense of camaraderie in the old days," recalled Lisa Kirk, the star of *Allegro* and *Kiss Me, Kate*. "We were all friends, and it was like one big family. Oh, sure, it was no picnic being out on the road; but we were working, and we had a lot of fun."

One of the many hit songs that Jule Styne wrote for Merman in *Gypsy* was "Everything's Coming Up Roses," a hymn to succeeding in the theatre. Every performer's dream is a successful opening night on Broadway. For Rosetta Le Noire, it was also a family experience. "My first show was with

The Up Side of the "Biz"

WHILE Anne Jeffreys found out how lonely life can be for an actor on the road, Susan Johnson discovered that there can also be a lot of laughs. She created the role of Cleo in *The Most Happy Fella*, and enjoyed a "unique" relationship with the show's creator, Frank Loesser.

"Frank was a good, loyal friend, and he also had a great sense of humor. One day in rehearsal our director, Joe Anthony, was working with us, and Frank came up on stage and said something to me. Well, that really pissed me off. I left the stage. He was giving me a direction in front of Joe, and that wasn't right.

"The next day, two dozen red roses arrived with a card from Frank which said, 'I apologize for talking to you during rehearsal. You're entitled to three Go Fuck Yourselves, but by the look you gave me when you left the stage, you've already used one of them up.'

"Then, when we were in Boston trying out, I was having dinner in the restaurant of the Ritz with some in-laws of mine I had never met before. They were kind of proper. One of them had written a book about classical music or something. I was trying to be respectable, but Frank was sitting across from me and kept sending me filthy notes. Every five minutes the waiter would give me a drawing of a penis or testicles with a note saying, 'I'll bet you can't show this to those people.' He was a funny man. I adored him."

---

my godfather, the great Bill 'Bojangles' Robinson. It was *The Hot Mikado*. I went into the show just to be in the chorus, but four days before we opened, the director called me and said, 'Rosie, go downstairs and get your costumes because you're going to be one of the Three Little Maids.'"

Craig Stevens, television's *Peter Gunn*, made his Broadway musical debut in *Here's Love*. "My agent, Milton Goldman, called me in England and told me they were interested in me for a Meredith Willson musical. I said, 'Oh, no.' I hadn't worked musically for four or five years, and I had very little time to prepare. Coming to Broadway tore up my life for a while, but it was worth it. I love the theatre. *Here's Love* was a disappointment, but I later did *My Fair Lady* on the road—and that was a wonderful experience."

Years later, John Schneider, one of TV's *Dukes of Hazzard*, made his Broadway debut in *Grand Hotel*. He had his doubts, but discovered he "loved the whole thing. Everyone welcomed me. There was no sense of 'Prove it, Mr. TV Star.' They just shook my hand and welcomed me as part of the company. I never thought Broadway would be as close-knit. We even played softball against teams from other shows in the Broadway Show League. It's presumptuous for me to think that I have a place on Broadway, but I love it."

After touring in *Purlie*, Ken Page finally had a glamorous opening night in the first major revival of *Guys and Dolls*. "I came to New York to be on Broadway, and that first night was really like something out of a storybook. It sounds like bullshit cliché stuff, but I was so familiar with the score—and then to find myself playing Nicely Nicely on Broadway was incredible. I couldn't have asked for a better Broadway debut."

Sally Ann Howes had a similar experience when she became Broadway's second Eliza Doolittle in *My Fair Lady*. "My actual debut was probably the most exciting day of my life, professionally. I was scheduled to open on a Monday, and Moss Hart decided that I should have one performance with an audience (one performance—very big of him!) to time the laughs before the critics saw me.

"So he asked Julie Andrews, who was the last of the original cast left, to give up the Saturday matinee so that I could go on. Moss himself made the announcement about the replacement, and the audience groaned and there was pandemonium. You could hear the audience muttering 'Sally Ann Howes? Who is she?'

"The overture started, and the audience was still furious. Fortunately, my father [British comedian Bobby Howes] and some of his friends were out there, and that helped. I had been hailed as a star in the West End, but at that moment I was totally unknown and unwanted. I thought, 'Well, I might as well just relax and enjoy this.' I'm always nervous before a performance, but I felt that I could only be better than their expectations. I didn't have to live up to anything.

"We stopped the show with 'The Rain in Spain,' and then again with 'I Could Have Danced All Night.' And the audience fell in love with me, and I with them. I've been in love with American audiences ever since."

Stopping the show is the fantasy of every performer. Styne and Sondheim gave Merman a showstopper in the perfect place when they wrote "Rose's Turn" for *Gypsy*. The relationship between the audience and the performer is ultimately what musical theatre is all about.

In 1969, Dorothy Loudon found herself in a turkey, *The Fig Leaves Are Falling*. "I'll never forget the matinee the day we closed. Everyone knew we were closing—and you know how people want to come to a show when they know it's closing. There wasn't a seat in the theatre—the show was sold out. I had a wonderful song in the show, 'All My Laughter.' And after I sang the number, they just wouldn't let me go on with the show. They wouldn't stop applauding. After the number, the phone would ring—and the applause was so loud you couldn't hear the phone. I kept saying, 'Is that the phone?' They didn't stop. Eventually, I had to start over and sing the whole thing again. And then they kept applauding. You don't sing encores in the theatre—you just don't do that. I don't think it would have happened if the audience didn't know that we were closing. But they wanted to show how much they liked the song, and the show."

On the opening night of Cole Porter's *Can-Can*, when Gwen Verdon finished her big first-act number, the audience wanted more. They insisted on it and wouldn't let the show continue. People have stopped shows before, but never like Verdon did that night. "Everyone else seems to know more about that moment than I do," says Verdon. "I had finished a dance and was offstage to change. Suddenly Michael Kidd [the choreographer] was standing in my dressing room. It was totally out of context—Michael didn't belong there, and I didn't know why he was there. Then he just grabbed me and pushed me out onstage into a set I'd never seen before, with the four actors playing the artists in the show. They were trying to go on with the show, and I just looked at the audience—and I had no feeling at all about what was happening. It was just very odd."

After the historic run-through of *Gypsy*, the audience of performers recognized that what they had seen that afternoon represented what they wanted in their lives. For that moment, unemployment, rejection, and separation from family and friends were all forgotten. All they thought about was why they had chosen a life in the theatre.

2

Situations Wanted

Trying to Get Work in the Theatre

audition for everything," says Dorothy Loudon. "It's safer. I figure if they don't like what you're doing, you can always say, 'Well, you auditioned me and you hired me.'"

Even stars with years of credits to their name are commonly asked to audition for a new project. Somewhere there may be people who enjoy auditions. But Phyllis Newman probably puts it best for all performers when she says, "I'd rather die."

It would seem that with experience, auditioning should get easier. It doesn't. June Havoc has been in show business since the age of two. "All auditions are terrifying. It's very scary to get out there. Sometimes you don't even know who's out front; you can't see, it's dark. And auditioning gets much harder—first of all, because everyone out front in the dark is ten years old. They probably don't know you anyway, if you're a leftover from the forties, the fifties, the sixties, or even the seventies. You wonder why fate hasn't been kinder to you and let them have seen what you've accomplished. I've done forty-four films and twenty-two Broadway shows, and endless television. They may not have even seen one of them. They're judging you on that one little thing—your audition."

Catherine Cox, with numerous Broadway credits, agrees. "I thought it would get better as I got older, but it frightens me every time. In fact, it gets harder as I get older, because as I've gotten more experience, I feel that every time, I have to go back to square one and prove myself all over again."

Nerves at an audition are as bad as or worse than performance jitters. Carole Demas once went to audition for Neil Simon: "It was a callback. That morning, I'd grabbed my vitamins from the counter and thought, 'I'll take these when I get to the theatre.' Just before I went out to audition, I remembered I'd forgotten to take the vitamins. So I grabbed the first pill and ran to the water fountain and took it—and then realized it was my cat's deworming pill. There was no way to get it back up, so I went out there thinking, 'Well, I may not get the job, but at least I won't have worms.' Neil Simon came down to the apron and asked how I was. I said, 'Fine, I guess.' He asked why I was so tentative, and I told him the story about taking the cat's pill. He thought it was hysterical. Well, I guess it was an icebreaker."

Mary Louise Wilson has been auditioning for decades. "Oh, God, I wish auditions would just go out of style." Fortunately or not, an audition can offer an advance glimpse of the show in question: "Actually, there are very few musical auditions nowadays. But I did one recently, I won't tell you what it was—oh, what the hell—it was *Meet Me in St. Louis*. And they gave me this song. It was about shillelaghs and all this Irish stuff. I took it to my accompanist, and he played it through. And he said to me very quietly, 'Mary Louise, does it seem to you that the American Musical Theatre has died?' He was very serious about it. The song was godawful."

Rita Gardner had found fame as the original Girl in *The Fantasticks*, directed by Word Baker. A few years later, she was up for the ingenue role in *A Family Affair*, also directed by Baker. "I had to audition for him! And he was my dear friend. But I never thought about it like that. I guess everybody has to do it. I'm not thrilled about it, but I don't think anyone is."

After sixty years in show business, Eddie Bracken is still called in to audition. A producer/director himself, he doesn't mind: "It's a comedown to an actor. They think, 'Don't they know my work after all these years?' But you continually change. Look, I've got gray hair now. I can't go back to high school. You have to just go up there and swallow your pride."

Young performers starting out commonly think everything is going to be easy. Before they know any better, sometimes it is.

Lee Roy Reams came to New York from Cincinnati. "I was fresh off the boat, and I got the very first job I auditioned for, which was working with Juliet Prowse in her nightclub act. Then I came back and auditioned for

An Audition Nightmare

AFTER singing such roles as Lucia, Gilda in *Rigoletto*, and Rosina in *The Barber of Seville* at the Metropolitan Opera House, Dolores Wilson turned her attention to musical comedy and was called in to audition for Richard Rodgers for the revival of *The King and I* the composer was producing at Lincoln Center.

"I knew Rodgers was a stickler about his music being sung exactly as he'd written it, with no frills or changes in any way. I had sung Mrs. Anna before, but I went to my accompanist and learned the score like it was a whole new piece to me.

"When I got to the audition, I started to sing the 'Soliloquy,' because I thought that would show that I could both sing and act. I got around four bars into it and they stopped me. 'Miss Wilson, can you sing something else? Mr. Rodgers doesn't want to hear that.' So I said, 'What do you want to hear?' and they said, 'Whatever you want to sing.' And I said, 'I started what I wanted to sing. You tell me what you want to hear.' So they said, 'Anything else.' I started 'Hello Young Lovers,' and they stopped me. They didn't want the introduction. So I went straight into the song.

"So I finished and I got the customary applause and the 'Thank you, Miss Wilson,' and I went off into the wings, where my agent was waiting for me. His face was ashen. He said to me, 'I just found out that they've signed Risë Stevens for the part.' This after I had gone to all the trouble and expense of getting ready for this audition! Well, I was mad, but still I said, 'What about Lady Thiang?' I had played that part, too. He told me that was also cast. By this point I was literally shaking. I was enraged.

"Without a moment's hesitation, I stormed right back out on that stage. There was a young girl out there auditioning for Tuptim, and I pushed her out of the way and said, 'Forgive me, dear, but this has to be done.' So I turned around and said, 'Mr. Rodgers, are you out there?' and he said, 'Yes, Miss Wilson, what can we do for you?' 'Well,' I said, 'I understand you've already signed someone for this part.' He admitted they had. So I said, 'What the hell am *I* doing here, and who the hell do you think you are? You asked me to come in here, and you could at least have been a gentleman and called me to say you had decided on someone else. I ask you again—just who the hell do you think you are?'

"The silence in that theatre was deafening. Nobody spoke to Rodgers that way, but I really didn't give a damn. As I was walking off the stage, I heard, 'You are absolutely right, and I apologize.' I turned to him and said, 'And well you should.'"

Wilson next met Rodgers on the first day of rehearsals for *I Remember Mama*, the composer's last show. The soprano had been cast as one of the Maiden Aunts.

"That frail old man with a cane was sitting there, and he said to me, 'You've never forgiven me, have you?' I said, 'I think I've forgiven you, but I've never forgotten. But I'm old enough to let that go by.' Actually, we became very fast friends after that."

Sweet Charity, and I got that. But then Juliet wanted me back again, and it was much more rewarding financially, so I turned in my notice right after *Charity* opened. Bob Fosse was furious. He said, 'How can you do this? People want to work with me, and I choose you, and now you're putting us all through so much trouble. The stage managers are tired, and everybody is tired, and now they're going to have to put in someone new—just give me one good reason why you're leaving.' I said, 'Juliet Prowse pays me three times what you do.' He said, 'I can't argue with that.' And that was it. But we remained friends, and later on, he asked me to do the film."

Marilyn Cooper's Broadway debut in *Mr. Wonderful* was just as uneventful. "I went to the audition. I stood in line. And then I sang. And I got it."

Gene Foote was once complimented at a "Cha-Cha Palace" by a table full of Jerome Robbins, Nora Kaye, and the like when he started his dancing career in summer stock. "I came back to New York, and there were two auditions that came up: one for the London Production of *West Side Story*, and one for *Li'l Abner*. So I went to *West Side Story*, and they kept me for eight days. On the eighth day I was eliminated because I couldn't do the New York accent. But I got *Li'l Abner*, and got to work with Michael Kidd. I don't know if Robbins remembered that night at the Cha-Cha Palace. I never got to tell him he was the reason I had a career."

When Ellen Hanley was still a student at Juilliard, she auditioned for *Annie Get Your Gun*—in front of a group that included Juilliard alumnus Richard Rodgers, one of the show's producers. "I went downtown with a friend who was going to audition for the chorus. I didn't know I was going

to be auditioning, and I didn't have any music. All the girls were so beautiful, and I felt like this tall, gawky kid. And I'd seen only one show on
Broadway before. So I got out onstage and sang 'Can't Help Lovin' Dat Man,'
and the next thing I know, Richard Rodgers and Irving Berlin were onstage,
talking to me. Dick asked me, 'Where did you learn to sing like that?' I'd
only been at Juilliard one year, and I was the bane of my teacher's existence.
But I said, 'Juilliard,' and he poked Irving Berlin and said, 'See, Irving, I told
you.' He asked me who my teacher was, and I said 'Nora Fauchald,' even
though she really never had a chance to teach me, and he said again, 'See,
I told you.' It turns out she had played the lead in the first show Rodgers and
Hart had ever written at Columbia University. So I got the job."

Rodgers also gave Nanette Fabray her first audition. Fabray had already
been a child star and in two Broadway shows, and Rodgers was thinking of
putting her into *By Jupiter*, opposite Ray Bolger. "I really didn't know how
to audition. I'd never had to do it. Later on, Rodgers used to tell the story
all the time, and he said it was the worst audition he'd ever seen; and if he
hadn't already seen me onstage, I wouldn't even have gotten into the chorus.
But I got the lead."

There is nothing like a bad audition to boost one's confidence. Jane Con-
nell went in to audition for Frank Loesser for Cleo in *The Most Happy Fella*.
"Right before me was this operatic guy who was auditioning for the leading
role. And of course, he was classically trained, and he said, 'My name is
Giorgio Scramoldi'—or whatever—'and I'm going to sing the aria from some
Mozart opera.' Then I came out and said, 'My name is Jane Connell and
I'm going to sing "Garbage," by Sheldon Harnick.' I wish I could have seen
their faces. Susan Johnson got the role."

Johnson's audition for *Most Happy Fella* hadn't, in fact, gone much
better: "I went down to sing for Frank Loesser, and I remember I had
this terrible, terrible cold. It was awful, and I sang a couple of songs, and
went immediately to the Warwick [Hotel] drugstore to get some cough
medicine. Well, Frank Loesser was living at the Warwick, and he came in
and grabbed my hand, and dragged me over to Frank Music on 57th Street
and played me this gorgeous ballad, 'I Don't Know Nothing about You.'
Later on he told me I got the part mainly because I didn't apologize about
my cold."

For the ingenue, Rosabella, Loesser auditioned a young singer named Jo
Sullivan—and auditioned her and auditioned her. "I auditioned six or seven
times for that part. Frank would always have you sing 'Happy Birthday.' He'd
have you sing it up, and up. Most people don't realize how hard that is.
When you auditioned for Frank, you were always in for a lot of carrying on,

shall we say." Loesser wanted a soprano for the part, but not an operatic soprano. He wanted her to sound like a waitress. "I guess I did—I guess that was a compliment." She got the part—and later became Mrs. Frank Loesser.

Every once in a while there is that audition in which everything comes together, and the result is a job that can change a performer's life.

Tammy Grimes was rehearsing for a television show when Barron Polan, her agent, called her out of the studio. "He was very excited: 'Listen, I've got this part for you—I mean, it's *you*, Tammy.' He came to pick me up, and I'm walking down Fifth Avenue, reading the script. It was called *The Unsinkable Molly Brown*, and I read about four pages and said, 'Barron, this girl is stupid; she's coarse and she's stupid—I can't imagine playing this part.' All of a sudden he grabbed me by the shoulders and said, 'Do you want to be a star, or don't you?' I said 'I want to be a star.' He said, 'Do you realize this character is offstage only seven minutes out of the whole musical comedy? You'd either sink or rise—and you'd be a star.'

"I was called onstage, and Dore Schary, who was directing, said, 'What are you going to sing for us?' I said, 'Melancholy Baby,' and they laughed, because it's an old joke. But I did. Then they asked me to read the soliloquy. Dore came up to the stage and said, 'Miss Grimes, would you have any objection to dying your hair red?' 'No, not at all, I love red hair.' He said, 'You've got the part.' I walked offstage, and Barron Polan was standing in the wings with tears streaming down his face. I owe him a great deal." *Molly Brown* made Grimes a star.

Gemze De Lappe continued a lifelong association with Agnes De Mille when she auditioned for *Paint Your Wagon*. "I was full of confidence. I wanted to prove myself to her, but it wasn't something that scared me. I knew I was her kind of dancer; I had seen her work, and I'd seen her dance. She was an acting dancer—that's what I was. I auditioned for her with Jimmy Mitchell. Jimmy and I had never met before, and we just clicked. We were the same kind of dancers; we breathed together; we moved together. So I was hired."

When Gwen Verdon auditioned for *New Girl in Town*, it was for some of the same people who had helped her become a star in *Damn Yankees*— George Abbott and Bob Fosse. But *New Girl* was based on Eugene O'Neill's *Anna Christie*, and Verdon had other things to prove. "I auditioned three times for that show. I wanted that part. Marilyn Monroe had auditioned for it, and Shelley Winters, and a whole bunch of people. I kept saying I wanted it, so I kept auditioning. I think everyone else turned it down, that's why I got it. I don't think they ever felt I had the talent to act it." Verdon won a Tony for the role.

The Ultimate Gypsy

*S*ILK *Stockings*, a musical written by Cole Porter with a book by Abe Burrows, George S. Kaufman, and Leueen McGrath, opened at the Imperial Theatre on February 24, 1955, and ran for 478 performances. It starred Hildegarde Neff and Don Ameche. The leading supporting role, Janice Dayton—the Hollywood star who also just happens to swim—was played by Gretchen Wyler. She opened to starmaking reviews after having replaced Yvonne Adair, Sherry O'Neill, and Marilyn Ross, all of whom had played the role on the road.

"I was really the 'queen of the gypsies' for a while because of the way I got the role in *Silk Stockings*. Feuer and Martin told me that they had a great job for me. They wanted me to understudy Yvonne Adair in this wonderful new Cole Porter show.

"So there I was at twenty-three, after only four years of chorus work on Broadway, and I said to them, 'No, no. I don't want to understudy anymore. I've done that on two shows, guys.' So I went off to Hollywood to try the movies.

"Then the show opened in Philadelphia and I got a call from Ernie Martin one night saying, 'How are things going in LA?' I was bemoaning the fact that things were terrible. Then he told me that the show was a big hit but Yvonne had gotten sick and her understudy, Sherry O'Neill, had gone on. Of course, that would have been me if I had taken the job. Then he told me that Sherry really wasn't right, and they didn't know if Yvonne was coming back, but they wanted me to come back and understudy the understudy, Sherry.

"Since I wasn't a Hollywood star, I thought this was a great idea. I was in Philadelphia in twenty-four hours. Then, once I got there, they started the most incredible search for someone else to play Janice. They started flying in all these Hollywood movie stars because the word was out that Yvonne would almost definitely not be coming back.

"They auditioned people like Virginia Mayo and Rhonda Fleming, who were the right age and beautiful and tall. The tall part was important. At that point, the producers were having a lot of other problems with the show. Hildegarde Neff was being hypnotized because she had such fear about going onstage. It was an amazing period.

"So here was Gretchen at age twenty-three, putting notes under the producers' doors saying, 'Please let me go on one night! I know that I'm right for this.' Meanwhile, I would sneak into the theatre, and try on the costumes and stand in the wings to try to learn everything I could in case I ever got the chance to go on. Finally, they brought in a girl named Marilyn Ross. I was really upset because she wasn't right for it either. She was a good belter and a pretty lady—she just wasn't a funny lady. Then they let her go and Sherry was going on again, but naturally she was unhappy because she knew that they weren't satisfied with what she was doing, and they'd never let her open the show in New York.

"We were in Detroit at that time and there had never been a Broadway show that had a tryout period as long as ours. We were out for fourteen weeks, and I was still in the back line of the chorus watching all these strange people they were bringing in. Then they found out that Yvonne was strong enough to come back. She rejoined us in Detroit and I stood in the wings and watched her, too. She really wasn't terribly healthy but she was doing a wonderful job.

"Ten days before the Broadway opening, I went to the theatre and at about ten minutes to eight with an eight-thirty curtain, Sherry O'Neill said to me, 'Gretchen, I'm going to New York. I'm catching a train right now. Yvonne's in and everything's all right.' She was going to audition for another show and then fly back to Detroit.

"She left. The show went on, and I was standing in the wings watching 'Satin and Silk,' Janice's last number in the first act, and Yvonne became very unsteady and looked like she was going to faint, which she did as soon as she came offstage.

"A few minutes later, I heard them calling, 'Sherry O'Neill, come to the stage manager's desk,' and I knew she wasn't around and they weren't going to find her. Then Henry Cooks, the stage manager, knocked on our chorus dressing room door and asked me if I could go on. He said he knew I hadn't been rehearsed, but they just wanted to keep the curtain up.

"It's amazing, but I've run into at least three people who were in the audience that night. Fortunately, Abe Burrows was also out there and Cole Porter and everybody else. They all came back afterwards and told me that I would be playing the part for the Broadway opening in ten days.

"In those days—and these days, too—chorus girls usually don't get breaks like that. I *was* brassy and young and very aggressive. There was poor Yvonne Adair collapsing, and Don Ameche throwing up, and Hildegarde being hypnotized, and I was perfectly cool. I couldn't wait to get out there.

"When I hear kids today—understudies—say, 'I hope I don't have to go on,' I want to kill them. For me, it's always been a matter of loving the business and wanting to be out there. And I was ready!"

Having a success in certain roles can be more hindrance than help when a performer tries to expand his vision and explore new ground. Knowing people sometimes just makes it worse. Lee Roy Reams had already done *Hello, Dolly!* and *Applause*—working with a number of the powers of *42nd Street*—by the time he finally got the role of Billy in the show. "They almost didn't let me audition for Billy. They thought I was too old. They wanted me to audition for Andy Lee. I was really mad, and almost didn't go to the audition. But I went in, and did my 'up' tune, then went right into a ballad, then did a tap routine with Toni Kaye, because I thought it was important they see me with a girl. They just saw me as the hairdresser from *Applause*. I finished, and it was a total silence. It looked like 'Springtime for Hitler.' Then this white-haired man walked down the aisle, and it was Gower Champion. He said I wasn't right for Andy Lee, and I said, 'I know. I'm right for Billy.' He said, 'Yes, you are,' and I got the job."

Champion had directed Susan Watson in *Bye Bye Birdie*, the show that made her a star. It should have been easy for her when she wanted to be cast in the National Company of *Carnival*, in the role created by Anna Maria Alberghetti. "Often, directors don't really see what you can do. He just saw me as this Sweet Apple, Ohio, pony-tailed girl—the comic, not the darker side of it all. For the audition, I did excerpts from *Candide*, jazz, everything—because I wanted them to know that I could do it vocally. Gower wasn't even at my first audition, because he didn't think I was right for it. It was for Jack Schlissel from the David Merrick office. I'll tell you, I pulled out everything but the kitchen sink for him. I pulled my hair back like Anna Maria had hers, and got black tights and a blue skirt, and a little white blouse. I costumed myself and came in and sang, and he said, 'Oh. I didn't know you could do that. Let me talk to Gower.' Knowing Gower didn't help at all. I had to shake up all of his ideas."

Ellis Rabb was casting *The Grass Harp* when he went to see Russ Thacker in *Life with Father* at City Center. The director didn't like Thacker, who remembers, "He thought I was too slick and showbiz-y. But I had an agent who was really an agent, and he persisted, so they saw me. I went in and sang something popular at the time like 'She's Having My Baby,' and Ellis ran up to the stage and told me I had the part. Then I wasn't sure if I wanted it. It seemed like it was too easy to get. It was what I had expected when I came to New York: I'd go in and sing, and get the job. Simple."

A first impression might land someone a job in the corporate world, but if that were true in the theatre, few people would ever work. Anne Jeffreys's Broadway debut was in *Street Scene*, Kurt Weill's adaptation of Elmer Rice's famous play, in which she played the simple little ingenue. Weill insisted on taking her to meet Elmer Rice, who was in the hospital. "I was all dressed up to go to a cocktail party, and I walked in there, this sophisticated young blonde in the high heels, with a black suit, and a big picture hat with a red rose on it, and the red lipstick and fingernails. And he shuddered."

Jerome Robbins and Hal Prince had spotted opera singer Dolores Wilson in her first Broadway role, as the down-home mother in *The Yearling*. They were sure they'd found their next Golde for *Fiddler on the Roof*.

DOLORES WILSON: "Unbeknownst to me, everyone who was coming in to audition for the role was in babushkas and dirndls and aprons. I was in a red chiffon cocktail dress because I was on my way to Frank Loesser's annual cocktail party at the Plaza. I had furs and the whole thing. Well, I came out and asked if the name was 'Muttel' or '*Motel*,' and they told me, and I went ahead and read. I really did have an affinity for the character. So they asked my agent if I would *sprechsing* it, like Rex Harrison. The only thing that worried them was the singing!"

Occasionally, who you know is important. Rene Auberjonois was a little boy when he first met Alan Jay Lerner. "I worked for him for two summers as a lifeguard/babysitter, and took care of his children around the swimming pool. And at ten o'clock every morning I would bring cantaloupe and coffee into his study, where he and Fritz Loewe were writing *My Fair Lady*." Years later, Auberjonois auditioned for him and was cast as one of the leads in *Coco*.

Zina Bethune joined *Grand Hotel* because a fan thought she should do it. "He said he heard that Tommy Tune was looking for someone to play the ballerina. I finally got Tommy's office, and I got a call back saying, 'Tommy wants to see you on Monday.' That was fine. But then he called me again on Sunday and told me to bring a song. I said, 'What?' He said, 'Bring a song.' Well, I hadn't sung in ten years, and I told him that, and he said, 'You have to sing. Bring a song.' I said, 'I'm not prepared to sing,' and he said, 'You have to.' So I stayed up all night and learned the song from the show—and it was a hard song. The next day at the audition, I went through the song with the pianist, and I said to Tommy, 'Do you want me to sing the song?' And he said, 'No, there's no need.' Then I put on my pointe shoes and they put on some music and I danced. Then Tommy ran up onstage and grabbed my hand and said, 'You have to play this role!' It was like a Mickey Rooney–Judy Garland movie. And he's literally 6'6", and I'm 5'4", and there I was, standing en pointe, trying to hug him."

Getting a job is not always the result of auditions—it can be inherited, as when the star breaks her proverbial ankle and the understudy takes over. There are also cases where stars are occasionally allowed to bypass the process—something most people dream about. Dealing with so much rejection, performers have a recurring fantasy about being begged by Cole Porter (Rodgers, Sondheim, whomever) to *please* do a show. It's like the constant dream most actors have: any performer who doesn't admit to having made up his or her Tony acceptance speech is a liar. The speech may never be given, but it's a part of the profession.

ALFRED DRAKE: "I was doing a show called *Joy to the World* when John Wilson, the producer, came back to talk to me about doing *Kiss Me, Kate*. So I went to Cole Porter and heard what there was of the score. Then they sent me the book, which I thought was inadequate, so I said no. But they kept coming after me, and my agent told me I should do it, so I agreed. Then, when we had the contract signed and everything, I got a copy of the supposedly 'rewritten' book, and it was worse than before. But I was confident about it. Cole, like Richard Rodgers, was very professional. He had very definite ideas, and he was always right. I knew we had a very good show. We all did."

During the period before and after World War II, available performers went from job to job—even during the war, when George S. Irving made his debut in *Oklahoma!* "I opened in it and played for three weeks. Then I got my draft notice. So I gave the show my notice. Then the draft board told me they didn't need me; but I was already out of a job. But I heard there was a chorus opening in *Lady in the Dark*. So I got the job in *Lady*, and rehearsed for a week. And the day I opened in that, I got the notice from the draft board: 'We want you . . . .' The company manager was furious. Well, what could I do? It was war."

A revival of *Oklahoma!* was being cast the day the closing notice went up for *Anya*, and Laurie Franks found she was about to be out of a job. "City Center was right up the street, and as soon as the notice went up, I went over to see them about auditioning. But I had to get back to do our matinee." The typically American *Oklahoma!* certainly required a look different from the one needed for *Anya*—a musical drama set in Europe. "After the matinee, I remember racing back up the street in full *Anya* makeup to audition for *Oklahoma!* I got the job."

"Gone are the days when you'd have auditions every day," says Sheila Smith, a Tony nominee for *Sugar*. "The day I auditioned for *Mame*, I also was up for *Sherry* and *Breakfast at Tiffany's*. And I did those on my lunch hour while I was rehearsing for another show. With all that going on, you were bound to get something."

3

Losing the Job

"WHEN a show is in trouble," according to noted musical director Buster Davis, "you always fire the ingenue. It's a very dangerous part to be in."

When Carole Demas was hired for the title role of *No, No, Nanette*, it was because producer Cyma Rubin had wanted a delicious new young face to surround her aging stars, Ruby Keeler, Patsy Kelly, and Hiram Sherman. She decided Demas was it. It was going to be Demas's first big break.

By the time the vintage revival opened out of town in Boston, Rubin had changed her mind. First she lined up Susan Watson. With credits like *Bye Bye Birdie*, Watson was the ultimate ingenue of her generation. She had also replaced Donna McKechnie when *A Joyful Noise* moved from summer stock to Broadway. Then, in one of the most well-publicized firings in the history of the Broadway musical, Rubin got rid of Demas.

CAROLE DEMAS: "It was just one of those things that happen. It was a battle. Some people wanted to keep me and some people didn't. My side lost. It's always a shock when something like that happens. But it was like they stripped my skin off."

Demas has since gone on to other successes, but she has never forgotten. For anybody, getting fired is at best traumatic; at worst, devastating. But it's

21

especially true for performers, whose lives are built almost entirely on acceptance. Losing a job doesn't mean just unemployment in a field where people
constantly wonder whether they'll ever work again—it involves loss of self-
esteem, sudden separation from a company that may have become close,
and often, public humiliation.

In her only Broadway musical, *Coco*, Katharine Hepburn dealt with the
"ingenue problem" with her usual directness, as featured performer Jeanne
Arnold recalls. "On the first day of rehearsal, poor Gail Dixon was late, and
Miss Hepburn had her fired on the spot. Her theory was that if *she* could be
there on time, everyone else could, too. Fortunately, this story had a mod-
erately happy ending. The girl who replaced her really didn't work out, so
Gail was back with us by the time we opened."

Stars will use their prerogative, which sometimes leaves other performers
helpless. Vivien Leigh made her musical debut in *Tovarich*. Among her
supporting cast were Taina Elg and John Emery, the elegant actor probably
best remembered as Tallulah Bankhead's husband.

Taina Elg had already starred in such films as *Les Girls*. "I was playing
the second female lead [in *Tovarich*]. Then, all of a sudden, when we were
out of town, Vivien got very nervous about everything—she had never done
a musical before. First, she had the director fired. It was Delbert Mann, who
was wonderful, and had been working on the show for years. She had Peter
Glenville come in, and he changed everything, including five of the actors.

"Apparently, I was the last one to know that I was going to be replaced. I
was devastated by the whole thing. But John Emery gave me some really
good advice. He said, 'When the producers take you out to dinner to fire
you, don't get mad and say you're quitting. Let them tell you that *they* don't
need *your* services. That way you can collect the benefits, because you never
quit.' " Both Elg and Emery were gone by the time the show left Philadelphia.

The reason why was never explained. Louise Troy, who originally auditioned for the part, was hired to replace Elg.

LOUISE TROY: "When they decided to replace her, I was asked to go to
Boston to see the show. When I saw Taina on the stage, she looked so much
like Vivien Leigh that it was shocking. Taina was beautiful, and wonderful
in the part. I had never seen her onstage before, only on the screen—but the
similarity between the two women was incredible, except that Vivien had
dark hair and Taina was redheaded. The haircuts, the features, the daintiness
were so similar. I was very upset for Taina. I'm sure Peter looked at the show
and saw Vivien, then saw Taina, and thought he had two of the same people.
Maybe Vivien thought so, too. I did *not* look like Vivien Leigh."

Unemployment benefits are small consolation for an artist. The next time Elg found herself in a dangerous situation—while working with Joshua Logan on *Look to the Lilies*, the musical version of *Lilies of the Field*—she was ready. "Joshua Logan had a tendency to pick a scapegoat in the production. He started to treat me badly, and I said to myself, 'No. I'm not going to let him do that to me.' I had been thrown out of *Tovarich*, and it was traumatic, and I was determined. So I decided to cry. I made up my mind. And I cried so hard, my tears were falling, and it was something. But it worked. After that, he was nice to me, and afterwards, whenever I met him, he was very kind. He even climbed all those stairs backstage at the 46th Street Theatre to come see me after a performance of *Nine*. He was not a well man, and I was very flattered."

Overwhelmed by a rash of firings in the mid-1970s, Actors Equity inserted a "just cause" clause in actors' contracts, preventing producers from arbitrarily terminating performers' employment. The major shows involved in the dispute were *Annie* and *Sugar Babies*, both huge hits.

Barbara Erwin created the role of Lili St. Regis in *Annie*, and stopped the show every night singing "Easy Street" with Dorothy Loudon and Bob Fitch. She left to join Loudon in Michael Bennett's *Ballroom*, and when that show closed, was happy to get her old job back in *Annie*. "The girl who was playing my part was leaving; and after all, it was a job—and a good job. Then, eight months later, they fired us all. I never really understood why Marty did that."

"Marty" is Martin Charnin, the show's lyricist, director, and co-producer, who fired a group of his cast members for reasons known only to himself.

BARBARA ERWIN: "At one meeting, I remember him saying that we were all stale. Most of the original cast was still with the show, and Reid Shelton, who was still playing Daddy Warbucks, spoke up and said, 'We are professionals, and we work on our craft.' He was right. If you get a show that's going to last, you want to stick with it—and you work at keeping it fresh."

Dolores Wilson, who was playing Miss Hannigan at the time, recalls the mass firings with dismay. "What did he expect? I was new to the show. I was doing extra work and thinking and talking about the role. But the others had what they were doing down pat. Did he expect them to be off in the corner working on motivations or something? Oh, please! I loved doing the part, but I left the show as soon as my contract was up."

ERWIN: "None of us really understood what was going on. We all got our notices at different times. Bob Fitch and I got ours at the same time. Then, a few weeks later, the others did. Finally, each of us had our two weeks' notice, and we had about a week to go, and the stage manager came to us one at a time and asked us if we'd be willing to stay an extra week. He said, 'The new cast members aren't ready to go in yet.' I was the Equity deputy then, and we had a union meeting, and then told them to forget it! It was really kind of ballsy of them to ask us to do that. I couldn't see the purpose in changing the cast. The show would have run anyway. Every kid in the world wanted to see it."

Erwin believes it might have been a financial move to keep operating costs down or some kind of power play. Charnin did call Erwin some time after she had left *Annie*. "He seemed mad at me. Somehow he'd gotten a copy of my picture and résumé, and I didn't have his name on it. He thought I was still mad about the firing, and he told me he didn't have anything to do with it. But who does the firing? How does this happen? To this day, I don't understand it. But I'll tell you—saying we were stale just wasn't true."

The ladies in the ensemble of *Sugar Babies* knew who had dismissed them. The hit revue starred Mickey Rooney and Ann Miller, and was produced by Terry Allan Kramer and Harry Rigby. There was a lot of television money invested in the show, and a long, publicity-filled road tour before this tribute to the "golden age" of burlesque reached New York. Most of the girls in the chorus were making their debuts on the Broadway stage. One of them was Terpsie Toon, who now works extensively as a director/choreographer. "I was one of four people who were let go, and it happened around the same time that the *Annie* people were fired. Mickey had a lot of control over the show as far as the gags went, but he and Annie [Miller] had nothing to do with what happened to us. Terry Allan Kramer really had all the power, and she used it.

"My grandmother always told me when I went into the business to beware of the casting couch. I realized six months into the road on this show that the girls didn't have to worry about it; it was the guys who had a problem. We didn't have to do anything except constantly go to parties. The producers were always entertaining. It was part of the way they were selling the show. I found that very, very hard to deal with. I don't know if they hired us because we were inexperienced, but we were all new blood, and we didn't know whether these parties were part of our job or not."

The parties were over when the show opened on Broadway.

"They fired four of us as an example to the company. We were told, by no one in authority, that we were being used as an example to everyone; that if they didn't do exactly what they were told, the same thing would happen to them. That sort of became a way of life with *Sugar Babies*. One of the girls in the chorus left to go home for a wedding and when she came back, she was out of the show.

Jack Schlissel / Jay Kingwill

226 West 47th Street
New York, N. Y. 10036
Telephone: (212) 354-1239

December 7, 1979

Ms. Terpsie Toon
c/o Tom McAteer
355 East 88th Street
#5D
New York, N.Y. 10022

Dear Ms. Toon,

In accordance with Actors' Equity Association rules, this
letter will serve as two weeks' written notice of the
termination of your contract with Sugar Babies Company
dated August 13, 1979 for SUGAR BABIES.

Your last performance will be Saturday evening, December 22, 1979.
Our best wishes for your future.

Sincerely,

Sugar Babies Company

JAY KINGWILL

JK:mf

cc/AEA

Courtesy of Terpsie Toon

"It was very hard. I'd lost my father two days before the show opened, and I was under a lot of stress. I remember going to Ernie Flatt [the choreographer] and asking why I was let go. He said, 'Well, you don't seem to be in the right frame of mind.' Probably I wasn't, but I was doing my job. I went to everybody, and nobody told me anything. Mickey didn't know, and the stage manager couldn't explain it. Nobody ever gave us a reason for why we were fired. We were just given notice that after Christmas we were through; don't come back to work. I saved that letter. I'll probably save it forever.

"Also, believe me, it doesn't make you tougher, and it doesn't help your self-esteem. There was no legitimate reason for it. It wasn't like we all weighed over four hundred pounds, or we weren't the right type. After all, they hired us!"

The reasons why noted dramatic actress Viveca Lindfors was replaced in the ill-fated *Something More* are no clearer. Jule Styne directed and co-produced the show, about the good life in Italy, which starred Barbara Cook. In the role of the Marquise, Lindfors was understudied by singer-actress Laurie Franks. "They did really a terrible thing to Viveca," Franks remembers. "We were in Philadelphia, and Viveca went back to New York for the weekend. Jule's secretaries, the Dicker sisters, thought I had cheekbones like Viveca's— I don't know where they got that from, because I don't look anything like her—but Jule had me read from the script, and they thought they would put me on in the role while they looked for somebody to replace Viveca. There used to be a rule that you couldn't fire anyone unless it was in the theatre. When Viveca came back from New York on Monday, they were rehearsing me onstage at the Shubert Theatre. She really had no idea what was going on, and she went to her dressing room, and the producers went in and fired her. I went on that night.

"It was a nightmare. There were lines pasted up backstage before every entrance I had to make, and I had lines pasted on my evening bag. While I went on every night, and also stood by for Barbara Cook, they kept auditioning people to replace me in the role."

Joan Copeland was finally chosen as the replacement. "*Something More* was something else! They hired me, and then kept me totally in the dark. They wouldn't even let me see the play. They were changing the script, and they said, 'Don't go to the theatre because we don't want you to see what's going on there. We don't want you to get the wrong idea.' They would feed me one line at a time.

"I finally got about four scenes, and they had me come in to rehearse. It was only like half an act, but they wanted me to go on that night. They said, 'Don't worry about it.' So I went on, and after the fourth scene, they brought the curtain down and the stage manager said, 'Miss Copeland is indisposed and her role will be played by her understudy, Laurie Franks.' Then, on the way back to the hotel, I stopped next door to get a soda or something, and some people from the audience came in and saw me, and said, 'Ha! Indisposed, indeed!'

"After a few days, I had the whole first act, and then I was only 'indisposed' for the second act. It was insane. I had some relatives in Philadelphia who called my husband to find out what was wrong, because they kept hearing I was 'indisposed.'"

Other performers find themselves out of a job—for better or worse, after being written out of the script during revisions. Patricia Marand, who starred as Lois Lane in *It's a Bird, It's a Plane, It's a Superman!*, saw her entire role eliminated from *La Strada* in Detroit. "What a disaster that was! And what a shame. I had a beautiful song in the show, called 'My Turn to Fail.' Everything was very dark, and I remember Shirley Eder, the Detroit columnist, writing about the number, 'If only people could see her as well as hear her.' It was a gem of a song, but one song does not a show make, and the whole thing was doomed from the start. They just wrote out my part, and I really don't know why." She was lucky. William Glover of the AP called the show ". . . a murky musical mistake." *La Strada* closed on its opening night on Broadway.

Another musical mistake was *The Utter Glory of Morrissey Hall*, a girls'-school spoof, which lost its original leading lady, award-winning actress Eileen Heckart, out of town. "I was quite terrible, and they asked me to leave. Originally, I did it because I loved the character. It was based on the character that wonderful English comedienne Joyce Grenfell always played. But the show wasn't wonderful; at least, I didn't think so. The music had a sameness to it, and as I worked on it, I became less and less enchanted. When they asked me to leave, they didn't have to plead."

With Heckart's replacement, Celeste Holm, *Morrissey Hall* opened—and quickly closed—on Broadway.

Latin bandleader Xavier Cugat was also respectfully asked to vacate the cast of *Oh Captain!* before it debuted on Broadway. Susan Johnson co-starred in the show, a musical version of the film *The Captain's Paradise*, directed by José Ferrer. "Cugie played the ship's mate, Manzini, and there was a scene on board in his cabin. At the first run-through, I was sitting out front, and Cugie had one of the chorus kids pull a violin out from under the pillow and ask Manzini to play! He'd just gone off on his own and arranged this.

"As soon as he started to play, Joe Ferrer got up and walked out. Everybody was shocked. I think Joe and Al Morgan [the librettist] went to the bar next door. Then Joe went to the nearest phone and called Ed Platt in California and told him to get on the next plane. So he came in and took over for Cugie. Nobody even knew Eddie could sing, but he turned out to be very good."

Carnival, based on the movie *Lili*, was produced by David Merrick and directed by Gower Champion. Anna Maria Alberghetti starred, and was originally understudied by Anita Gillette, who had left *Gypsy*, another Merrick show, to join the company. Gillette regretted her decision. "I thought Gower was going to fire me. In fact, he did fire me, when we were in Washington at the National Theatre. He had decided I was too American-looking for the role. I had one of those contracts where they can decide after five days whether or not to pick up your option; and on the fifth day, they didn't pick up mine, and I was devastated.

"The way Gower fired me was very crude. He was directing a scene with Kaye Ballard and Jimmy Mitchell. Neil Hartley was our stage manager, and he told me that Gower wanted to speak to me. And God bless him, Neil did try to prepare me for what was going to happen.

"So I went out into the theatre, and sat down next to Gower. As he was directing the scene, he said, 'Anita, we've decided you're too . . . No, Kaye, I want you to cross on that line. Okay, Jimmy, go on . . . We've decided that you're just not right . . . No, Jimmy, not that line. We want you to cross there . . . We've decided that you're just not right for the role. Of course, you can stay in the chorus if you like.'

"It was one of the cruelest things that ever happened to me. I've never forgotten it. He treated me like nothing, like a fly on a garbage pail. It was horrible—a really big thing for me. I didn't know whether to stay in the business, or leave. But I decided to stay and tough it out.

"The only thing Gower had based firing me on was walking through a room when we were having an understudy rehearsal, and at that point, none of us knew what we were doing. I would get all these letters from girlfriends in New York saying, 'I just auditioned for your job.' It was rough, but I stuck it out."

Amid all the pressures of getting the show ready for New York, the producer and director failed to hire another understudy. When Alberghetti went into the hospital shortly after the New York opening, Anita Gillette went on in her place, and received rave notices. In a shower of publicity arranged by Merrick, Gillette was photographed in front of the Imperial Theatre sign with her name on it. What Merrick didn't know was that just before Gillette had to go on, she had turned in her notice, having signed to do the new Schwartz/Dietz show, *The Gay Life*. When he found out his new star was leaving, Merrick was furious. Gillette recalls: "I got a bill from the Merrick office for ninety dollars to pay for hanging the sign. Then I got a bill from a sign company in Paramus, New Jersey. But it worked out. I went to do *The Gay Life*, and my part was cut in Detroit. So when David needed me to fill in again in *Carnival*, I came back."

Gower Champion's indecision led to multiple firings during *The Happy Time*'s pre–Broadway tour. It was all complicated by the fact that his concept for the show, which was about a photographer's homecoming to a French-

Canadian town, centered on a series of photographs of the cast to be projected on the back wall of the set. It may have been a good idea . . . once. But not after his original casting choices started changing and the photographs had to be changed just as frequently. June Squibb was one of the cast members who made it all the way to Broadway. "We had three different leading ladies. Then they also flew out three or four other ladies from New York to audition for the role."

The show starred Robert Goulet and David Wayne. At Champion's insistence, the production rehearsed in Los Angeles.

SQUIBB: "Willi Burke was first. She sang like a bird; what a beautiful voice. But she just looked too mature for Bob Goulet. I don't know why she left. Then we had Linda Bennett. She went in very quickly, and did a nice job. I don't really know what happened to her. Then Julie Gregg was hired, and she went with us to New York. But by then it had become something of a joke."

Three leading ladies, three different sets of photographs for the rear wall, when Champion decided to replace Gene Scandur, who played Bibi, Goulet's nephew. *The Happy Time*'s chorus was filled with young performers, most of whom were making their Broadway debuts. Among them was Mary Ann O'Reilly. "According to Gower, Gene Scandur just wasn't working out; the same as with Willi Burke. He was very specific about what he wanted. So Gower just pulled Mike Rupert out of the chorus and put him in the lead. Scandur did look a little older than Rupert. But I remember he was devastated by the whole thing."

So it's not always the ingenue who gets the ax. But it's still not the best position to be in. Diane MacAfee found this out playing Eve Harrington during the out-of-town tryout of *Applause*, the musical of *All About Eve*. Lauren Bacall was the star, and the cast included Laurie Franks. "We got to Detroit, and it was obvious Diane just wasn't strong enough for Lauren. So she was out, and Penny Fuller came in."

PENNY FULLER: "I was hired on Sunday, went to Baltimore on Monday, rehearsed with the understudies on Tuesday and Wednesday, when I learned the two musical numbers. Then, on Thursday, I worked with the regular people. I had a full orchestra rehearsal on Friday, and went on Friday night.

"Eve makes her entrance from the front of the house. I went out to the front of the house. I had on my predecessor's gown, and they had no time to get me a wig, so they put a turban on my head—a white turban, with a jewel. I was sitting there in the front row of the Morris Mechanic Theatre in Baltimore, ready to go on with only four days' rehearsal, and I remember thinking quite calmly, 'I'm going to get up and walk out the door, and

Talent Will Out

FTER her much publicized dismissal from the title role in the revival
of *No, No, Nanette,* Carole Demas was cast in the title role of *The
Baker's Wife,* with music and lyrics by Stephen Schwartz, produced
by David Merrick. Demas and Topol opened in California as the stars of the
show on May 11, 1976. The show never reached Broadway. *The Baker's Wife*
closed in Washington on November 13, 1976. The final performance starred
Paul Sorvino and Patti LuPone.

CAROLE DEMAS: "I guess I was a little paranoid after the *Nanette* experience, but things were going well. One day after rehearsal, Lucia Victor
[David Merrick's assistant] came up to me and said, 'Carole, no matter what
happens with *The Baker's Wife,* all the problems and the birth pains—whatever—you are wonderful.' I was so relieved to hear that.

"We opened in LA, and the reviews were good for me. But the day after
the opening I was locked out of my apartment, and trying to get a window
opened, my hand slipped and went through the glass. At that point, subconsciously, I might have been trying to beat myself up—I was under a lot of
pressure then. But the reality of the situation was that blood was spurting out
of my artery.

"I got to the theatre that night and I was in real pain, but my understudy
wasn't ready to go on. So I had to do it, and I did. I did a damn good job,
too. Topol came up to me after the show with tears in his eyes and told me
what a wonderful job I had done and what a brave woman I was. Believe
me, I was just happy that I had gotten through it.

"At that very moment, the producers had Patti LuPone in a hotel room
in LA, and they were getting ready to cut my head off. The day after the
accident, my manager, Bob LaMonde, told me they were firing me. Equity
told me to go to the theatre every night and prepare to go on. So I did. I put
on my makeup and set my hair. I got pretty good at doing that with one
hand. Then the stage manager came to me and told me they didn't really
think I was up to going on. He and I both knew that if I could go on right
after the accident, I was damned well up to it the following night. They were
trying to build a case that I was unable to play and live up to my contract.

"Equity knew by this time that Patti was there and they were rehearsing
her, and they couldn't have two of us under contract for the same role. Then
David Merrick arrived. Bob [LaMonde] had been very discreet up to that

point, but he finally said, 'You want to fire Carole, fire her, you want her to go on, then let her go on. But this charade has got to stop. We know that Patti is here.'

"I think that Merrick had been told that I was a complete disaster, and there I was, ready and willing to go on, and Merrick was very upset. I was injured. It hurt like hell, but it was getting better and it didn't look that bad. Our director had said some of the company complained about it, but they assured me they didn't. They all thought I was doing a good job and it didn't bother them a damn bit.

"Well, Mr. Merrick was very nonplussed and he said, 'This is my show. I'm the producer and she's not fired.' This was the big time, and all of this was going on! Finally Merrick left town and they officially replaced me.

"Equity set up a hearing to determine whether I had been fired because I was incapable of doing the job or because they just wanted to replace me. Mr. Merrick is really an amazing man. I had been doing battle with his lawyers all day, and then he came up to me and offered me another job in a Broadway show.

"The union settled in my favor, and when I walked out of there, my head was just reeling. For a long time after that I would run into other actors in the street, and they would thank me for standing up to the system, or whatever. But the whole experience cut me deep, and it scared me. I don't think there's anyone who's had a career as a performer who wouldn't say it's been pretty bloody at times. I don't know that it's been as bloody as mine, but there's pain with all the joy."

---

nobody will notice.' Then they made the announcement that I was going on. And there I was, thrown on in a white turban with a jewel."

When it finally reached Broadway, No, No, Nanette was a phenomenal hit, and Susan Watson in the title role had a huge popular success. But in Don Dunn's subsequent book about the production's troubles, The Making of No, No, Nanette (Citadel Press, 1973), Carole Demas got a whole chapter to herself. Fortunately, by that time Demas's career was moving in a more positive direction, but the whole episode did get her a lot of attention.

DEMAS: "Well, it's a sort of strange way to attain fame!"

4

Stars Are People, Too

W E need stars," says Beulah Garrick. "We really need to have a star system for commercial theatre to work." Miss Garrick began her career in England and later worked in improvisational theatre with producer/director Joan Littlewood and the Irish playwright Brendan Behan. When she moved to America, she shared the stage with more glamorous types, such as Rosalind Russell, Beatrice Lillie, and Zero Mostel.

GARRICK: "You have a star like Rosalind Russell: many people found her difficult and unpleasant. I found her one of the greatest professionals I'd ever worked with. Tough, yes—very tough. She would not take nonsense. You would be warned one time not to do something, and the second time you were fired. That's just the way it was. But she created great professionalism because she was a great pro, and she demanded it from others."

Movie stars have always liked to try their hand at musical comedy. Katharine Hepburn was no exception when she took on *Coco*, but she was a movie star with a long history of stage experience. *Coco*'s cast included David Holliday, Jeanne Arnold, and Rene Auberjonois.

JEANNE ARNOLD: "Hepburn never behaved like a 'movie star.' When we traveled coach, she traveled coach. I remember on one flight Emlyn Williams [the Welsh actor/playwright] was on board, in first class, and she went up to see him; but she sat in coach with us."

DAVID HOLLIDAY: "Hepburn has her own world, her own world of thinking. She made a policy of not signing autographs only because she couldn't figure out what people did with them. It wasn't about stardom or anything. There was one time when she came out of the theatre and there was a lady in a wheelchair, and she signed, then turned to the crowd and said, 'She's in a wheelchair, that's why I gave her my autograph'—as if it made sense. And I'm sure it made perfect sense to her."

ARNOLD: "There is a sweetness about her. One time in rehearsal, before I was really used to her, she said something to me and it really jolted me—not that I probably didn't deserve it. But she felt that she had hurt my feelings, and she had. Then she surprised me. She came over and apologized. That's good stuff."

HOLLIDAY: "It had been published that she took her brother's birthday when he died. So when that came up, I racked my brain to come up with something for her. So I went over to Tiffany's and found a little glass egg with her birth sign, and I sneaked it into her dressing room during rehearsal. Around ten minutes later, she came up to me and said, 'It's not my birthday, and I don't accept gifts.' I was flabbergasted. I didn't know what to do. So I went back to her dressing room and left a note saying, 'Well, if it isn't your birthday, let this be for *Lion in Winter*, and thank you.' Another five minutes went by, and she came to me and said, 'You dear, sweet man. My niece, Katharine Houghton, gave Spencer one of those eggs and I've always admired it.' She was in many ways like a little girl."

ARNOLD: "In the show I had one scene about my fat daughter eating too much, and the scene just wasn't working. Days went by, and Alan [Lerner] and the director said, 'Oh, yes, we have to do something,' but they had a lot on their minds, and nothing happened. So finally I went to Kate and explained the whole thing to her. Well, she got up early the next morning and came in to work on that little scene, and gave me new lines, and really worked to set it up so it would work. I said to her, 'Oh, Kate, I'm so sorry to bother you about this,' and she said, 'Don't worry. They always treat us actors like this. They always think we don't know what we're doing, and they always think it's ego. They don't realize that we only want to do a good job.'"

In order to do a good job, it's almost always essential for a star to display some ego—which is often confused with temperament. This was not the case with Hepburn.

Smith's Follies

W HILE standing by for Jane Russell in *Company*, Sheila Smith was also playing the role of Meredith Lane in *Follies* with a star-studded cast that included Alexis Smith, Dorothy Collins, Yvonne DeCarlo, Ethel Shutta, and Fifi D'Orsay.

"Hal Prince had asked me to stand by for Yvonne, but also for Fifi, who was considerably older than I was. I had always wanted to work with Hal. So I went to the audition looking a little bit older but still good enough to stand by for Yvonne DeCarlo.

"I got the job, and then, on the first day of rehearsals, I was put into the 'Mirror, Mirror' number, and they gave me a character name. So I was in the show, too.

"Originally, Yvonne was supposed to stand by for Alexis, but she had so much trouble learning her own lines they took that away from her and I became Alexis's standby also.

"Let me tell you—that was a really strange group of people. I think Ethel was seventy-five, and Fifi was eighty, and they both needed a babysitter. They really acted like kids. Hal was always reprimanding them: 'Now, Ethel, don't move there . . . Now, Fifi, don't keep waving your finger.' It was hysterical— all these stars and all this confusion. It was very hard for Hal. Out of town, I said to Yvonne, 'It's the photographer scene,' and she looked at me as if she didn't know what I was talking about.

"At that point, in Boston, I wasn't officially covering for Alexis, but she began having problems with her voice, and I thought it would be a good idea to be ready. So I went to the Beef and Ale and had a vodka gimlet and went back to the hotel and stayed up all night learning the script.

"Then I came in at nine the next morning and did a run-through. I was singing 'Leave You' and saw a flash of red at the back of the theatre and knew Alexis was there. Needless to say, I never got to go on.

"Alexis was really the 'Ice Goddess,' but she did want to be a part of things. If we all cracked up onstage—and we did—she'd never participate, but she always wanted to know what was going on when we came off. Yvonne was famous for being great in rehearsal out in the hall. She would tap dance her little heart out and then change her shoes, go on stage, and lose it. She also used to put all these hairpieces on, and they'd fly all over the stage. Dorothy Collins would crack up at that, and then we'd all be gone. Dorothy worked really hard, and in my opinion she was the 'ticket' on that show. People came to see *her*, even though Alexis and the others were great.

"What an experience! When I left the show, they bronzed my tap shoes and sent them to me for the opening night of *Sugar*."

RENE AUBERJONOIS: "Kate has this really phenomenal ego, but it's wonderful. It's like a child's ego. It's very benign. It's an absolute sureness; but she also has a lot of humility."

ARNOLD: "When we were touring, we played Cleveland, and it was in one of those theatres where they divide it in half and put a steel wall up to separate the houses. And the night we opened, on the other side was a concert by the rock group Three Dog Night. It was our opening—and Kate didn't say a word. She went through the whole show. But at the end, when we were taking our bows, she stopped the applause and asked the audience if they had heard all that racket, and they shouted back 'Yes!' She said, 'Well, go and get your money back.'"

Coco had been constructed around Hepburn. When she finally left the show, the producers hired French movie star Danielle Darrieux to replace her.

ARNOLD: "Danielle was also wonderful, and there is no way to compare them. Kate had the magic, and worked like a dog, and filled the house and never let down for a second. But Danielle was French and she could sing. And to come in after Kate took a lot of courage. She was so gracious, and always tried to defer to us. We would say, 'Miss Darrieux, do whatever it is you want to do. We'll adjust to you.' She got wonderful reviews—they were like her mother wrote them. But they never advertised the show with Danielle, and that was really a shame. Kate was the draw. She filled the houses across the country, and that was it."

Applause was a vehicle for another strong movie personality, Lauren Bacall. Penny Fuller was intimidated, coming into the show to replace the fired ingenue. "I usually don't bother God. I figure He has more important things to do. But I remember saying to Him when I went into that show, 'Please, God, if I'm any good, please let Lauren Bacall know that it will only make her look better. The better I am, the better she'll look, because it will give her something to play against.'"

The cast also included Lee Roy Reams and Gene Foote.

GENE FOOTE: "Bacall knew she was in very deep water when she walked into that rehearsal hall. We were introduced to Lauren Bacall, and she turned to all of us and said, 'The name's Betty.' During rehearsals she was very friendly—not outgoing, but friendly."

LEE ROY REAMS: "The show was very difficult for Bacall, and people were a little bit afraid of her. She had never sung and danced on the stage before. But she really cared about the work."

FOOTE: "She was just there, being Bacall. The Look was there. She could give you that, and you were done for. She was working with wonderful people who knew what they were doing. She really needed us. Then, when we opened and she got her reviews, she didn't need us anymore. She was the Queen of New York, and she would slam that scarf on her head and walk by the fans, never giving autographs, and get right in that limousine. She didn't seem to be having any fun, and that's what I always thought it should be about."

Some stars need strong people—or the *right* people—in command, especially if they're on unfamiliar turf. A strong director or producer, or someone who knows how to coax and cajole a good performance out of someone, is essential. Shelley Winters went back to the musical stage after a long absence to do *Minnie's Boys*, about the Marx Brothers. The show was a bomb, and Winters was a nervous wreck. The cast included Carole Schweid and Julie Kurnitz.

CAROLE SCHWEID: "I used to stand in the wings and watch Shelley Winters, and she was driving the Marx Brothers nuts. But she was incredible. She was an actress who needed someone who could speak her language. She was willing, and I guess she was scared to death."

JULIE KURNITZ: "She'd be wearing her mink coat, and a couple of times, when something was going wrong with the show, she'd say, 'I'm a very gifted actress. I've won two Academy Awards.' I thought, this is so sad she has to say this. But she had to do it to bolster her confidence."

SCHWEID: "She was doing fine—she just had nobody helping her. She would say, 'What am I doing here?' And they'd tell her to just say the line and get to the number. You can't do that with Shelley Winters. She's a fanatical person who works in a certain way, and you have to give her what she needs and wants. Lauren Bacall, I'm sure, was given everything she needed, and *Applause* was a hit. We were in the same season. Shelley could have been just as good. She didn't sing well, but she was very believable, and there was a lot of fun in the show."

Occasionally, stars from other fields entirely come to Broadway for a shot at a musical, as ballerina Natalia Makarova did for a revival of *On Your Toes*, where she danced "Slaughter on Tenth Avenue," partnered by Lara Teeter.

LARA TEETER: "It was one of the most exciting things you could ever imagine. Touching her lower back was like plugging into an electrical socket. We had everything—and nothing—on each other . . . because she had never done a musical comedy before, and I had never partnered the greatest ballerina in the world before."

Opera star Teresa Stratas made her musical comedy debut in *Rags*, which struggled for a time and then closed. Michael Cone was in the cast. "Stratas was very cooperative, and offered to take a cut in salary to keep the show going, just like everybody else did. The only night she was uncooperative was opening night in New York. She refused to go on until the stage was warmed up. So they turned all the lights on, and the audience waited, and we waited, wandering around until it was warm enough out there for her to go out and be comfortable and sing."

A beginning performer can learn a lot from an accomplished star. Jo Sullivan appeared as Polly in Kurt Weill's *The Threepenny Opera*, which starred the composer's widow, Lotte Lenya. The German star was fanatical in her dedication to her work.

JO SULLIVAN: "She was a very serious person, and never clowned around on the stage. I learned by watching her. She had this incredible discipline, and was always at the theatre to get ready by six o'clock. Because she'd been there when Weill had created the piece, she really understood it. And if you wanted to learn, she could teach you a lot."

Bette Davis once said that Lillian Gish invented the closeup. When Gish made her musical debut in *Anya*, the musical version of *Anastasia*, directed by George Abbott, she shared the stage with Constance Towers, Michael Kermoyan, Laurie Franks, and Maggie Task.

CONSTANCE TOWERS: "Lillian Gish was so fragile and delicate, I was just so overwhelmed to be in her presence. But then I found her to be one of the strongest women I'd ever met in my life. Every night before the show began she'd be dressed, in full makeup and costume, sitting in a chair in the wings, ready to go on."

LAURIE FRANKS: "She was as spry as a little bird. You never had to worry about her. In a blackout, she was up and out of there faster than anybody. She had this big entrance on a grand staircase, and one night she stumbled a bit, but caught herself. Well, the next day there was a five-pound box of chocolates backstage for all of us, with a little note saying, 'I'm sorry.' She just didn't want to do anything to upset anyone."

MICHAEL KERMOYAN: "I remember one day in rehearsal Abbott wanted her to do something, and it was a little off—most of us would have asked, 'Why?' But not her. She'd try it, and if it didn't work, it didn't."

The Star Who Came to Dinner

O NE of the perks that comes with working in a big musical featuring a major star is that occasionally a supporting player develops a friendship with a star that manages to last after the show closes. This happened to Michael Kermoyan when he worked with Richard Burton in *Camelot.*

"My wife and I were both in the show, and we got to know the Burtons. Richard was really lovely to watch every night and lovely to work with, and my wife and Sybil [Burton] became good friends."

Then came *Cleopatra.*

"The next time we got together he was doing *Hamlet* and was married to Elizabeth [Taylor]. My wife and I had tickets for the show, but he called and said he wanted us there the next night and he had already left tickets at the box office for us. So we saw the show and went backstage, and met Elizabeth, who was very nice to both of us. Then Richard said, 'I want my girl to taste some of your Armenian food.'

"Well, this was fine by me, and I told him I'd cook an Armenian dinner for him after the show a week from Saturday. So we invited some friends in. It wasn't a big crowd, but he was coming with Elizabeth. We made one mistake: we told our son, who was about twelve or thirteen, that they were coming, but he wasn't to tell anyone. It didn't work. Elizabeth and Richard were having a lot of problems with crowds then.

"When they got to our apartment, Richard said to me, 'What's going on here? Your elevator operator is all dressed up in a long black dress with a corsage and her hair all done up,' and I said to him, 'We don't have a female elevator operator!' He looked at me and said, 'Well, you do now.' It was the super's wife. Our son had told people that Elizabeth Taylor and Richard Burton were coming, and the word spread. Now, she didn't know who the hell Richard Burton was, but she sure as hell knew who Elizabeth Taylor was!"

Towers: "As a young person in the theatre, she gave me great encouragement and great support. And she always continued to support me. When I did *The King and I,* I wanted her to come and see it, and she did come. But she insisted on buying her own ticket, and she gave me a check. And I said, 'I'm glad you wrote that check, because it will never be cashed. It will be framed and put on the wall as an autograph.'"

Maggie Task recalls the closest Gish got to star temperament: "At one point, she didn't like the way the show was going, and she turned to George Abbott and said 'George—' and Abbott just threw his hands up and said, 'Lillian, why don't you just ride the bus and leave the driving to me.'"

Task also shared the stage with Eileen Heckart, Morris Carnovsky, and Shelley Berman—three names not usually associated with musical comedy—in A *Family Affair.* "Eileen used to go out with us after the shows, and she was always asking a lot of questions about the singing things. And we'd say, 'Forget trying to sing it. Just go out there and act it.' She had a wonderful song, 'Autumn Is Over.' I still hear it on Muzak. Then she and Morris and Shelley Berman had a trio, and Morris used to call it the 'trio for three basses.'"

Applause had been tailored for the talents of Lauren Bacall. When she left the show, the replacement brought in was Anne Baxter, who on film had played the conniving actress trying to unseat the star, portrayed by Bette Davis. Now Baxter was the star and Penny Fuller was playing Eve. "Anne was thrown into the show. She was a big star, but she didn't have the experience of being thrown on like I had so many times. I remember everyone was trying very hard to help, and everyone was telling her what to do and saying things like, 'Bacall does this or that.' I went down to her dressing room and knocked on the door and said to her, 'Every movie star in the world wanted to play this part, and you're the one who got it. Nobody can play Margo Channing better than you can. You know what to do, now you just have to do it.'"

Gene Foote: "When Anne Baxter came into *Applause* it made so much sense, because she was a real actress. She was wonderful, but they didn't make any changes in the show for her, which was unfortunate. She was a very small woman, and she had to run across the stage because Ron Field didn't change any of the patterns. Bacall was tall and could take four steps and cover the whole stage. It was like Annie was running all the time."

Fuller: "For my opening night, a friend had given me a picture of Anne as Eve, holding up the dress in front of the mirror. Well, when I started rehearsing with her, we got to the scene where I'm holding up the dress— and Anne came to the door as Margo, and I looked at her, and she looked back, and I didn't know whether I was Eve, or she was, or what. It was such a strange moment—and she came over and hugged me. She knew exactly what had happened."

If that wasn't disorienting enough, everybody remembers the day Bette Davis came to watch.

REAMS: "When Bette Davis came, Anne was a wreck, and she went up on her lines. But there was Eve Harrington at last being Margo Channing and having to face the first Margo—it was really too much."

FULLER: "I was onstage, and there was a buzz around the theatre, and I looked off into what would be the opening on the set for the bathroom—and there was Bette-fucking-Davis standing there watching me, with all those bracelets jangling. The real Margo Channing was standing there watching us! (I never used the word 'fucking' until I heard Margaret Leighton say it—and there never was a finer, greater lady in the theatre. So I thought, if she can say it, I can say it. Sometimes it's the only word that fits.)"

FOOTE: "As I was standing there in the wings next to Bette Davis, ready to make an entrance, she said to me, 'Take me out there with you. Take me out there.'"

What Ann Miller knew about Broadway she had learned in the movies. When she came to Broadway to play Mame, Laurie Franks was playing the companion, Agnes Gooch. "The first day she came in, Ann Miller said, 'She can't play Gooch. Her complexion's too good.' I don't know what that meant, but I think she was trying to say I wasn't the right type. She wanted me out from the beginning, and they wouldn't do it. This was Ann's first Broadway show, and she wasn't getting the cooperation she wanted from everybody, because we were a pretty tight-knit group.

"She wasn't really interested in her acting, but in getting to the song-and-dance numbers. And she was terrific in those, and they put a tap number in for her, and they were giving her oxygen offstage.

"We weren't really too pleased with her. In the scene when they were talking about getting me dressed, she would sometimes 'tap dance' with her fingers on the back of my neck. Maybe she was thinking with her fingers, I don't know. But it was really disconcerting for me.

"She tried to get rid of me when we moved to the Broadway Theatre. She said she'd sign her contract if they got rid of Laurie Franks. They said they couldn't get rid of Laurie Franks! So she said, 'Well, then, I'll go back to LA.' So they said they'd put me back to playing Cousin Fan, which was all right with her. I gave my notice, but I had to stay for two months so they could replace me. It was breaking my heart to be out there onstage playing Cousin Fan. It was really rotten."

Liv Ullmann was another movie star out of her element when she was given the starring role in the Rodgers/Charnin musical *I Remember Mama*. Elizabeth Hubbard was playing one of the aunts. "Liv Ullmann had no experience in the form, and very little confidence. The whole thing became very, very difficult. It was a wonderful idea for a musical, and it had some really wonderful songs. But for one thing, it was strange to me how Liv could be doing that wonderful role, which was really perfect for her, and never even look at the children. Warmth is what that show was about, and warmth is what wasn't there."

There are certain stars practically born in the theatre: old-time musical pros like Bill "Bojangles" Robinson and Eddie Foy, Jr., came out of vaudeville and were most at home in a spotlight.

Robinson had become one of the most famous performers of his day through his work in films, in clubs, and onstage. His goddaughter was Rosetta Le Noire, whose first Broadway show was Michael Todd's *The Hot Mikado*. She remembers: "It was so wonderful to work with Uncle Bo. Every night after the show he would do a little bit from his nightclub act, and he'd usually grab one of the girls—me, usually—and do the Lindy. Then, as he was going offstage, he would lean out and say to the audience, 'Thank you all, thank you all. I've never had such a good time since I've been colored.' The audience would scream and applaud. He was very generous to all of us. It was a real eye-opener for me. Up until that time, the only discrimination I had experienced was within my own race. But going out on the road and seeing my godfather, who was a big star, not being able to stay in third-rate white hotels was shocking to me."

Eddie Foy, Jr., was literally born in a trunk, to the ultimate vaudeville family. He never quite managed to shake off his roots when vaudeville died and he took to the musical stage. After hits like *The Pajama Game*, he found himself in a disaster called *Rumple*, with Gretchen Wyler. "Eddie was very charming onstage," Wyler remembers. "We were just stuck with a rotten show. It just wouldn't work, and Eddie knew it, and my memories of him were just as a kind of beaten little man."

The critics loved Foy in *Rumple*. His last chance at Broadway stardom was in *Drat, the Cat*, which also featured Jane Connell. "He was filled with all sorts of stories about the old days and vaudeville. He was also quite deaf, and he refused to wear a hearing aid. I don't think he really understood a lot of direction, so he didn't take it. Eventually he was replaced."

Shirley Booth, known to all as television's Hazel, was an Oscar and multiple Tony winner when she took on *Look to the Lilies*, a musical based on the film *Lilies of the Field*. In it she and Taina Elg played nuns.

ELG: "The show didn't work because Shirley Booth had her own ideas. She wanted to be different from Lilia Skala, who had played the part in the film, and the whole point was that here was a tough Mother Superior who was very determined to build this chapel in a very difficult terrain. Very determined and very tough. Then this nice, charming black boy comes wandering through, and is coerced by this strong woman into building the church. The contrast worked very well. But Shirley Booth wanted to be a nice Mother Superior—and you couldn't have two goody-goodies. There was no conflict."

Kelly was a nightmare for everyone involved, but especially for Ella Logan. She had starred in such shows as *Finian's Rainbow* and was fired from *Kelly* out of town, cast member Maggie Task recalls: "She was a darlin', as the Irish would say. She would always say things like, 'What is the Mother doing here? You don't need me in this scene.' The creative people were all very nice to her, and telling her everything would be all right. Then, three days later, they came to her and told her she was being let go. It wouldn't have been so bad if they hadn't been giving her this song and dance about how they were going to fix things and build up her part, and all that encouragement."

Kelly starred Anita Gillette. "Anita was a doll," Task continues. "I remember walking out onstage in this very low-cut dress, and Anita was singing something about tomatoes, and all of a sudden she looked at my chest and started giggling—in character, of course. In a show like that, you laughed whenever you could."

Sometimes working with certain people is the most memorable thing about a show. Andy Griffith starred as the sheriff in *Destry Rides Again*, with a cast that included Rosetta Le Noire. "On the road, he would not go to any hotel, or any place we all weren't allowed to go. He used to come to the theatre early and play the guitar, and Libi Staiger and I would come in early and sing with him. He always called me 'Rosella.' He said, 'Down South, where I come from, they called you Rosella, not Rosetta.' Just a heavenly man to work with."

The Unsinkable Molly Brown was Tammy Grimes's first starring musical vehicle. Gene Foote danced in the show. "I had a lot of trouble with her in the beginning. I don't know why, but she took a dislike to me, and it took about six months to end. She accused me of trying to upstage her. In one scene I was a drunken miner, and she was playing the piano, and there was a part where I would take a grape off the waitress's tray and eat it. This was constant. One night after the scene she found me and grabbed me, and said, 'What were you eating onstage? That's very rude!' I said, 'I wasn't eating onstage.' She said, 'Well, I saw you,' so I explained to her that the same thing happened every night. She had her hand on me, and I said, 'Look, I know there's something about me you don't like, but I was not doing anything out of the ordinary, and if you ever have any problem with me again, you go to the stage manager.' So I made my change, and went on in the Monte Carlo scene. And onstage, in front of however many people were in the whole theatre, Tammy walked out in that red dress, walked directly over to me, and said, 'I'm sorry, Foote.' Then she went right on in the scene. From that moment on, I could do no wrong. And she had hit me with a broom when I played one of the brothers in the opening scene—she had really hated me."

In *42nd Street*, Tammy Grimes was cast as the star who breaks her ankle.

LEE ROY REAMS: "There are hundreds of stories about Tammy. Gower used to send her off alone to rehearse, and one night a few of us were taking a cab uptown after rehearsal, and we remembered that nobody had thought to tell her that we had broken for the day, and Tammy was probably still down there in a rehearsal room, working by herself.

"There was also this one dress that she wore backwards because she thought it looked better. And then she complained about it, and we said, 'If you wear it backwards, what do you expect?'"

GENE FOOTE: "Tammy can be strange, but she's a fascinating performer. She had studied with Sandy Meisner, and with his technique, everything was new to her every night, even though she was very consistent."

Carol Haney had danced in films like *Kiss Me, Kate* (partnered by Bob Fosse) when *The Pajama Game* made her a star. She went on to do the movie. Zoya Leporska was Fosse's assistant, and the dance captain on the show.

LEPORSKA: "When that voice came out, the house fell down. And she wasn't pretending. Then she took Broadway by storm, and everyone was imitating her haircut. Even I wanted to do it."

Chita Rivera's haircut in *Bajour*, a show about urban gypsies, improved out of town.

GENE FOOTE: "Chita was playing a very hard character. Michael Bennett, myself, and three other dancers came in with her father. In Philadelphia, he announced her, and I had to throw open the door—and Chita was standing there in her best gypsy pose, in this black dress and long black wig. She looked just like the Wicked Witch of the West, and I gasped when I opened the door. Chita just stood there and looked at me and said, 'Shut up.' And she went on. She was very game about it. She really scared me! The next night the costume was gone and the wig was shorter."

When Jerry Bock, Sheldon Harnick, and Joseph Stein got together and created the role of Tevye in *Fiddler on the Roof*, they came up with one of the greatest leading roles in the history of musical theatre. They also created a potential monster. The role is a star part; it has attracted many different actors, all of whom brought their own qualities to the role. But actors are only human, and any actor lucky enough to be cast as Tevye knows that the success or failure of the production rests on his shoulders. Unfortunately, for whatever reason, actors who play Tevye are not always the easiest to work with.

Maria Karnilova won a Tony for her portrayal of Golde, Tevye's wife in the original Broadway production of *Fiddler on the Roof*: "I've never been fortunate enough to have a great male star to work with. Zero Mostel was dreadful; Herschel Bernardi was a disturbed and unhappy man. Then Luther Adler came in, and he was such a Jewish Theatre actor, you could never find him on the stage. He was always holding up the scenery. He was already an old man, and he had these high Adler elevator shoes, so he walked kind of funny."

Ruth Jaraslow is in the *Guinness Book of World Records* for the number of performances she has given as Yente. "The personality of each of the men came through the character. I think Topol, knowing that Zero had created the role, tried not to do comical bits, and whatever humor came was out of the script. He tried to be as straight as possible. It's a funny role, but Topol tried to avoid some of the schtick that Zero used."

BARBARA COLTON: "I also did Golde with Robert Merrill. He was a total male chauvinist, and vulgar; an unfeeling man with the attention span of a small termite. I was always in the wings, waiting for an entrance when Hodel sings 'Far from the Home I Love.' Right after the song, Tevye has one of his conversations with God—'Take care of her, see that she dresses warm,' or something. Well, six or eight weeks into the run, Merrill looked up and said the line, then proceeded to pick up Hodel's suitcase that had been left on the stage by accident, and walk offstage! Now, it defies my imagination to know how an actor—how a human being with all of his marbles intact—suddenly has a prop in his hand that hasn't been there through the three weeks of rehearsal and however many weeks of the run, and not realize that it had never been there, and it wasn't supposed to be there. That's what I mean about his attention span."

Some Tevyes were easier to work with.

KARNILOVA: "I loved Paul Lipson and Harry Goz. I had five husbands in the show—and all those daughters, including Bette Midler."

DOLORES WILSON: "Luther Adler was my first Tevye, and in my opinion he was brilliant. He was really nervous about the singing, and started rehearsals with a scarf around his throat—he was afraid of losing his voice. We made a deal: he asked if I could listen to him and tell him if he was doing anything wrong vocally, and I told him I would if he would watch and tell me if I was doing anything artificial or wrong as the character.

"Then Hal Prince asked me to go back into the Broadway company, with Harry Goz. I did one rehearsal on Monday and I was opening on Tuesday. He had both my name and Harry's above the title. It was the first time in the history of *Fiddler* that any actress playing Golde had gotten that."

Carol Channing owns the roles of Dolly Levi and Lorelei Lee, having taken them around the world. Eddie Bracken played opposite Channing's Dolly for four years, on Broadway and on tour. "Sometimes it was difficult, because I didn't want to do anything that would upset her rhythm or her performance—I wanted to do things her way. But one day she didn't like something I did. See, she's playing the role, she's getting some laughs—but unless Horace reacts, it really doesn't work. I think at the time Carol forgot that. It got me a bit peeved—and it's practically impossible to get me upset. So I just decided to do it my way—and the laughs came up. And later on, she came to me and asked me if there were things she could be doing that could help. I told her a couple of ideas, and she tried them, and they worked, and got a hand afterward. When you play something so long, it's easy to forget."

Lee Roy Reams played with Channing both in *Hello, Dolly!* and in *Lorelei*. "Carol is a theatre actress. I used to stand in the wings every night and watch her. She was like clockwork. Her closing nights were like her opening nights. I loved going to the theatre knowing that you were going to get the same performance every night.

"Every night after the show, she would analyze the audience: why this laugh was bigger or smaller, or, God forbid, was not there.

"I learned a lot from Carol: a lot about the business, about PR. I became part of her publicity machine. In Oklahoma City we both got fur coats, and we had pictures taken getting on the bus. Of course, I was taking the bus and she had a limo. But it was all very glamorous, and lots of fun."

Gwen Verdon became a star the moment she stopped the show in *Can-Can*. She took on more and more challenging parts throughout her career. Theatre people consider her the ultimate gypsy.

ZOYA LEPORSKA: "When I first met Gwen Verdon in *Damn Yankees*, I was so completely in awe of her, and wanted her approval and acceptance.

I was almost afraid to give her notes. Gwen goes very deeply into character, down to the minutest detail. She does that with everything. That's what made her real, and good. That's what made her great."

PATTI KARR: "Gwen is such a lady. She works so hard, and is always like one of the gang. You can take the girl out of the chorus, but you can't take the chorus out of the girl."

Describing what makes the Fosse style, Verdon says, "In Bob's work, the movement has to come out of the acting. If you don't know how to 'act' the number, you won't be able to dance it."

Elaine Cancilla is known as a "Fosse dancer." She moved from the chorus of *Sweet Charity* to playing the title role in regional theatre. "Of course I was influenced by Gwen. Anybody who's worked with her wants to emulate that style. She is the greatest. If I were to start dancing again today, it would still have a Fosse look to it."

Though Jerry Orbach works successfully in films and television, he followed in the tradition of leading men like Alfred Drake in becoming one of our few true male theatre stars. Adrienne Angel has worked with Orbach in shows like *Promises, Promises*: "Jerry Orbach wasn't really right for the part in some ways. But he was such an ingratiating personality, and such a gifted comic performer, that you accepted him.

"One night, in previews, the scenery fell down. And he just talked to the audience, and said, 'We're having a little problem here,' and he would just go on. He could forget lines and it wouldn't bother him at all. Whenever I forgot lines onstage, I would go to pieces. Nothing seemed to affect him. One night there was a fire in Shubert Alley, and smoke started filling the theatre. The audience was murmuring, and getting nervous, and Jerry was told by the stage manager to make an announcement. So Jerry just stepped out of character and said, 'I've been asked by the management to tell you that there's no fire in the theatre. It's in some garbage out in the alley, so let's just go on with the show. But let's take it from after where he hits me. I don't want to do that again.' He even made that work for him."

When British performer Robert Lindsay arrived on Broadway in *Me and My Girl*, he created an instant sensation. Jane Connell was featured in the cast. "I had shared a dressing room with Maggie Smith in *New Faces of 1956*. Recently, I was talking to her about the fuss we made over Robert Lindsay. He won every award. He had never danced, but he won the Fred Astaire Award. People were mad about him. And Maggie said, 'You know, we don't do that in England.' Then I remembered Robert's girlfriend sitting in his dressing room and opening his telegrams, and I said, 'Oh, you must be used to this by now.' And she said, 'No, we don't do this in England.' Maggie then told me that when she won the Academy Award, they didn't bother to tell her. They just don't think things like that are very important. In fact, she said she was playing someplace over there recently, and the exits were through the house. She ran out the exit, and she heard a man say, 'Thank God she's gone.'"

5

They Sing, Too (Sometimes)

W HAT are the differences between playing in a musical and playing in a straight play? According to Jack Gilford, "In a musical, you get to face front more and look at the audience."

Everyone secretly wants to be a song-and-dance man (or woman). When we think of musicals we think of Verdon, Channing, Merman, and Martin. But the lines between musicals and straight plays are not so tightly drawn. According to Tony winning actor Barnard Hughes, "After all, who wouldn't want to get up there and do the things they've been doing for fun at parties and get paid for it?"

So actors like Hughes, Rex Harrison, Eileen Heckart, Glynis Johns, Julie Harris, Philip Bosco, Ruth Ford, Barbara Baxley, Farley Granger, Frances Sternhagen, and Tony Randall—along with many others—have plunged into musical comedy, while singing actors like Carol Channing, Jerry Orbach, and Joan Copeland, for example, make the move effortlessly from one form to another.

JOE BOVA: "There's a big difference for me in preparing for a musical or a straight play. The whole theatre is bigger than life anyway, but a musical is even bigger than that. It's always been interesting how many musical stars never really became noted for acting in straight plays. Mary Martin, Ray

Tony Meets Annie

A Tony winner for *A Delicate Balance* and a nominee for *Deathtrap* and *Father's Day*, Marian Seldes has also propagated the dramatic tradition by teaching at Juilliard. Her career started in the classics, with Katherine Cornell and Judith Anderson. Eventually, when she took on the role of Marietta Christmas in *Annie II*, she found herself on the musical comedy stage.

"There were interesting things that were tried that never would have happened in a play. Martin Charnin tried to figure out what the final exit of my character would be. They all wanted it to be very funny. The last scene was on a yacht. They thought maybe the character could get sort of pulled away up in the air on a rope, but there were so many other things going on that the rehearsal where I had to test the rope never happened.

"Then we got an idea that Punjab might carry me off, so we practiced a way where he could pick me up and turn me upside down. He swung me around, and it *was* funny. The only thing is, when we did it at the first preview, as I was being swung around, my head hit the rail of the boat and I thought for a minute that either my brain was being dislodged or my head was coming off. There was no damage done and it never happened again. And the exit worked.

"On December 31st, New Year's Eve, the company sang 'Auld Lang Syne' with the audience. Things like that don't happen in a straight play."

Bolger, and all those people who were wonderful performers never made the transition."

Ruth Ford, who made her reputation doing Tennessee Williams and William Faulkner, made her musical debut in *The Grass Harp*. "I always wanted to do a musical. When I was at the University of Mississippi, I used to sing at all the fraternity dances. So after many years of talking about doing a musical, I finally decided I should do something about it. . . . So I started taking voice lessons with Ron Claremont, who was a graduate of Juilliard. Then I started auditioning for musicals whenever I could. I would have my agents get me auditions for things that I was right for. I never got one, but each time I realized that I'd learned something and I was getting better."

Glynis Johns made her Broadway musical debut in A *Little Night Music* after a career of straight theatre and film roles. "My whole background on my mother's side was musical. My mother was a concert pianist, and my grandmother was a first violinist in Australia, and played every musical instrument. All the family sang. Then my grandmother inherited a musical company; it was very much like a stylish music hall. I watched numbers as a child, like 'Burlington Bertie' and 'The Man Who Broke the Bank at Monte Carlo,' and all of those. I used to do them. I won Junior Cups. I had twenty-five gold medals by the time I was twelve."

John Cunningham has moved back and forth between musicals like *Zorba* and plays like *Six Degrees of Separation*. "I caught the tail end of the good years. In that era of the American musical theatre people had more of a chance to go back and forth. I sing well enough so I can do things, but it's not so frequently now that I do a musical. Now it's more production oriented, rather than story oriented. I like being able to lose myself in the character. The best results are when acting is not apparent, when you just *are* the person. That usually requires some belief in the scene and the situation, rather than having it so theatrical that you're an outsider."

After a nonsinging theatre and movie career, Farley Granger made his musical debut in *First Impressions*, then came back for more. "The singing is difficult, but the acting in a musical is the same as being in a straight play. I did *The King and I* with Barbara Cook at City Center. *The King* is such a great joy to do, because it's such a well-made piece. When we did it, we were both too young for the parts; but since we both were too young, it worked. That was an absolutely thrilling experience."

Tony winner and noted Shakespearean actor Philip Bosco took on the Victor McLaglen role as the brother in *Donnybrook*, the musical version of *The Quiet Man*. "I do remember one thing really well. When we opened in New York, it was during a cold spell. I had to fall into a tub of water during the show, and I would get totally drenched, and I'd take the curtain call and all that totally drenched. The show ran twelve weeks, and I was out of it with this terrible cold from two or three days after we opened until the end of the run. I never got back to it."

Actress and comedienne Thelma Ritter was the most often-nominated supporting actress for an Academy Award, for roles like the dresser in *All About Eve*. She made her stage musical debut with Gwen Verdon in *New Girl in Town*.

GWEN VERDON: "She did a kind of talk–sing. If she was nervous about doing her first musical, she surely didn't show it. One night out of town, the steam heat in the theatre went on and she was supposed to sing a song. She'd get a bell tone from the orchestra; but she took the heat pipe as her bell tone. It was so high, she realized halfway into the song that there was no way that could possibly be right. She looked out at Hal Hastings, our conductor, and said, 'My dear, I think we better start this over.' She was just so at home onstage. Nothing ever seemed to throw her."

Except for the extra physical stress of singing and dancing through a story that one would otherwise stand around and talk through, many actors approach their roles in a musical in the same way they would approach a straight play. For some it takes getting used to.

Julie Harris is much better known for dramatic portrayals like Emily Dickinson in *The Belle of Amherst* than for her musical comedy career, but she tried out her singing and dancing in *Skyscraper*, the musical version of Elmer Rice's *Dream Girl*. "It's another world, but at the same time, actresses should be able to do that. The approach is cartoony, in that it's broad strokes. There's not much time for subtlety, although that can come with time. But it's the broad strokes that count. At the end of a number, there's a 'button'—a sort of exclamation point at the end of the scene—that makes the statement. You're always looking for that, and you don't have that so much in plays. And those strokes have to be real; they can't be manufactured."

JOAN COPELAND: "In a way, you have to capsulize the characters in a musical more than in a straight play. You have to get to the character more quickly and precisely. You have far less dialogue to establish and develop the character. If it's a good musical, you can develop it musically with a song; but you don't always get everything you need in the songs. So as an actress, often you find that you can express things better in words, and you're more restricted with a song than you are in spoken dialogue. In a song, there are certain beats, and things that the composer and lyricist want to say, with the meter and dynamics—that provide certain restrictions and affect what you're doing. With spoken dialogue you can pause and modulate it on your own. There is more freedom. But in a musical, there are a lot of forces telling you what to do. You have very little control, and you should have very little, because in a musical, it is the composer who is God."

Apart from a stint as Julie in a summer-stock *Show Boat* early in her career, Marian Seldes encountered the musical stage for the first time in the ill-fated *Annie II*. "It takes so much longer to find your place in the scheme of things in a musical—because the scheme keeps changing. I don't think I had any idea how little control I had. For instance, I did not have my costumes until the day I left New York for the Washington tryout. Incidentally, the shoes didn't feel comfortable and I mentioned it. For the first few weeks in Washington I was almost on the brink of tears every time I wore the shoes, because they were so painful. They were absolutely perfect for the character! In the hugeness of the musical, I could not choose my own shoes, and they did not get me new shoes until other, much more pressing problems were solved. You have to focus on your own contribution. It is such an enormous undertaking, and it is so easy to lose your way in it."

When Tony Randall made the jump to musical comedy in *Oh Captain!*, he was not isolated in a sea of song-and-dance people. The show had as its director one of the leading theatre men of the day, José Ferrer.

TONY RANDALL: "I take a different view than almost anyone else. I don't think there's any difference in acting, no matter where or how you do it. Acting is acting. People say you act differently onstage than you do on film. Olivier certainly said so, but I've never agreed. It's exactly the same job. Your job is always to make it come alive, and to interpret the material. In musical comedy, it's exactly the same—except you sing."

BOSCO: "When you act, you act. It really doesn't matter whether it's a musical, or a drama, or a farce, or whatever."

When she did *70, Girls, 70!*, Mildred Natwick had been absent from the musical stage since her stint in the chorus of *Stars in Your Eyes*, over thirty years earlier. "I don't think I prepared any differently than I would for a regular play. You just try to find the character and go from there. *Stars in Your Eyes* was a lot different—they spent so much time on the stars, and the rest of us were sort of just there. But the Kander and Ebb we really worked on like a play. I always enjoyed trying to act, and that's what it's all about, isn't it?"

June Havoc has been equally active in musicals and straight plays. "There's a balance you have to find. Projecting is different, being with each other on the stage is different. In a straight play, you're not selling anything. It's an old-fashioned word, but in a musical comedy, there are certain things you really have to 'sell.' With a big musical, if you're the star, you have to make sure the audience is focused on you. There are other people on the stage doing all sorts of exciting things, but you're the guy who must command attention. I don't understand how people can say there's no difference."

Frances Sternhagen made her musical debut in *Angel*, based on Thomas Wolfe's *Look Homeward Angel*. "I approached *Angel* right away from the point of character. I just wanted to play Eliza Gant. The only thing that bothered me in the beginning was that I didn't think Eliza would really sing that first song, 'Bring a Little Sunshine,' because the character wasn't that sort of person. But I found that I could do it because you could rationalize it—certainly for a musical. When you read the book, you can't really picture

Eliza Gant coming on and bursting into song. I really had to shift gears and tell myself, 'Well, this is the part of the show that is a musical.'"

Angel also starred Fred Gwynne. Joel Higgins played their son: "Frannie's part was definitely a character part. They weren't there to be John Raitt and Shirley Jones; they were Mom and Dad. They were used and battered people. Fred actually had a wonderful, huge, booming bass voice, and Frannie has a very gentle, nice character type of voice. It wasn't required that she be a diva. There should always be people like that in a musical."

JOHN CUNNINGHAM: "For an actor who hasn't done much singing, it can be, 'Oh my God, now I'm singing—now I'm me—I can't do it, I'm locked up.' But if they can have something to act while they're singing the song as the character, they forget about it."

After achieving success in Tennessee Williams's plays and other classic dramas, Barbara Baxley tested the musical waters off-Broadway, taking over for Lotte Lenya in *Brecht on Brecht* at Lucille Lortel's Theatre De Lys. She went on to do *She Loves Me* on Broadway. "In the approach, there is no difference. Speaking in acting terms, you have to be specific; you have to make acting choices both in a straight play or a musical. During rehearsals, you have to make the right choices for your character, the natural and correct choices for the playwright. I had been trained by Sandy Meisner, and I hope I'd always done that."

Eileen Heckart had already sung "Zip" in the City Center revival of *Pal Joey* when she starred in John Kander's *A Family Affair*. "The book scenes were acting—only I cared about them more than the people who were musical people cared about them. But the emphasis was on the musical numbers—and that was my problem; it wasn't anybody else's. When something is wrong with a play, you work on the things that are wrong in a particular scene, or maybe a new scene is rewritten. And you spend two or three days rehearsing it. In a musical, they say, 'Well, that number's out, and this is a new one we put in tonight.' Well, when you're not musical, that's frightening. It's the unfamiliarity. I had five numbers. It was agony; I was frightened all the time. You can be a pro at what you do, but when you know you're out of your element, doing something else is not that easy."

Barnard Hughes was one of the most experienced and recognized actors on the American stage when he went into his first musical, *How Now Dow Jones*. "I remember I was moving, and there was a great big number going on behind me, and I was watching, fascinated. And the stage manager said to me, 'You better move faster, or you're going to get killed.' The next night I watched, fascinated, and one of the dancers came flying at me like he was shot out of a catapult. And if I'd slowed down, it looked like he would have hit me right in the head.

"The most terrifying thing for me was getting hit by a follow-spot. My God, I've never felt so alone in all my life—out there, with this light hitting you. The night I went into the show in Philadelphia, I thought about Ethel Merman and all the people I'd seen there. They all looked so much at home, and I'm sure I didn't look anything but terrified, and wondering about how I was going to get off."

Two unlikely candidates for musical comedy stardom would certainly be Lauren Bacall, starring in *Applause* and *Woman of the Year*, and Katharine Hepburn, who "sang" in *Coco*.

Bacall had been away from the stage since before she began her movie career: "I started to prepare six months before rehearsals. I took a two-hour dance class with Ron Field's [the director] assistant every day and singing lessons daily, working with Peter Howard on songs in the show. I'm lucky that I am musical. I'm not a singer, and I'm not a dancer, although I studied dancing for thirteen years. I am still very musical, so it all came to me fairly naturally. Except that of course I did have to work on my singing, and I was using muscles I didn't even know I had."

Added to the pressures on Bacall was the task of erasing from the public's mind Bette Davis's portrayal of Margo Channing (just as in *Woman of the Year* she had to overcome the fact that Tess Harding was one of Katharine Hepburn's signature roles). "Bette Davis was totally identified with the character—and will always be, because she was perfect and it is on film. But I just plunged ahead anyway, because I have more nerve than brains, I guess.

"I absolutely would not think in terms of Bette Davis—or Katie Hepburn in *Woman of the Year*. Number one, I couldn't—there was no way I could do it as well as they did. What I was doing was completely different. The musical form has no bearing on either a straight comedy or a dramatic piece. I just jumped in with both feet and hoped I wouldn't drown.

"I didn't look at *All About Eve*. I worked with the book we had. Comden and Green, two of my oldest friends, were writing it, Charlie Strouse and Lee Adams wrote the score, and Ron Field was a first-rate choreographer and was directing for the first time. It was a happy group, and we all agreed on what it ought to be."

The show's original Eve, Diane MacAfee, was replaced out of town by Penny Fuller.

BACALL: "Diane MacAfee was very good. I had no idea she was going to be replaced until Ron came to me one morning and told me. Penny Fuller took over, and was wonderful. She was more experienced—a little older than Diane—and created a threat to Margo Channing. We needed that. The audience had to believe she could manipulate Bill Sampson, my director and the man I was in love with."

PENNY FULLER: "I had no idea of what to think about her, because she was a movie star. She was 'Lauren Bacall.' I was fortunate in the fact that she was smart enough to know that I wouldn't be dangerous to her, I would only be helpful; that what was good for the show was good for her, too."

Lee Roy Reams played the role of Margo Channing's hairdresser. "The show was difficult for her, and people were a little bit afraid of her."

BACALL: "My focus is on being good—and being part of the company. I cared very much about being accepted by the dancers—wanting them to know that I would work as hard as they would; that I'd do everything I could to make the show the best show ever. Quality was first. I don't go into a show thinking I'm doing it all myself. That's impossible, anyway. The theatre is a cooperative effort. So many people contribute to the success of a show, that's the way it has to be."

REAMS: "When we rehearsed the first big, long scene, I really had nothing to do. So I asked Ron Field if I could come on with a comb and a hairbrush, and go over—and I wouldn't touch Miss Bacall's hair, but just mime fluffing it in the back. He agreed, and I went and told her what I was going to do, and she looked at me like, 'Who the hell is this?' Then Ron told me to go and sit by the closet. And I said, 'I thought this guy had been out of the closet for a long time,' and Betty roared, and a bond was established. We became inseparable after that. I could always make her laugh, and that would help her to relax."

In *Woman of the Year*, Bacall did something unusual for a star: she gave up a number, "The Grass Is Always Greener," to share it with Marilyn Cooper.

BACALL: "I love talent. Marilyn Cooper is talented. In our scene, there was no doubt that Coopie would score heavily. That was great—for her, for me, for the show."

The number helped Cooper earn rave notices and a Tony. Recalls Cooper: "We had a great time together."

BACALL: "I do not have a killer instinct, which has probably held me back to some degree in my career. It's that the whole piece is more important than one individual. I love the contribution made by other actors—I look forward to it. The only time I have a problem with another actor is when that other actor becomes a problem. I love professionals. If I have the opportunity to work with talented people who are professionals—boy, I'm in clover."

In *Woman of the Year*, Bacall played the role that Katharine Hepburn had originated onscreen. In *Coco*, Hepburn portrayed designer Coco Chanel. Nobody recalled ever having seen Hepburn sing and dance in a musical before.

KATHARINE HEPBURN: "What's the difference between a straight play and a musical? Having only done *Coco*, I'm hardly an expert on the musical theatre."

Even though Hepburn was a newcomer to the field, the cast, which also included Jeanne Arnold and David Holliday, remembers that she was in no way intimidated by the challenge.

DAVID HOLLIDAY: "Hepburn would drop little notes to me, and one of them said, 'Upstage me totally. I can take care of myself.' She wanted to shine in a particular moment."

JEANNE ARNOLD: "Kate was the leader. She took responsibility. She took care of the cast. She liked a very cold rehearsal hall, but she brought sweaters and heaters and things for everyone. She wasn't a bitch, like 'I want this, so you've got to live with it.' She would get Eric Harrison, who was George Rose's dresser, to get champagne and cheese and things, and after the show she would come up to the second floor and we would all stand around and have a drink together. That's classy! When we were on the road, she would give a huge party everywhere. When we were in Toronto, she hired a bus and we went to Niagara Falls, and she had a huge party for us. She really knew how to head a company."

HOLLIDAY: "One night, she came out and packed all of her friends who were with her into her limo, and then she realized that there wasn't any room for her. They were all going back to her townhouse. So she had the driver open the trunk and with all these people watching, she crawled into the trunk and they drove off with her holding on to the trunk door. She was amazed when people started laughing, and said, 'There's no room up there,' as she rode through Manhattan in the trunk of her car."

AUBERJONOIS: "It was funny, because she really wasn't a singer. When the album came out she said, 'I sound like Donald Duck!' And in fact she does, kind of, but that's not the point. I suppose in years to come people will listen to the album and say, 'Why did people bother going to hear her?' But they will have missed what she was all about. Ellis Rabb said he went to see the show and sat there cynically, with his arms crossed, thinking 'What is this?'— but at the end found himself standing and cheering for her. That was the kind of thing that she was capable of doing."

Singing onstage for the first time is a great leveler. The most dramatically accomplished stars have to swallow their pride and work on getting the voice to come out on cue, on pitch. Rex Harrison may have devised a talk–sing that worked for him in *My Fair Lady*, but everyone else has to prepare.

BARBARA BAXLEY: "Most straight actresses find getting up to sing terrifying. They'd rather be murdered."

For help, Baxley went to vocal coach David Craig. "When I was doing *Brecht on Brecht*, and I had to sing Lotte's songs after she left, that's when I really spilled blood on the stage. It was terrible. But by the time I auditioned for *She Loves Me*, it wasn't that horrible feeling. There was a voice there that could be heard. It wasn't pretty, but it could be heard."

Ralph Williams, also a nonsinger, was cast with Baxley in *She Loves Me*.

WILLIAMS: "Baxley and I were really embarrassed about being around all these people with wonderful voices. I had met her only once before, and I remember thinking, 'I hope I never have to work with her.' Then it couldn't have been more than ten days later that we were starting rehearsals. A cab pulled up and Baxley got out, and she grabbed me, and her nails sort of dug into my palm, and she was shaking all over. I was so grateful that there was someone there as nervous as I was."

Julie Harris did not consider herself a singer when she auditioned for *Skyscraper*'s creators and producer Cy Feuer. "Cy kept saying, 'Oh, she's perfect, she's perfect.' And I said, 'But how am I going to perform eight times a week? I'm not a trained singer.'"

Feuer sent Harris to Keith Davis, who also taught Eileen Heckart how to sing.

HARRIS: "I studied with Keith for several months before rehearsals began. I began to improve a little, get stronger. Everybody kept saying, 'Oh, the thrill of it, when the first orchestra rehearsal you hear those first chords . . .' I thought, 'I'll go out of my mind with fear.' But the orchestra rehearsal was held in some little place in Detroit, where we opened, and I survived it. Cy kept saying that I had 100 percent perfect pitch, so I had to trust that, and I took daily lessons with Keith throughout the whole run.

"I only lost my voice once, when we were in previews in New York. That was the night of the big blackout. I missed one performance. Otherwise, for the ten months we ran, I never did. And I really wasn't a trained singer. I had no business to try to do something like that."

EILEEN HECKART: "Keith Davis was a darling. Opening night of *Family Affair* he rode on his little motorcycle to Philadelphia, and knocked on the door and said, 'Half hour.' And my maid opened the door, and there he stood. I said, 'What are you doing here?' And he said, 'Well, I've got my pitch pipe—how were you going to go on if you didn't warm up?'"

Rex Harrison and his "talk–sing" in *My Fair Lady* has inspired countless unmusical performers to try musical comedy. "I am not by any stretch of the imagination a singer," Harrison observed, "in fact, I don't think you would find anyone who would argue with the fact that I'm basically not a very musical person."

Going into *My Fair Lady*, Harrison should have been the nervous one— since Julie Andrews's musicianship has never been a problem. But it was Andrews who was worried. "First I thought, 'What are they going to do to poor George Bernard Shaw?' Then I was very nervous about working with Rex. One always heard these things about Rex—how rude he is, and all that. If it hadn't been for Moss Hart, they would have sent me back to England. It was really Pygmalion and Galatea—Moss made me be Eliza."

HARRISON: "I had the great good fortune of having sterling colleagues and a foolproof role. When I started on the project, I had enormous difficulty with it, and went to a singing teacher who was highly recommended. And it did no good at all. I have a range of about one and a half notes, and that's that."

Though she'd been singing on the stage since childhood, Andrews was not immune to the strains of performing *My Fair Lady* every night. "My voice was ragged from belting. Then I had my tonsils out in my early twenties, and I thought I would never sing again. I took on *Camelot* very tentatively. I got my voice back, but there was an enormous period of anxiety. But *Camelot* was a good level for me, just my size and weight. I enjoyed it much more than *My Fair Lady*."

Musical comedy performers going into straight drama or comedy are just as nervous facing roles without the security of being able to burst into song or dance.

Louise Troy has had success on both stages. "My debut was in *Pipe Dream*, and I really did not want to do musicals. I was an actress. So that was a really strange experience. There were sixteen of us—sixteen—in the bowels of the Shubert Theatre. Sixteen ingenues in one dressing room. Because I was much more of an actress than a singer, I was coaching some of the girls on the sly."

Chita Rivera has stepped off the musical stage to do such dramas as Tennessee Williams's *The Rose Tattoo*. "Fear is always of the unknown, until you get there and you must go ahead and do it—open your mouth and let the first words come out. I thought I'd die in rehearsals for *The Rose Tattoo*. I had to wipe out of my head the great women who have done that role yet keep some of the images, because Anna Magnani was so brilliant. Then, going back to musicals, I was more confident. I felt like more of a person, a stronger person."

Musical performers who want to stretch into straight theatre are also subject to prejudice and stereotyping. Gwen Verdon starred on Broadway in a short-lived mystery with no music or dancing, *Children! Children!*, and on film in *Cocoon, Cocoon, the Return*, and Woody Allen's *Alice*. "I'm still waiting to be considered an actress. I don't think I'm accepted as *just* an actress. People think of me as Lola. They still don't think I was acting in between the song and the dance numbers. It's much easier to make the transition from singer to actress than from dancer to actress because people think of dancers as being mute. I can't tell you how often I've heard people say, 'Oh, she can't open her mouth. She can't talk.' I must have been saying *something* up there on that stage for all those years. *Children! Children!*, unfortunately, only ran three weeks in previews and then closed on opening night in New York, but all the prepublicity that came out was about the fact that Gwen Verdon was acting for the first time, and I became a little belligerent about it, which I shouldn't have. But people still feel, Oh, she's just a dancer."

JOE BOVA: "Carol Channing is one who never really crossed over to the realm of doing straight plays. Her whole focus is much bigger. The fact that you have to fill a theatre creates a certain style that does become larger than life. You can't define it.

TAMMY GRIMES: "The change is mostly physical and vocal. It's much bigger. If you have a big, big part and you have to do a lot of singing, a lot of dancing, that means you are the main focal point of that musical. And that means if you don't do it all, the musical won't work. It's all going to be down the tubes. You have an unbelievable responsibility. When you do a musical, you must really be very, very disciplined."

Chris Sarandon moves around in film, drama, and musical comedy. "Getting ready for a musical is like preparing for an athletic event. You have to go into training. I think doing Shakespeare is simpler. Here [in musicals] you have to get your voice, your body, and the whole thing together. You can't be a reprobate and do musicals. Well, the theatre is full of people who have been reprobates and have done musicals and Shakespeare. But for me, I have to be in a disciplined state of mind. You can't stay up late, or smoke or go out partying."

BACALL: "Musicals are very tiring; the effect is cumulative. So by the end of a week you're weary. One day is not enough time to regroup—to rest and then build yourself up again. If you really collapse, you'd need a week to recover. The minute I stopped playing *Applause*—which ended in London and had taken five years off my life—my body fell apart. Because that daily discipline was over."

Most actors survive their brush with musical fame, and many of them—secretly, or not so secretly—want to try it again.

GLYNIS JOHNS: "I would love to do another musical. I'm really only happy when there's music around me. I can still dance, you see. At Stewart Granger's birthday party . . . they had a Highland piper in, playing the bagpipes in full dress. I just threw off my shoes and did the Highland Fling, and they all nearly fainted because they didn't know that I won All-England four years running for the Highland Fling, and I could do the sword dance. Jimmy Granger kept saying, 'My God—you've got to do another musical.'"

BARNARD HUGHES: "I think I went into the business because I wanted to be able to do a soft shoe. It's the perfect fantasy."

6

Trouble Away from Home

W E had fourteen weeks out of town in *Kismet*," says Alfred Drake, "which is a long time. But actually, Jack Cole never even finished doing the choreography. There wasn't time to do all the work he wanted to do."

Kismet survived its out-of-town troubles and went on to become a hit, thanks in large part to Drake. It was lucky. Out-of-town tryouts are supposed to be a time for miracles, but it doesn't always work that way.

NANETTE FABRAY: "The thought was always, 'Well, we'll open out of town and we can fix it.' But now we know that's not necessarily true. There are a lot of shows that can't be fixed. You think you can work on it for the six weeks out of town, but when you're committed to those theatres, you have to give a performance every night and there isn't all that much time to work on fixing the show."

Hot Spot was the vehicle dreamed up for Judy Holliday, to follow *Bells Are Ringing*. It had foolproof ingredients, with a score by Mary Rodgers (*Once Upon a Mattress*), lyrics by Martin Charnin, a book by Jack Weinstock and Willie Gilbert (*How to Succeed in Business without Really Trying*); it was directed by Morton "Tec" Da Costa (*The Music Man*) and choreographed by Onna White, with Holliday as a bumbling Peace Corps

61

volunteer. The supporting cast included Joe Bova, Mary Louise Wilson, Sheila Smith, and George Furth. It turned into one of the biggest nightmares in Broadway history.

To try and fix a show that just wasn't coming together, Morton Da Costa was replaced by a series of directors.

JOE BOVA: "We had a succession of people like Bob Fosse, Abe Burrows, Jerry Robbins—the best people in the business. They'd make a speech to the company and say, 'I know what the problems are, and I'll be with you in the morning and get right to work on them.' Then the next morning we'd show up for rehearsal and there'd be no one. I guess there would be a disagreement behind the scenes between the new director and Judy and the writers, and the new director wouldn't be able to do what he wanted, so he was gone."

SHEILA SMITH: "When they'd bring a new director in, everyone would make a bet about what song we would start off with. If it was the one number that really worked, we knew we'd have to wait for a new director. They finally brought in Arthur Laurents. He arrived onstage, and there was all this kissing and hugging, and Arthur looked wonderful—he'd been skiing in Switzerland—and we were all told to go home and take the day off. When we came back on Monday, there was not a word about Arthur. Then they started with the same opening number—and we knew he was gone."

Herbert Ross was the last director to file through. The Philadelphia *Evening Bulletin* wrote, "*Hot Spot* is a show unworthy of the talents of its star, and in its current tangled and tasteless condition, a dim prospect for success."

During the pre–Broadway tryout, the show was being rewritten and changed around so drastically, and by so many different people, that even the cast had no idea what was happening in the show.

SMITH: "Poor George Furth didn't know who he was playing. One week he was a newscaster, and the next week a senator's son. At one point, they changed the characters' names for no apparent reason."

MARY LOUISE WILSON: "I had a scene with George Furth, and they had changed his name—and he didn't know what his name was. There were scenes that weren't even a part of the book, but they kept them in because Judy needed time to change her costume. For a while I was given a lot of new material; then, right before we opened, it was all taken away from me. On opening night I actually walked into a piece of scenery because everything had been changed at the last minute."

Here is *Hot Spot*'s synopsis of scenes as it opened at the National Theatre in Washington in February 1964, and as it landed at the Majestic in New York in April, the same year:

WASHINGTON	NEW YORK
ACT I	ACT I

1. The 6:45 report	1. The 6:45 report
2. A Corridor in the Pentagon	2. Peace Corps Headquarters
3. Idlewild Airport	3. National Airport
4. In the air over D'Hum	4. In the air over D'hum
5. The D'Hum airstrip	5. The D'hum airstrip
6. The American Consulate in D'Hum	6. The American Consulate in D'hum
7. The Infirmary	7. The market place
8. The Palace	8. The Clinic
9. Snapper's apartment at the Constable	9. The D'hum airstrip
10. The D'Hum airstrip	10. The Palace
11. The market place	11. The 6:45 report
	12. A Beauty Salon in Washington
	13. All of D'hum

ACT II	ACT II

1. The 6:45 Report	1. Exterior of Yakacabana
2. A beauty salon in Washington	2. Interior of Yakacabana
3. The Reception room at the Palace	3. Moscow
4. A Sidewalk cafe	4. A street in D'hum
5. Berlin	5. The back room of the Clinic
6. Moscow	6. Snapper's apartment at the Consulate
7. The market place	7. Outside the Yakacabana
8. Snapper's apartment at the Consulate	8. The Yakacabana
9. A street in D'Hum	9. The 6:45 report
10. A night club	10. The Consulate yard
11. The 6:45 report	11. Peace Corps Headquarters
12. D'Hum airstrip	
13. The Consulate Yard	
14. The Reception room	

M. L. WILSON: "Opening night we sat in our dressing rooms and heard an overture we had never heard before. It was like being in the wrong theatre."

"It is difficult to conceive a property which can smother the prodigious and ebullient Miss Holliday," wrote John McClain of the New York *Journal-American*, "but *Hot Spot* gets the job done." The show closed after five weeks.

When Carol Lawrence joined the cast of *Shangri-La*, she assumed it was going to be a blockbuster. James Hilton's *Lost Horizon* had been a bestseller, and Frank Capra's film version a classic. *Shangri-La* had music by Harry Warren (of "Jeepers Creepers" fame), book and lyrics by Hilton (who died in the process), Jerome Lawrence, and Robert E. Lee. The dances were choreographed by Donald Saddler, with costumes by Irene Scharaff.

CAROL LAWRENCE: "Trying out any show is always a nightmare. I had three understudies in *West Side Story*, and you were always under the gun of being replaced. You have to be running at 200 percent all the time."

Lawrence was one of the few people in *Shangri-La* not to be replaced. Originally directed by Marshall Jamison, the show starred Lew Ayres, the movies' original Dr. Kildare.

LAWRENCE: "*Shangri-La* was the perfect example of people floundering around and not really knowing what they were doing. How could you not have a great musical with *Lost Horizon*? The basis was there for what all great musicals need: magic and fantasy, with still the kernel of reality."

The show had elaborate special effects, and started with an onstage plane crash. "If the book of this musical matched the lavishness of its scenery and costumes, this would be a terrific show," wrote *Variety* when the show opened in New Haven. The director was replaced and the show completely rewritten, with portions thrown out, and new lyrics added by Sheldon Harnick.

LAWRENCE: "They tried to include the original essence of the story, but they diluted it by bringing it out of the thirties and into the present, and including Chinese communists—and that had nothing to do with what the play was about. It bastardized the piece, and I think the audience saw that."

In Boston, leading lady Susan Cabot was replaced by Japanese movie star Shirley Yamaguchi. Lew Ayres was then replaced by actor Dennis King. King had trouble learning the show's mountains of dialogue in time for its reopening in Philadelphia.

LAWRENCE: "He had a prompter behind him at all times. They put a curtain down, and he'd be philosophizing away, and the prompter would be right there. Then he'd go, 'What did you say?' The audience knew exactly what was happening. Audiences are really very smart. The last preview before we opened in New York, he came out calling his own name in the show. The audience thought we were doing a farce. It was so sad."

Peter Larkin had designed elaborate sets, including a panoramic vista of the Himalayas made out of Lucite, which stood behind a scrim.

LAWRENCE: "Lucite had just come out then, and he had carved it into shapes of mountains, with snow on the top. When you looked at it, you felt like you died and went to heaven. The day of the opening in New York, at rehearsal, the entire company had just done a cross in front of this, and the two largest pieces of Lucite fell from their moorings and started crashing through the scrim and falling on us. It was like God saying, 'I don't want this production!' It finally stopped falling, and we all just stood there looking at the devastation. We got hysterical, with that whole speech about 'My God, Mr. Chang, this is the most incredible vista I've ever seen in my life! What do you call this paradise?'"

The New York critics called it everything from "deadly" to "ghastly." It closed after twenty-one performances.

LAWRENCE: "We were always so embarrassed by that show. You really had to work hard to mask your humiliation."

"I don't know anything more painful," says Brenda Lewis, "than having to get up on the stage in something that you're ashamed of doing, and then, good God, you have to do it. It's your nightmare come true."

Sigmund Romberg had been dead three years when opera singer Lewis found herself in *The Girl in Pink Tights*. The show had been pasted together from music out of Romberg's "trunk," with a book by Jerome Chodorov and Joseph Fields. The producers imported French ballerina Renée "Zizi" Jeanmaire to head a cast that also included English comedian Charles Goldner, David Brooks, and Michael Kermoyan. *The Girl in Pink Tights*, the story of putting on the first American musical, was in trouble the moment it hit the road.

LEWIS: "We opened in New Haven, and that book was changed every night. The designer had fantastic, megalomaniac ideas. There was one piece called 'The Elevated Railway,' and they had a mock-up of an elevated railway made, a big stage set—and they brought it into the theatre in Philadelphia, and couldn't erect it. It was just too gigantic. Thousands of dollars, God knows how much, was wasted on these wild ideas."

"Brenda Lewis . . . puts zest into the part of a femme theatre owner," wrote *Variety* after the New Haven opening.

LEWIS: "*Pink Tights* had an awful lot of music that was better left in the trunk. The music was not real music. I wound up in the show as a comic instead of a singer. And Jeanmaire, who came in as a dancer, wound up as a singer. It was a totally disorienting experience. There was no fixed script, no fixed songs; and if you had a song, you weren't sure what the key would be. Everything was shifting under your feet."

The director and producer was Shepard Traube; Agnes De Mille was credited with choreography. As the show moved from city to city on its way to Broadway, things weren't getting better.

"The hysteria was mounting, because it was just so bad, and nothing was coming together. At one point Shepard Traube jumped up on a pile of scenery that had been scrapped and was lying around backstage. He had totally lost disciplinary control, directorial control. And in an absolute bug-eyed fury, he pounded his chest with both fists, like King Kong, screaming 'I am your God! You do what I say! I am your God!' I remember all of us looking up at him, jaws hanging, transfixed. So much was at stake: big stars, lots of scenery, Romberg—and nothing was happening. That was the good part. It went downhill from there."

Traube decided the answer was to replace romantic lead David Brooks, which meant he had to find a legal way of breaking Brooks's run-of-the-show contract.

LEWIS: "They started following him around with psychiatrists—a man and a woman with a pad and pencil. And we were being accosted in corners, asked our impressions of why this or that happened in this particular scene— in the hopes of finding material to use against him. One of the complaints against David was that he wore bobby pins, and that you could see the bobby pins shining in the spotlight—and that men didn't wear bobby pins. It was insane."

MICHAEL KERMOYAN: "I always went to the theatre early, and I saw David come in and walk by—and he never came in that early—and he said hello, and five minutes later he came by and said, 'Goodbye, Mike,' and he told me they had just told him he was being let go. The replacement took over that afternoon."

On the sly, the producer called in David Atkinson, who was ready to replace Brooks.

LEWIS: "They kept David Atkinson totally out of the rehearsal place, under wraps, and we would rehearse with him at night after we played—so that David Brooks would not know that he was there."

The Girl in Pink Tights finally opened on Broadway, but it didn't stay long. Brooks Atkinson pointed out in the *Times* its "lust for mediocrity. . . . The score . . . overflows with mechanical melodies out of a departed era."

For Brenda Lewis, the experience was not a total loss: "The only thing I got out of it was my first mink coat, by my own honest labor. I'm one showgirl who earned her mink coat legitimately."

Another Romberg musical, *My Romance,* had similar problems, mainly that it was an operetta and the form had been dead for years. The plot dealt with a minister who falls in love with an Italian opera singer. It had already been a play and a movie with Greta Garbo, and producer J. J. Shubert loved the project so much, he hired Denes Agay and Philip Redowski to write a score.

Unfortunately, *My Romance* opened to mediocre reviews on the road, and Shubert decided that what the Romberg-style show really needed was Romberg. The composer sent in the new score, song-by-song, from California.

The show starred Anne Jeffreys. "There had been a beautiful song called 'No One's Heart,' and the one thing I insisted on was that they weren't going to take it out. Well of course Sigmund Romberg had clout, and he wanted the whole score to be his own. We went round and round about that number. He was insistent, and pleaded with me—got on his knees—that everything in the show should be his. He cried alligator tears, and then started getting angry like a little boy, when he didn't get his way. He wrote a song to replace 'No One's Heart,' and I said to Rommy, 'I'll learn it, and we'll put it in and see how it goes.' I did, and it didn't have the same effect at all. We ended up putting 'No One's Heart' back in, and Rommy was never really happy about it."

Shubert went all out to make *My Romance* as lavish as the Romberg operettas, like *Blossom Time,* that he and his family had produced so successfully a few decades earlier.

JEFFREYS: "You hear all these terrible things about J. J. Shubert, but he was always a perfect gentleman. The show was his baby, and as far as he was concerned it was my show. My costumes were absolutely gorgeous. The chorus people may have had fake ermine, but mine was real. The costumes were real velvet and satin that he had brought over from Paris, with gold and silver thread that had to be wrapped in paper so it didn't tarnish."

When *My Romance* opened in New York, John Lardner of the *Star* suggested that "Shubert had called in all the thirty-nine previous Romberg shows, from the turnpikes of South Dakota, the ice-packed trails of the Yukon, and the buffalo wallows of Burma, and put them on the stage together in one big wad to celebrate the occasion." It closed after ninety-five performances.

People like to say that every show is in trouble out of town. Rodgers and Hammerstein had already done *Oklahoma!* when they found themselves in

Barely Walking

WALKING HAPPY (1961) was a show that in preproduction had everything going for it. A production at Britain's National Theatre, starring Michael Redgrave, Joyce Redman, and Frank Finlay, had been a huge success—but that was the musical's source, the play *Hobson's Choice*, by Harold Brighouse. Producers Cy Feuer and Ernest Martin announced the musical as a Broadway vehicle for Mary Martin, and with a score by Sammy Cahn and Jimmy van Heusen, it had every sign of being a hit. Then Mary Martin dropped out. The setting, which had been changed from Lancashire, England, to Pennsylvania, went back to the industrial English town, and the search was on for an actress who could sing and act the role and handle the regional accent. Louise Troy was the eventual choice.

"I adored playing the part, and I did learn the North Country accent, but *Walking Happy* was not a happy experience. Bob Fosse was a big part of the show at the beginning, when I first auditioned. When I was called back and he wasn't there, they kept me there singing the same song over and over until Bobby finally came in and gave his approval—it was a really grueling audition.

"While we were still in town, Bobby would quit periodically. Then he left the show; but he did come back after I called him one night and asked him to come in and help me. He said he would be there at four o'clock the next day, and he walked in at four o'clock right on the dot. And he was great, because he told me it was going fine, but I—or the character—had to take over more.

"When Bobby left the show, one of the things he wanted was to get rid of my two sisters in the play. I don't know how he thought he could do that—but then, he also saw himself playing the lead, and he would have been wonderful in the part. Also, all the time we were on the road, they were bringing people in to see the show to replace me. I know Sally Ann Howes came out to see it, but I learned later that Ernie Martin insisted that I stay. Well, we all survived.

"I was thrilled to be nominated for a Tony for the role, and the funny thing about that whole experience was that I worked so hard to get that accent, I couldn't get rid of it. I went to London after the show closed, and a cab driver asked me how long I'd been gone from the North Country."

On Broadway, *Walking Happy* closed after 161 performances. While critics loved the work of Troy and George Rose, British comedian Norman Wisdom did not have the charisma to carry a big Broadway musical.

———

trouble on the road with *Carousel*. The show starred John Raitt. "Work on the show was very slow and laborious," Raitt recalls. "When we opened in New Haven, the curtain came down at a quarter to one. After the show every night, Oscar would write until three or four in the morning, and then at nine o'clock we'd get the changes, and rehearse until five, and then play the show. Mr. and Mrs. God were still in the show, and when we got to Boston, I remember the *Christian Science Monitor* saying you couldn't have a Mr. and Mrs. God. Well, Dick and Oscar were walking across the Common from the Colonial Theatre to the Ritz Carlton after the show, and Dick, with that wry sense of humor, said, 'Oscar, we've got to get God out of that park. Put him on a ladder. Put him anywhere.' And that's how the ladder scene—the Starkeeper—evolved."

Carousel was adapted from Ferenc Molnar's play *Liliom*. It was directed by *Oklahoma!* director Rouben Mamoulian.

RAITT: "We had a problem about ending the show, and it was Mamoulian's idea when the Starkeeper said, 'Time's running out, Billy,' and Billy says, 'I want an extension.' And it really worked. They wanted to go on to Philadelphia, but in this business, if you postpone the opening, people really think you're in trouble, and it affects the way you're received."

Carousel opened at the Majestic Theatre and ran 890 performances. The film version was less than successful. Later on, Raitt and his original Julie, Jan Clayton, recreated the Bench Scene ("If I Loved You") for a Rodgers and Hammerstein celebration on television's *Ed Sullivan Show*. Fortunately, a classic moment in musical comedy has been preserved in its entirety.

Another adaptation, *The Gay Life*, imported Walter Chiari to play Anatol, the Viennese rake of Arthur Schnitzler's turn-of-the-century comedy. Chiari was an Italian movie star, best remembered for his affair with Ava Gardner. In *The Gay Life* his leading lady was Barbara Cook. "He was thought of as the quintessential Latin lover, which was one of the reasons he was cast," Cook remembers laughingly. "But he wasn't one of those 'Let me take you to the Casbah' Latin lovers. He was actually like a little bunny rabbit that had to be taken care of. He was very helpless."

The musical had a score by Arthur Schwartz and Howard Dietz.

COOK: "From the very beginning, there were problems with Walter. He had terrible trouble sleeping, so we didn't start rehearsals until noon—or one, even. He was taking all these sleep suppositories, or whatever, that he would send off to France for—and that still wasn't working. He was the sort of man who needed lots of attention. He wasn't used to the kind of discipline that was needed. I just adored him, and it has nothing to do with what I thought of him personally. His experience in Italy had been mostly as an improvisational comedy actor. They never did the same thing on successive nights. But that doesn't necessarily give you the kind of discipline you need to do the same show eight times a week with the same dialogue. In fact, it makes it more difficult. He had a great deal of charm, but it was lost on the audience because he was hard to understand. He didn't sing terribly well— he had a kind of raspy sound. But he had a great, great comic sense, and he was very sexy."

The cast included Anita Gillette as one of Chiari's women. "I had only one scene and one song, and the most beautiful gown in the whole show. I had the first scene, where Jules Munshin tries to convince me not to commit suicide by jumping off the bridge. My song was 'I Lost the Love of Anatol.' It was a beautiful song. Then you never heard about me for the rest of the show."

In Detroit, the producers decided to cut Gillette's part completely.

GILLETTE: "They tried to bring me back in the second act, but there were just too many women in the show [also featured were Elizabeth Allen, Jeanne Bal, and Yvonne Constant]. They didn't know what to do with me, and Kermit Bloomgarden [the producer] took me aside and said, 'You're just too strong.' He said it was too much, it was out of balance. And I believed him. At least, I wanted to believe him."

But this was a minor problem. The show lacked focus, and in Toronto, director Gerald Freedman was replaced by Herbert Ross, who was already doing the choreography.

COOK: "The show was episodic. I played the young girl who's sort of like Gigi. There were all these vignettes with all the other women he's involved with. One idea Herbert Ross came up with—which, naturally, I loved—was for me to play all of the women's roles. But there were protests about giving me all that responsibility, and they also got cold feet because they felt there really wasn't time. It was an interesting idea. It might have helped."

The Toronto *Daily Star* called it "a *Gigi*-like musical with a Viennese accent. The accent in *The Gay Life* is uncertain and excessive, like virtually everything else in the busy and gluttonous production."

Cook: "We all worked so hard on that show. You just can't let yourself get down. I always have to have hope that you and the people around you can pull this off. It's always disappointing when a show doesn't work. No matter how hard you prepare yourself, you're never really prepared."

When it opened, Walter Kerr wrote in the *Herald Tribune* that the librettists' flair was "approximately as continental as a box of Cracker Jack." But Barbara Cook got unanimous raves: "As she lifts her sweet, precise voice and opens her earnest child's eyes," wrote Walter Kerr, "all of the atmosphere that has been lying in wait, unused, now wraps itself around her. . . . Whatever those other people are in, Miss Cook is in a success. . . ."

The Gay Life was closed down after a few months on Broadway. "Magic Moment," Cook's big ballad in the show, was recorded by Nat King Cole.

Anita Gillette was cast as New York Mayor Jimmy Walker's mistress in *Jimmy*, which co-starred nightclub impressionist Frank Gorshin and Julie Wilson. "Julie Wilson and I had to work very hard," remembers Gillette, "to make those parts come alive."

With music and lyrics by Bill and Patti Jacob, the show was produced by Jack Warner, who had insisted on Gorshin for the role.

Gillette: "Personally, I think Frank Gorshin was miscast. I don't think he had anywhere near the qualities Jimmy Walker needed. He was more like a punk from Philly. But Jack Warner loved Jimmy Cagney, and when Frank came in and did his Cagney thing, Jack said, 'This is my man.' They said, 'But he's not Jimmy Walker,' and Jack said, 'I don't care—I won't put my money in the show unless he does it.' That was it."

Not the least of the show's problems was the clash of personalities between Gorshin and director Joseph Anthony. Julie Wilson, the quintessential cabaret artist, had already been proclaimed a star on the London West End stage when she was cast as the neglected first wife in *Jimmy*.

Julie Wilson: "Frank was very reticent to accept Joe Anthony's direction. And Joe got so upset, he wound up in the hospital with pneumonia.

"Frank was unhappy, because he felt he didn't have a song with great quality. Anita didn't either. I was the lucky one. I had a great torch song called 'I Only Want to Laugh' and a marching song called 'The Charming Son of a Bitch.' Then I had another ballad, called 'Jimmy.' Egos were flying, and everybody wanted something better. Joe Anthony came to me and said, 'Frank wants your song "I Only Want to Laugh."' I said, 'Give it to him. I want a job, and I want this to be a hit, and I want to run on Broadway. So if it'll make it work, try it out.' They tried it out in Philadelphia. Then Anita was unhappy, so they took 'Jimmy,' my torch song, and rewrote it for her. It was okay—it worked out. So they gave me back 'I Only Want to Laugh.'"

Jimmy arrived at the Winter Garden theatre in October.

WILSON: "Opening night, we were all called onstage five minutes before the curtain went up. Mr. Anthony addressed us all—terribly elegant, very well spoken. He said, 'Ladies and gentlemen, I wish to thank you all for treating this production as a hit show, and for working very hard. You have my respect and admiration. To continue, I am sure that all of you are aware that Mr. Gorshin and I have never seen eye-to-eye. So tonight is the test: it's all right that he could not abide by my direction. So, Frank, have it your way. Do it your way—but for God's sake, do it with conviction. Good luck to you all.' Now, is that a speech two minutes before you go onstage opening night? The show went straight downhill. It was like we were in quicksand."

GILLETTE: "That night was hard, hard work for Julie and me."

The critics spent almost as much time sympathizing with Wilson and Gillette as they did berating the weak book and score. "This was not the kind of show that could be stopped," wrote Clive Barnes in the New York *Times*, "but every so often both of these girls threatened to start it." Richard Watts, Jr., of the New York *Post*, wrote, "Julie Wilson has the most difficult and unrewarding role as the discarded wife because she must chiefly stand around and look nobly sacrificial, which she does with credibility."

Pleasures and Palaces was Frank Loesser's follow-up to *How to Succeed in Business without Really Trying*. *How to Succeed* had won the Pulitzer Prize and almost every award imaginable; *Pleasures and Palaces* never made it out of Detroit. Loesser had teamed up with playwright/librettist Samuel Spewack (*Kiss Me, Kate*) for the story about Catherine the Great and John Paul Jones based on Spewack's bomb of a few years earlier, *Once There Was a Russian*. Featured in the show was Phyllis Newman. "I must say, when I read the script, I did not think it would work. I thought my role, and the show, had problems. The story was told in a disjointed way; the numbers were sprawling."

Loesser wrote a score that was on the operatic side, and hired Bob Fosse to direct and choreograph. They scheduled an April 19, 1965, opening at the Lunt–Fontanne Theatre on Broadway, and headed out of town. When the show opened in Detroit, Newman, as a nymphomaniac countess, was supplying most of the laughs.

NEWMAN: "The character had wonderful things. Frank Loesser wrote an eleven o'clock number for me out of town called 'Pleasures and Palaces.' Just working on that number with Bob Fosse was worth the whole price of admission. He was a wonderful director, full of humor."

Also in the cast was Laurie Franks: "We had a nine-day technical rehearsal; it was incredible how long it was before Bobby got the show the way they wanted it."

The Detroit reviews were devastating. The *Detroit News* ran the headline "Palaces, Da, Pleasures, Nyet," and critic Jay Carr went on to say that *"Pleasures and Palaces* is lesser Loesser . . . a stultifying scissors-and-paste job."

After changes in the script, score, and cast, Loesser decided that *Pleasures and Palaces* couldn't be saved.

NEWMAN: "It was horrible—everybody had worked on it for such a long time. I was surprised when I heard that we were going to close on the road and not come to New York."

FRANKS: "We were all called in to the theatre, and Bobby was sitting on the edge of the stage with his legs dangling over, and his hands resting on the stage. He said, 'Well, kids, this is it. We're not going to Boston, and we're not going to Broadway. We're not going to make it. The only good thing I can say is that since we're not giving you a week's notice, you can get the extra week's pay'—or whatever it was back then. I think he felt like we were all family and he had let us down."

Franks was in the singing chorus. But by this stage in his career, Fosse had already adopted a family of dancers—gypsies he used over and over again.

FRANKS: "These kids went up onstage, and went through a number he had been working on. It hadn't gone into the show yet, but they knew the show was closing, and they wanted him to know that they had learned it for him."

Frank Loesser died four years later. Had he lived, *Pleasures and Palaces* would no doubt have lived on in some form; the score recycled and songs found their way into other works. Loesser wasted nothing, as Laurie Franks recalls. "The day we got the closing notice, I ran into Frank Loesser on the way up to the dressing room. He was talking about what could happen to shows, and how things could change. Then he told me how 'Standing on the Corner' was written originally for *Guys and Dolls*, but it was cut. Then, when they were in trouble out of town with *Most Happy Fella*, he just put it in."

The Rothschilds found success only in its second incarnation, twenty years after its 1970 Broadway premiere. Originally, the Jerry Bock/Sheldon Harnick musical came into New York a very expensive disappointment. In the story of the Rothschild family's rise, Leila Martin played the role of Mama Rothschild: "On the road, two songs of mine were cut. Believe me, those two songs would have made my role much more important. The director didn't think my character should be that important. There was one wonderful song where Mama Rothschild talked about her children being dispersed to different parts of the world, and it centered around a map. Well, the director said, 'I will not have this number end my first act.' The composers said, 'Try it in Detroit.' But they had cut all the dialogue explaining it—so it really wasn't allowed to work."

Bock and Harnick's last project had been *Fiddler on the Roof*. After *The Rothschilds*, they never worked together again.

MARTIN: "We never saw any friction or anything. But what do you do to follow *Fiddler?*"

In Detroit, director Derek Goldby was replaced by Michael Kidd. Chris Sarandon, who had been playing one son, was switched to the role of another. There were a lot of radical changes.

CHRIS SARANDON: "Being new to the business, it never occurred to me that all this wasn't normal. There's always some drastic change. Derek's being fired was ours."

Out-of-town reviews were mediocre to deadly. In Detroit, Jay Carr of the *Detroit News* wrote that Kidd wasn't "able to escape the fact that stage Jewishness is becoming as hackneyed by cliché as stage Irishness was a generation ago. . . . I found its chassidic timesteps embarrassing."

The Philadelphia *Evening Bulletin* called it "leaden" and "pompous."

SARANDON: "With the change in directors, the show moved away from the family. Derek was a director of straight plays. He had done *Rosencrantz and Guildenstern Are Dead*. Michael Kidd was much more a person of musical comedy. He was a very pragmatic guy, and that's how he approached the show. How do we get from A to B, and C to D. It was more about how we get the scenery moved. I can understand where people who had bigger parts and found things missing would have been really upset."

MARTIN: "The damage was really done to the show in Detroit, and there wasn't enough time to fix it. If they had been able to close down and work on it for another few weeks, it would have worked. It was almost wonderful. The music was terrific, and there was the basis of a really good story. But we lost the intimacy, the reality."

When *The Rothschilds* opened on Broadway, Martin Gottfried wrote in *Women's Wear Daily*, "This lead-footed and overstuffed musical, oldest of old-fashioned, only represents the vulgarity of money and the vulgarization of Jewishness." Some critics found that "making money" was not an endearing theme for a musical. *The Rothschilds's* backers didn't make any at all. It closed in less than a year. But there was a happy ending: twenty years later,

The Rothschilds was revamped and scaled down for an off-Broadway production. Finally it was a hit, and ran for almost two years.

Perhaps the most legendary out-of-town fiasco was *Annie II*, the Martin Charnin/Charles Strouse venture. It's predecessor, *Annie*, complete with orphans and dog, was a colossal hit. The sequel should have been easy.

Marian Seldes played a character called Marietta Christmas when *Annie II* opened in Washington. "I had no idea on opening night, when my character chose to sing 'The Sun Will Come Out Tomorrow' for the audition scene in the show, that the audience would be appalled; that in a sense, the song had become an anthem, it had become a part of people's childhoods, something that represented all good things to all people, and my character almost made a mockery of it."

Dorothy Loudon had made a huge success in the original as the villainness, Miss Hannigan. "We never had a complete run-through until the first paying audience came in Washington. Down at the rehearsal place, we were all doing things in separate rooms. When you see things in segments and you don't see the whole thing, you don't realize that the whole thing isn't working. So it was shocking to realize after that first performance that we were in an awful lot of trouble."

Michael Cone played Fiorello LaGuardia, and was eventually written out of the show. "It was like a *Forbidden Broadway* version of *Annie*, sort of like the *Annie* that they always wanted to see, like a *Saturday Night Live* version of the original. They were really setting themselves up. One of my favorite lines was Miss Hannigan's 'Hey, Annie, tonight you're going to see Sheepshead Bay from the bottom!' In an interview, Tom Meehan [the librettist] talked about the little girls in the 'velvet dresses' and how scared they were by the show, because they were trying to kill Annie."

SELDES: "The stronger Dorothy Loudon was, the less the audience responded to her character. Dorothy did some marvelous things on the stage—she had to carry the show."

CONE: "They made Hannigan much more matronly and warm. Dorothy called it her 'Shirley Booth.' And they gave her a really touching number called 'You Go On.' You realized what a hard life she had had. Then they pulled the plug. It was just starting to work."

LOUDON: "I hate to say this, because it's like I'm cutting my own throat, but I think it was a mistake to put the emphasis on Miss Hannigan. It just didn't work. They gave Miss Hannigan a boyfriend! Right away they were in trouble. The reason people rooted for Hannigan in the first place was that she didn't have anything; she was trapped. Now she had everything, and she was going to marry Daddy Warbucks—and there was nothing to root for."

The show closed in Washington. It was resurrected several months later in workshop at the Goodspeed Opera House in Connecticut. Marian Seldes came back to find her part completely altered. "I was no longer a high-class Connecticut congresswoman. I was someone named Miss Stark, a rather low-class lady from the Bronx. Toward the end of the workshop I felt that most of my contribution to the character was diminished, that they wanted a more clichéd, or recognizable, 'heavy' character. But I had learned from the Washington experience that in a musical you must allow yourself to be a puppet and do what the puppeteer wants. It's very humbling and hard to learn."

Annie II had begun as a shoo-in, and at a cost of six million dollars, a very expensive one.

SELDES: "I smile when I remember it, because my first reaction to the script was so positive, and I had to sign a very long contract. I thought, I suppose the only problem I'll ever have is finding a way to leave this, because it's going to be such a big hit!"

It Really Should Have Worked

NANETTE Fabray was at home in California in 1961 with a newborn baby when she got a call one day from Irving Berlin: "'Hi, Nan, this is Irving.' I pulled my usual 'Irving, who?' but he said, 'No, this is serious.'" Berlin wanted to know if she would like to play the lead in his new musical, *Mr. President*. Joshua Logan *(South Pacific)* was directing. Howard Lindsay and Russel Crouse *(Call Me Madam*, Pulitzer Prize winners for *State of the Union)* were writing the book. Leland Hayward *(Call Me Madam, Gypsy)* was producing. Fabray did the only thing she could do: "We rented our house to Imogene Coca and took a year's lease at the Carlyle Hotel in New York."

To sign with *Mr. President*, Fabray turned down a movie role and the chance for immortality as the voice of Wilma on *The Flintstones*. The family went to New York.

FABRAY: "I was out doing major preshow publicity when the script arrived. When I got home my husband said to me, 'Do you have a copy of your contract?' I said, 'Why?' and he said, 'Because we have to get you out of this show!'"

That *Mr. President* turned out to be a disappointment surprised a lot of people. Considering the legendary talent involved, it really should have worked, though it's not that unusual when a great-*sounding* project fails to work. Many factors can hurt a show: a good idea can be executed in the wrong way; talented people can be given an idea they don't know how to deal with; something that looks good on paper can fall flat when it is put up on the stage. A superteam putting together any project brings its own set of problems: all those egos bumping into each other, more inflexible and stubborn just because they're used to being so great.

The main problem with *Mr. President* was its book by Lindsay and Crouse.

FABRAY: "It took Josh Logan two weeks just to get all of the first names out of the script: whenever anyone would come on, they would say, 'Hello, Bob,' or 'Hello, Nell,' or whatever our names were in the show. We were in terrible trouble, but we couldn't get Lindsay and Crouse to change a word."

The authors' biggest hit had been the long-running *Life with Father*, and it almost seemed that for *Mr. President* they were trying to take *Life with Father*'s Day family and put them in the White House. It didn't work. They also insisted for the most part that the way they wrote it was the way it was going to be. (As it turned out, Crouse was seriously ill, and he died shortly after the show opened.)

FABRAY: "They just wouldn't make any major changes, which the show needed. Irving Berlin was wonderful. He was running around all the time trying to change things and make the show work."

The Kennedys were at the height of their popularity when *Mr. President* was being assembled. Robert Ryan played the title role.

FABRAY: "Maybe *Mr. President* could have been saved. But there were dumb things in the show. Like at the beginning of the second act, Robert Ryan walked over to a typewriter and put a piece of paper in it and said he had to write his memoirs; then about five minutes later he pulled the piece of paper out—and it was like he had given it his best shot. There were just so many things in the show that were obviously wrong, and they just wouldn't change them."

The First Daughter was played by Anita Gillette, who had an especially warm relationship with the composer, whom she always referred to as "Mr. B."

GILLETTE: "We got awful reviews in Boston; Elliott Norton talked about how corny it was. Everybody was worried about Mr. B's state of mind. So Josh and Leland told us to be very careful and not talk about the reviews— talk about the weather, whatever. Well, the day after the reviews came out, we were walking across the Commons, and Mr. B said, 'Well, what did you think about the reviews?' And we just all went 'blah, blah, blah, and who cares.' Finally, he said, 'Listen—I know my songs are corny. "White Christ-

Ethel Merman as Rose in the first scene of her last Broadway triumph, *Gypsy*.
(Billy Rose Theatre Collection. The New York Public Library for the Performing Arts, Astor, Lenox and Tilden Foundations)

Dainty June and her "best friend," Caroline the Cow, in *Gypsy*. Merle Louise and "Friend."

The electrifying stripper, Electra (June Squibb), teaching the art of burlesque to the title character in *Gypsy*.

Susan Johnson (r.) and Jo Sullivan in the opening scene of Frank Loesser's musical *The Most Happy Fella*.

Jerry Orbach: "I like long runs. . . . I can walk to work and I'm home in time for the 11:00 news."

Gretchen Wyler: "I'm really glad I was born when I was. I really think that was the 'Golden Age.'"

Carole Schweid in character as Morales in *A Chorus Line*.
(Photo courtesy of Ms. Schweid)

Tony winners Marilyn Cooper (r.) and Lauren Bacall stopping the show in *Woman of the Year*.
(Photo from the authors' collection)

Maggie Task: "*Greenwillow* was a charming show. We need music like that these days. Now it seems they're trying to make the voice do terrible things. They seem to hate big voices, or good voices."

Carole Demas: "There is nothing that has given me as much joy as the theatre, and there is nothing that has hurt me as much, except maybe for the death of relatives or close friends."

Willi Burke: "There was no choice for me. It was either go on the stage or go into the convent. Also, I wanted to get out of the small town I grew up in, and it was always New York. Hollywood was never my dream."

Patricia Marand (on *Wish You Were Here*): "If you didn't have a good memory with that show, forget it! Harold Rome [the composer] would grab anything he could write on while he was watching rehearsals. I got all sorts of changes on little scraps of paper, and these were things that were going in that afternoon or evening."

A quiet moment from *She Loves Me,* featuring
Barbara Baxley (l.) and Barbara Cook.
(Billy Rose Theatre Collection. The New York Public
Library for the Performing Arts, Astor, Lenox and Tilden
Foundations)

Eddie Bracken and Carol Channing in
the 1978 revival of *Hello, Dolly!*
(Photo from the authors' collection)

Peg Murray leading the chorus in a production
number from the ill-fated *Something More.*
(Photo from the authors' collection)

Elaine Stritch and friend (Donald Barton) in the Jean and Walter Kerr musical *Goldilocks*.
(Billy Rose Theatre Collection. The New York Public Library for the Performing Arts, Astor, Lenox and Tilden Foundations)

Backstage at *A Joyful Noise*, John Raitt with his leading ladies, Karen Morrow (l.) and Susan Watson.
(Billy Rose Theatre Collection. The New York Public Library for the Performing Arts, Astor, Lenox and Tilden Foundations)

As a prize for sticking with the tour, Harold Prince rewarded Dolores Wilson with star billing for her Broadway debut in the role—the first Golde accorded the honor
(Photo courtesy of Ms. Wilson)

June Havoc in *Sadie Thompson*, the musical version of Somerset Maugham's *Rain*. (Photo courtesy of Ms. Havoc)

Zoya Leporska (at right), Bob Fosse's assistant, teaches the title role in *Redhead* to Taina Elg. (Photo courtesy of Ms. Leporska)

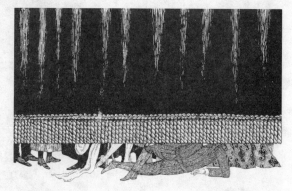

After the premature closing of *Gorey Stories*, artist Edward Gorey provided a postscript for the production showing the curtain coming down.

(Postcard from the authors' collection. PLAYBILL is a registered trademark of Playbill, Incorporated, New York City. Used by permission)

Gwen Verdon, winner of four Tonys, in the title role of *Redhead*.
(Billy Rose Theatre Collection. The New York Public Library for the Performing Arts, Astor, Lenox and Tilden Foundations)

mas" is a very corny song, and so are "Blue Skies" and "Easter Parade"'—
and he began naming all these classic standards. Then he looked at us and
said, 'But so is "My Old Kentucky Home."' His timing was so perfect, we all
roared with laughter. He wasn't upset at all."

At the time, the show had the biggest advance sale in Broadway history.
With the talent involved, everyone's expectations were high. A variety of
show doctors were brought in out of town to try and save *Mr. President*.

FABRAY: "Another big problem was Robert Ryan. As someone who came
in to help us said, he just didn't know how to come in after a laugh, or ride
it and make it work. . . . It's a funny thing about doing musical comedy."

But when a show isn't working, every performer in it has his own personal
complaint.

GILLETTE: "Nanette may not have had nice things to say about Robert,
but I loved him. And I'd like to say here that it was Nanette Fabray who took
all my good clothes away; she didn't want my dresses to be better than hers.
Theoni Aldredge [the costume designer] told me years later, when we were
doing *Moonstruck*, and I said to her, 'Remember that beautiful dress? Why
did it get cut?' and she said, 'Miss Fabray requested it.' Oh well!"

When *Mr. President* opened at the St. James Theatre in October 1962, it
was panned by everyone. "There is just no way to be charitable about *Mr.
President*," John McClain of the *Journal-American* began; he went on to
demolish Lindsay and Crouse's book, Berlin's music and lyrics, and Logan's
direction. Fabray got the best notices: "They provided a First Lady as pretty
as Jackie, as much a homebody as Mrs. Nixon and a lot livelier than both
in Nanette Fabray," wrote Norman Nadel of the *World-Telegram*. Taubman
of the *Times* added, "If it weren't for her effervescent charm . . . *Mr. President*
would be as diverting as a budget message."

The show ran for nine months on the strength of its $2,000,000 advance
sale. The day the advance ran out, the closing notice went up.

FABRAY: "It was very hard, trying to make the show work when we knew
it wasn't good. When a show is not well received, and it's going to run, you
just have to get over the pain and do the best you can. And hope by some
magic you can make an audience love it."

Earlier in her career, Fabray had had an experience similar to *Mr. President*. *Love Life*, with music by Kurt Weill, book and lyrics by Alan Jay
Lerner, direction by Elia Kazan, and choreography by Michael Kidd, opened
in 1948 and ran for 252 performances, losing money. The show had a limited life after the original production.

The book was confusing, and the librettist and director didn't seem to
know how to fix it.

"Even Legends Can Have a Bad Day"

WITH a score by Richard Rodgers and Sheldon Harnick and a bankable and controversial star like Nicol Williamson well cast as King Henry VIII, Penny Fuller had every reason to believe that *Rex* would be a smash hit when she was offered the female lead.

She would be playing two dream parts for an actress, Anne Boleyn and her daughter, the young Queen Elizabeth I.

"That show became one of the most difficult experiences one could ever go through. This may not be true, but it seemed to me that there were always two camps working on the show, the musical comedy group, and then those who were into legit theatre. It was like my feet were on two different ice floes and they were going further and further apart until I was almost doing a split.

"I thought, what better part could there be for Penny Fuller? I got to use my classical background, the legit training, and my singing. This had it all—all the magic, everything anyone could ever want. But right from the beginning it turned out to be one of the most difficult things imaginable.

"I really didn't believe the show was going to work, but then I thought, 'What do I know? It's Richard Rodgers and Sheldon Harnick!' I didn't even ask to hear the music. What was I going to say, 'I'm not doing it until I hear Richard Rodgers's music'? Well, then I heard it and I thought, 'Oh my God,' but still I thought I must be wrong. I just didn't understand how I could be right and all of those people wrong.

"I don't think the show could even have been fixed. In my opinion, you can't have a musical about a king who kills all his wives. A theatre piece, yes. An opera, yes. But there are too many mixed metaphors there and it just didn't work. It was basically a 'show,' and the subject didn't fit the mold.

"They never resolved the problem of why there was one actress playing both roles, and we never learned anything about Anne; what was she thinking, what was she feeling. All we knew was that she wanted to be queen.

"I had one big number in the first act right after a confrontation scene between Henry and Anne, and I could never get through it. She had just defied the King of England, and yet it was a love song and that was the time for an 'I' song, something about how she was feeling. I kept trying to do it, but I could never really begin the song.

"So one day they brought me in to see Mr. Rodgers, who said, 'I hear you're not pleased with the song.' I tried to explain my feelings to him and they did write a new song, but it never did work. They threw it out.

80

"The story just wasn't being told, and in a musical you have to know who are the good guys and who are the villains. It's so simple, but people muck around with that and forget it. That's why *Applause* worked. In *Rex* the hero was a villain, and we weren't dealing with the irony that there is a villain in all heroes.

"All the time, hope, money, and caring that went into that show, and it still didn't work. How can that happen? I don't know how so many people can go to work on a show that has that many problems. I guess they think they'll just fix it in Boston or whatever the equivalent of Boston is nowadays."

FABRAY: "Friends who came to see the show out of town kept telling Alan that he had to make it clearer. The show went from 1776 to the present, and he just wasn't helping the audience know where the time changes were.

"I think Elia Kazan is one of the greatest directors who has ever lived and I love him dearly, but he just didn't have the magic touch that was needed for that show. He wasn't a musical comedy director.

"We ran a year and got pretty good reviews and I won a Tony for it, so I can't say that the show was really a disappointment to me. We never made an album. The show did have one hit song. Alan lifted it and put into *Gigi* as "I Remember It Well." Everyone knows the song now—but no one knows it was mine!"

First Impressions opened in 1959. It was a year when *My Fair Lady* was still selling out, and *Gypsy* and *The Sound of Music* were about to open. It was a banner year for musical theatre, and it seemed a good idea to adapt Jane Austen's *Pride and Prejudice* for the stage. The music and lyrics by Robert Goldman, Glen Paxton, and George Weiss managed to have commercial appeal while retaining the subtlety of Austen's book. The sets were by Peter Larkin and the costumes by Alvin Colt. Both men were award winners and seemed perfect for the period musical. Producer Jule Styne chose for the show's librettist and director Abe Burrows—the man who was identified with the classic New York musical, *Guys and Dolls*. The cast was headed by Giselle MacKenzie, who was then a star on TV's *Hit Parade* and thus guaranteed to draw the crowds. Under the act of God clause, she left the show because of her pregnancy, but Styne replaced her with Polly Bergen, a recent Emmy winner and another box-office name. Bergen's costars were Farley Granger and Hermione Gingold. Also featured in the cast were Hiram Sherman (replaced in Philadelphia by Christopher Hewett), Phyllis Newman, Ellen Hanley, and Adrienne Angel.

Granger was making his musical stage debut after starring in films, but from the beginning, once the show was put together and they were in rehearsal, he was realistic about the show's prospects.

FARLEY GRANGER: "It was very miscast. A lot of the people in the show were wrong for the parts, because it was a period piece. Polly was wrong for the part. She was just too contemporary. Some of the daughters even had Brooklyn accents."

The mismatch of styles in *First Impressions* was the big problem. *Pride and Prejudice* is recognized as one of the wittiest novels ever written. Despite their love for the material, it is difficult to understand why two "Broadway" stalwarts like Burrows and Styne would want to musicalize it; but they did. Burrows was brilliant and literate, but he had trouble with the Georgian style of the piece.

Christopher Hewett was brought in for his ability to work with both Gingold and Bergen. "Hiram Sherman came up to me and said, 'You know my part, right?' I had been watching the show, so I said, 'Yes, I know everyone's part.' He said, 'Well, I have a feeling I'm going to be out on Monday. My heart is having a little tremor.'"

Sherman had gotten all the good reviews, but he managed to get out of his contract.

HEWETT: "I got into *First Impressions* because Jule Styne called me and said, 'Polly Bergen and Hermione Gingold are not speaking, and you're friends with both of them, and we want you in the company to keep them apart.' I said, 'Well, I'll do the best I can, but that's something you really can't do.' I had worked with Hermione for about six years in England. She was one of my oldest and dearest friends. When I went on for Hiram, we had a terrible row. I think I had mentioned to her that something wasn't really in the period, the style. And she said, 'What would you know about the period? Anything you know about the period I taught you!' I think Hermione should have played Lady Catherine. Imagine Hermione being the mother of five daughters! It truly stretches the imagination."

Out of town, *First Impressions* wasn't going well.

HEWETT: "When Noël Coward came to see it, he said, 'I don't think this marriage between Abe Burrows and Jane Austen is really going to work.' Abe Burrows was a brilliant Austen scholar and a brilliant man. But he was very nervous about the English style. I remember at the beginning, he said he had no intention of doing this in a 'Cyril Ritchard style.'"

GRANGER: "I think when we opened in New Haven we had a much better show than we did when we came into New York. They start making changes, and everybody gets into the act, and people lose the concept of what they had originally intended to do."

The show's creators were devoted to the material and knew it was good—they just didn't seem to know how to make it better.

Adrienne Angel was in the chorus, and understudied Phyllis Newman: "Out of town, I knew it was going to be a bomb. I remember one of the chorus dancers, Janice Gardner, said to me, 'Adrienne, you're so negative. How can you be so negative?' But I can tell. When you see people sitting around in rehearsal and not being used, you know you're in trouble. There was nobody directing, because Abe Burrows was writing. There was nobody minding the store. Abe was just wonderful, and had a great wit and loved Jane Austen, and really wanted to do it—but it wasn't the ideal marriage."

Phyllis Newman was cast as Jane, the pretty, conventional Bennett daughter, after having worked with Jule Styne in *Bells Are Ringing*. "When I do a show, and work so hard on my character, I don't judge how the show is doing. I just don't know. Out of town, we would rehearse new things during the day, and do the old stuff at night. I had one song called 'I Feel Sorry for the Girl.' It was a rather charming song. It was in the first act. Then they had it in the second act, because a scene changed, and they had to cover it. Then they asked me if I could sing it very slowly—until they could get the scene changed. So every night I'd sing this song very slowly, and the audience is going, 'What is she doing?' But you learn a great deal: I learned that I had to make it as important and fresh as if it were going to be in the show forever."

If the creative decisions involving Newman weakened the show, a bigger mistake was made in the casting of the female leads.

GRANGER: "Hermione was not Mrs. Bennett for a second. Hermione was always Hermione—and she knew it, and she said it. She said, 'If you want Mrs. Bennett, I'll leave the show, but if you want Hermione Gingold, that's what you're going to get.' So it started off on the wrong foot."

In the classic MGM film, Greer Garson had played Elizabeth, the second daughter, opposite Laurence Olivier. In *First Impressions*, the role went to Polly Bergen, who had just gotten attention doing *The Helen Morgan Story* on television.

HEWETT: "The part was actually written for a coloratura soprano, and bless her heart, Polly Bergen was not a coloratura soprano. So when she and Hermione sang together, she was quite a bit lower than Hermione. I had to do a number with Polly that was called 'Fragrant Flower'—and all she had to do was trills—and you can't trill an octave lower, you just can't."

When Bergen was cast, Ellen Hanley had also been in the running for the part. "Jule Styne called and said, 'I know you want the part of Elizabeth, and you'd be wonderful, but we have to have a name—the theatre party people want a name. So Polly Bergen's going to do it.' So I said, 'What did you call me for, then?' He said, 'Don't be upset. We want you to understudy. We want you there for insurance.' I was livid. I went home and cried. But I went into the show and played Charlotte, the plain friend. In rehearsal, I was just sitting around watching Polly rehearse and eating my heart out."

Shortly after *First Impressions* opened in New York, Bergen was out.

HANLEY: "One night I was home having dinner, and Abe called me and said, 'Hi, doll, how are you doing? How soon can you get down here with a script in your hand . . .?' I panicked, but I did it, and it was a great success. I stopped the show when I sang. The next thing you know, Polly was in the hospital with a tubular pregnancy. I played it for a week at first, at which point Kermit Bloomgarden called me to ask me to replace Barbara Cook in *Music Man*. But I adored playing Elizabeth, and that same week we were told Polly was not coming back."

HEWETT: "When Ellen Hanley went on for Polly, it was a completely different show. She sang the score the way it was written, and it had a truly beautiful score."

By that time, though, the show had already been reviewed unfavorably. Walter Kerr called it "quite dreary."

First Impressions closed after eighty-four performances at the Alvin Theatre. It was not the first time Burrows was out of his element with a new show. Several years earlier this ultimate show doctor of the day was brought in by the producers out of town to fix *Three Wishes for Jamie*, an Irish musical fable. With music and lyrics by Ralph Blane, the book was by Charles O'Neal (father of actor Ryan), who had adapted it from his own award-winning novel *The Three Wishes of Jamie McRuin*. The show starred John Raitt and Ann Jeffreys.

JEFFREYS: "When we opened in New Haven, the critics and everyone were on the floor. They loved the show, and it was a new *Oklahoma!*, and a new *Carousel*, and I couldn't believe that we had just opened out of town and we actually had a hit. Everyone said it was just twenty minutes too long."

The producers brought in Abe Burrows to "tighten it up."

JOHN RAITT: "It was badly produced. First of all, they oversubscribed it— they went 120 percent over. The producers got put in jail. That New Haven version was the best the show was ever done. It was about 80 percent. We got to Boston, 70 percent, by the time we got to Philadelphia, 60 percent, and by the time we opened in New York, 49 percent. Burrows just wasn't right to do it—he didn't believe the flahooley story. He's writing gags, he's writing exit lines—and it's not that kind of a musical. It's a romantic musical."

After New Haven, it was decided that the leading lady, Jeffreys, still didn't have a great number.

The Wrong Time for Singing

TELEVISION'S beloved Althea from *The Doctors*, and Lucinda, the woman viewers love to hate on *As the World Turns*, Elizabeth Hubbard, appeared in the musical version of Richard Llewellyn's novel *How Green Was My Valley*. The book had already been turned into an Academy Award-winning film by director John Ford, and the musical that opened in 1966 had every sign of being a huge success. The score was considered good, if not great, and the original story told from a young boy's point of view as he grew up in a Welsh mining town had all the earmarks of an ideal plot for musical theatre. Hubbard played the boy's sister-in-law (an important character in the book and film). The show closed after forty-one performances.

HUBBARD: "They cut the subplot totally, and that was, of course, the part of the show that involved me. It was really working out of town, too. I don't know why they did it, but I guess they had their reasons. Everything shifted away from the boy and the family to make the show into a love story between the daughter and the minister. The show even ended with a tableau that had them reaching out to one another. It led the audience to believe that there would be a happy ending, and that was ridiculous.

"The book and the movie were so well known that it was crazy to mess with the basic plot. My husband in the show and I had a duet, and we got good reviews for it in Boston. It was working, but they gave it to the character of the minister, which really didn't make sense. It's fascinating and puzzling what people will do to make or try to make a musical a hit.

"One night I was told that I was supposed to go out and sing one bar or something of a new song, and then break down and cry about my husband's death. Then they told me that the duet was cut. That night I went out there and *really* cried!"

JEFFREYS: "Ralph Blane dug down into his trunk and came up with a couple of songs. One of them was good, and we put it in. But the other one was questionable, so it didn't go in right away. Meanwhile, we were making the show longer, instead of shortening it. So when we moved on to Philadelphia for even more work, we were now thirty minutes long."

In Philadelphia, choreographer Eugene Loring was replaced by Herbert Ross.

JEFFREYS: "I didn't like what Herb Ross did with the show. He took numbers out of Act One and put them in Act Two, and out of Act Three [and] into Act One. He played musical chairs with the material. He took the marvelous Irish wake out altogether, with the keening and the wailing, and replaced it with a ballet with boys running through the woods and hitting each other with towels and playing horsey.

"Then they put in the song that I thought was questionable, called 'My Home's a Highway.' It was a good song, and jazzy, and maybe it could have been a hit record. But I didn't think it was right for my character. Then they wanted to make me more sexy, which was hard with the long period costumes. So they put me in riding breeches with a crop, and had me coming in on a horse as a horsewoman. It all seemed so out of character to me. Opening night in Philadelphia, I came out in this outfit, with the long hair, and leading the horse. And in the dialogue before the scene, the horse did what horses will do, and let fly. The audience was convulsed. I looked over and said, 'Well, horses will be horses, somebody get the rake.' And at this time I heard somebody screaming and running down the aisle. It was our producer, and he screamed, 'You can't do that when my leading lady is onstage!' and he was standing there shaking his fist at the horse, in front of the whole Shubert Theatre. I went right on with the song."

When *Three Wishes for Jamie* opened at the Mark Hellinger Theatre, critics agreed that, as Brooks Atkinson of the *Times* put it, it "has a more immediate Broadway than Irish ancestry."

JEFFREYS: "The charm was all taken out of the show. If we could have gone back to what we opened with in New Haven, I think we really would have had a hit."

Walter Kerr had not only been one of the country's foremost drama critics for a decade, he had already written, with his wife, Jean, the material for three Broadway revues, directing the last two himself, when he embarked on *Goldilocks*. His first book musical, its star was Elaine Stritch, the score was by LeRoy Anderson, the choreography by Agnes De Mille.

ELAINE STRITCH: "I had a terrible time in that show. The book was smart and witty, but it kept getting weaker and weaker. Walter Kerr was doing his first musical, and he was confused. I really didn't know what I was doing. Everyone was confused except Agnes. She sort of took over. She didn't understand the sophisticated book, being the *Oklahoma!* lady, so she kept demeaning the book and promoting the dances. If everyone had been a little more sure of themselves and less confused, *Goldilocks* could have been a big hit."

Russell Nype had already won a Tony for *Call Me Madam* when he took a supporting role in *Goldilocks*. "I thought the script was terrible. I thought there was so much about the script that wouldn't work. And Agnes said, 'Why are you doing it if you feel this way,' and I said, 'How often does a role come along that you're right for?' So I went ahead and did it, and I was proved to be right."

In Philadelphia, leading man Barry Sullivan was replaced by Don Ameche. The show still wouldn't work.

STRITCH: "I had such a facade; the only defense I had was to pretend I knew everything. It was like the President of the United States reporting for rehearsal. But this was my first time out in the big time, and I had to be funny and romantic. Everyone kept trying, and trying, and the show just didn't work. I was a wreck."

NYPE: "One of the problems was Elaine. She just wasn't right for it, and they tried to replace her, but no one would take the part. They flew down Dolores Gray, and all these people."

STRITCH: "I couldn't make it work, and I thought it was my fault. It was like being sent to your room for something you didn't do. I was crying every night in my dressing room, because I was scared, and they weren't sure about me. They were taking a chance with me, and they were nervous about it. I need someone to know that I can do it, and then I'm okay."

NYPE: "I don't think Walter ever gave me a single direction. He was so worried about sending Elaine to the dressing room because she wouldn't follow his directions, and so many other things, that I just walked through doing my thing. And they kept cutting my role because the audience liked it. [The show may have been running long—cuts were always made out of town.] It's never the size of your role that makes the impact, it's what you do with the material you have."

When *Goldilocks* arrived in New York at the Lunt–Fontanne Theatre in October 1958, it was Walter Kerr who was taken to task by his colleagues. "It is so lacking in a sense of direction that it never develops a personality of its own," wrote Frank Aston of the *World-Telegram & Sun*. Added Richard Watts, Jr., of the *Post*, "What made the dissatisfaction all the more upsetting was that the weaknesses of *Goldilocks* appeared to be chiefly in the writing contribution of the Kerrs." Elaine Stritch, who among other things onstage danced with a bear, got great reviews.

STRITCH: "In a way, great reviews don't do you any good, because you get so many people sore at you. The only way you can make friends with people like that is by making money for them, and you don't make money for them by getting all the notices. It made people come to see me for six months, but that wasn't long enough to pay for *Goldilocks*."

It ran 161 performances. But the show changed the course of Stritch's career, because one night, during its blackest days in Philadelphia, Noël Coward came to see it.

STRITCH: "I was in my dressing room after the show, having a large drink and crying, because I never thought I did it right, and Noël came backstage. And he was really angry; I never saw him that mad. Walter and Jean Kerr were there, and Agnes, thank God, was there to hear it. And there's Noël Coward, and I'm drying my tears and opening the door, and he said, 'What in Christ's name is the matter with you?' I said, 'Nothing, I'm fine.' And he said to the powers that be, 'You have no book, forgettable tunes—the only good thing in your entire production is Elaine Stritch, and she's crying. Something has got to be wrong.' It was like a wonderful movie—'Not guilty!'"

Coward went home and wrote his next musical around Stritch. *Sail Away* was about a cruise director who falls for a younger man. But it didn't start out that way. Originally, there were two leads, Stritch and opera singer Jean Fenn, who got the guy.

STRITCH: "In the opinion of this reviewer, the comedy lead is the woman who doesn't spend quite as much time onstage as the leading lady, and makes everyone laugh, and sings the funny songs, and she exits as everyone's laughing; and you never know what happens to her. This was my part in *Sail Away*. I was the funny cruise director, and I had to take care of the children, and the old ladies, and walk the dogs and make everyone behave, and do everything on the ship."

In true Coward style, he wrote the book, music, and lyrics to *Sail Away*, and directed it as well. The show began its pre–Broadway tryouts to standing-room audiences, but it became obvious that the love story wasn't working.

STRITCH: "Audiences just didn't care. Jean had a perfectly glorious voice. Something I think about now is that the funny girl falling in love is a lot more interesting than the serious one. When you discover that the girl who's a million laughs, this fun-loving, hardworking broad sees this young guy and falls for him, and gets nervous about feeling that way, you have a lot more dramatic shit going on than with Madeleine Carroll in the long pearls."

In Philadelphia, Coward decided to cut Fenn's part completely, and give the guy to Stritch.

STRITCH: "I was having a ball, partying every night, and just doing my part, having the best time in the world doing this Noël Coward musical and singing the song that always stopped the show—'Why Do the Wrong People Travel'—I'd get standing ovations. So one night after we'd been playing for a few weeks, Joe Layton [the choreographer] came back and said, 'Mr. Coward would like to see you in his suite.' It was 'Mr. Coward' then. Well, let me put it this way: if someone walked in here now and said someone robbed the Chase Manhattan Bank, I would feel responsible. I always took the blame for everything. So I thought, what have I done? He wants to see me in his suite! I thought, I'm going to get the sack. I'm stopping the show every night, and they're going to get rid of me. But they really wanted me to play the lead, and wanted to know if I had it in me to work all day Sunday and Monday and learn all the lines and the songs.

"I did it. We opened Monday night, and I don't know why this happens in the theatre, but it was all so thrilling, that something came out of me I didn't know I had before. I was terrified. I went out that night and had six beers. I was never so happy to be off a stage in all my life."

By the time *Sail Away* opened at the Broadhurst Theatre, it had racked up a $1.4 million advance sale. The opening night party at Sardi's was attended by everyone from Adlai Stevenson to Marlene Dietrich and Myrna Loy. Reviews were mixed; Stritch's reviews were ecstatic: "Her performance is glorious," raved Nadel of the *World-Telegram & Sun*.

But *Sail Away* didn't run. As its advance was used up, the new ticket sales weren't there. The critics had attacked Coward's story and dialogue as "sodden" and aimless. "Noël Coward's *Sail Away* easily could have qualified as the musical of the year if it had opened in 1936," sniped Nadel. What had looked like a solid hit turned into a six-month run, and *Sail Away* closed. The London production ran slightly longer, and made Stritch a transatlantic star.

Truman Capote's novella *The Grass Harp* had already been a straight play for twenty years when it was musicalized by Kenward Elmslie and Claibe Richardson, and after several productions, made its way to Broadway. The story of people climbing a tree to escape the world was directed by Ellis Rabb and starred Barbara Cook, Ruth Ford, and Karen Morrow, who replaced Celeste Holm out of town.

CELESTE HOLM: "The show had a lovely, lovely score, and they offered me the part of Baby Love. Of course, everything of Truman's was so delicate. But it all went wrong. This is funny: when we were playing, Helen Hayes came to see the show, and she said, 'Where's your part?' I said, 'Well, there's the song . . .' and she said, 'It's not enough.' And she was right."

Russ Thacker played the youth who barricades himself in the tree with spinster Cook and the maid, played by Carol Brice.

THACKER: "The tryout in Ann Arbor was a series of disasters. Carol's part had been played by Muriel Smith, and at the dress rehearsal, she literally flipped out, and then she disappeared. She refused to get up in the tree, and it was like, 'Did you read the script? It's about three people up in a tree.

Where were you for the last three weeks?' But she refused. Then Carol Brice just walked in, and she was incredible. On opening night I was terrified, and Barbara was scared, too—she'd been away from the stage for a long time, and Carol said, 'You children just be calm. It'll be fine."

Reviews in the Detroit papers were not good. "Warmhearted but feeble," wrote one critic, who went on to say Holm was miscast.

HOLM: "I thought that Dolly Hart [Barbara Cook] should die at the end, as she did in the book. I didn't want one of those official happy endings. The book was sort of 'Disney cute'—but there were wonderful possibilities there. So anyway, I was asked to leave, and they paid me quite a bit of money for that. It was a disaster, and it was all so sad, because the relationships in the show were so good. When you see things that are potentially marvelous mangled by competitiveness and silliness, and just a lack of maturity, that really is the saddest thing to me."

THACKER: "They wouldn't go for the things in the novella, like the fact that the two women die at the end. They didn't want to deal with the negative element—or what they thought was the negative element. There was really no way you could tell it was all a memory. The only thing they did was, at the end, the lights went out and I was lying on my back like it was all a dream. But it really wasn't clear."

BARBARA COOK: "Ellis Rabb didn't have that courage. He was so new to all this. I think what happens is they don't have the courage of their convictions even if it occurs to them, because they think, 'Well, I'm so new to all of this. What do I know? Maybe I'm wrong.'"

Although Celeste Holm's name was in the original ads for the Broadway production, when *The Grass Harp* opened at the Martin Beck Theatre, Karen Morrow was playing the evangelist Baby Love.

She was warmly welcomed by Colin Duffy, who was in the children's chorus: "I was in love with Karen Morrow. I had this horrible crush on her for years and years."

KAREN MORROW: "I came in and learned it in two weeks. I was having such a hard time, I said to Ellis, 'There will come a time before we open when I probably will burst into tears and have a little breakdown.' And he said, 'All right.' It's usually because I don't know what I'm doing, or I haven't gotten a handle on it yet. So it happened. One night I just sat down in the middle of the stage and just cried and cried. Then I heard this voice from the back of the house say, 'Is this it?' And I laughed and cried at the same time. But I felt then that the show really wasn't going to make it."

Ruth Ford, veteran star of such dramas as William Faulkner's *Requiem for a Nun*, had broken a contract for a road tour to do *Grass Harp*. "Inspiring is the word for the play. It really had a message that everyone could relate to and understand. The New York previews were wonderful. All of the professional people who saw it loved it. It was a very happy company. Barbara Cook was really the only musical comedy name in the show, but she wasn't really the star; we were all starred."

After five previews, *The Grass Harp* opened in New York, and the reviews ranged from tolerant to disastrous. Some critics, like Martin Gottfried, were particularly vicious. Watt of the *Daily News* called it "A handsomely produced bit of cloying nonsense." Notices for the cast were all good. Watt went on to say that "Barbara Cook sings as affectingly as ever as the spinster, and Ruth Ford offers an amusing portrait as the practical-minded sister," and "Russ Thacker sings and dances agreeably as the youth." Karen Morrow was singled out all around: said Watts of the *Post*, "Miss Morrow makes the most of the five or six numbers that have been wisely allotted to her." None of that helped *The Grass Harp*. It closed after seven performances. There was a cast album, however, and because of it, the show has developed a loyal cult following, as Karen Morrow can attest: "Wherever I go, whatever city I'm in—all over the United States—there are always a bunch of people who come back with the album for me to sign. God bless them! The album has given the show real life."

8

It Didn't Work

"I NEVER really was very smart," says Karen Morrow, "I was just kind of talented. I never even heard of musical comedy until I was in one. And then I just did it."

Karen Morrow probably has starred in more musical flops than any other Broadway performer. She has always gotten excellent personal reviews. Critics and audiences love her, but she has never had a hit show. "I have a wonderful ability to block out things that are unpleasant—and when I look back at my Broadway shows, most of them were worthy of being blocked out. It's selective amnesia. Then people remind me, and it comes back, and I say, 'Oh my God!'"

When she auditioned for *I Had a Ball*, the first of her six bombs, she auditioned simultaneously for *Kelly*, which would turn out to be a one-performance disaster itself.

"I got both of them. They gave me ten minutes to decide and call them back. Well, *Kelly* had been hyped so much that I thought there was no place to go but down. So I chose *I Had a Ball*."

Set in Coney Island, the Jack Lawrence/Stan Freeman musical was a vehicle for comedian Buddy Hackett.

MORROW: "Buddy was very insecure; but I came to find out that comics generally are. He was great to me, but he was very difficult. I had a beautiful ballad that was cut because it was just before his eleven o'clock number. I thought that was kind of mean, but I understood. It was definitely a star vehicle, and the rest of us were just there to keep the plot going."

"I loved Karen Morrow, she's a darling," says Rosetta Le Noire, who was also in the show. "Oh, we suffered. I'll tell you, my friend Buddy was something else. I had a scene with him, and he had a rubber chicken coming out of the fly of his pants, and he was making up lines that weren't in the script. And you know, I just got so tired of all that, I just looked at him and said, 'Let me ask you something. Since you're giving birth to chickens, do you give eggs, too?' Well, the audience applauded and screamed, and he fell to the ground kicking his legs in the air. That was the last time he ever did that to me. I was so shocked at myself that I went to my dressing room and cried. I was so ashamed, but everyone else was thrilled, and the pranks sort of tapered off."

MORROW: "It just wasn't very good material. Buddy kept the show open single-handedly, and did his nightclub act at the end. There was a scene at the end where we all went into the Tunnel of Love—and we had nothing but black light onstage and everything glowed. Then we would come out and I would end up with Richard Kiley, and there was a kiss, and everyone lived happily ever after. Well, Buddy used to invite his cronies, like Steve Lawrence and Sammy Davis. At the end, I never knew who I was going to come out with. One night it was Jan Murray, another night with Sammy or Dick Shawn. Buddy thought that was a hoot, and of course, the audience loved it."

Not enough. Karen Morrow found herself out of work after about six months, when *I Had a Ball* closed.

MORROW: "I was really, really rudely awakened. To me, it was all magic. God chose people to be in a musical. I thought, 'I must be chosen.' It doesn't work that way. Luba Lisa [the ingenue] got the Tony nomination. It was just stunning, we couldn't figure that out. That's when I realized it has to do with other things. It's taken me all these years to figure out what the other things are."

The awards system is extremely political, and recognition often has nothing to do with talent or reviews. Morrow's inspiration, Susan Johnson, never got a bad review. For her performances in such shows as *The Most Happy Fella* and *Donnybrook*, her notices were never less than ecstatic. She received only one Tony nomination.

Harold Rome adapted *Gone with the Wind* for the musical stage. It never made it to Broadway. Some novels were never meant to be sung. *Angel* was a musical adaptation of Thomas Wolfe's novel *Look Homeward, Angel*. It had already been a Pulitzer Prize-winning play, and the musical had as its star dramatic actress Frances Sternhagen: "The music was relatively unsophisticated, and I remember that when I heard it, I thought, 'This isn't really going to work.' It shouldn't be a Broadway musical, I didn't think it was Broadway material. But I loved the material, and the cast, and loved working on it. And I remember when we opened, and we were grousing and saying, 'Oh, they don't appreciate us,' and all that; my husband said, 'Remember what you thought when you first heard the music?' We didn't get good reviews, and I wasn't surprised, but I was sad."

The cast had good notices, particularly Joel Higgins. Wrote Christopher Sharp in *Women's Wear Daily*, "Higgins is one of the few performers who can tie all the loose ends of his character together when he sings. His voice is outstanding."

JOEL HIGGINS: "Sometimes when you're offered a show, you just think about the part that was offered to you. I loved the idea of doing this doomed guy, Ben Gant. I loved the challenge of dying of consumption while at the same time I had to sing big enough to fill the whole damn house."

When *Angel* arrived at the Minskoff, it was with the addition of cast member Patricia Englund and an elaborate boardinghouse set.

PATRICIA ENGLUND: "When it came time for us to go into the Minskoff, I walked into the theatre and my heart sank. And I knew we didn't have a chance. The set was beautiful beyond words—but it was a doll's house. You could see every room of the boardinghouse, but it was constricting, it was cramped. You couldn't perform that show in that, it was very soaring music. I instinctively knew it was wrong. It was the first time I began to realize how important production values were."

STERNHAGEN: "The funny thing was that we had positive reactions to it; the negative reactions were from the critics. And I think if we had played it in regionals, or smaller cities, it would have gone over very well. We put in a lot of good work, and had a lovely bunch of people. If they'd had more money for advertising, I think we could have run, because it was a good family show. A *Meet Me in St. Louis*, or an *Angel*, if you can keep them open, are very good things for Broadway."

Another classic that met with disaster was *The Yearling*, a musical based on Marjorie Kinnan Rawling's Pulitzer Prize-winning novel about a boy and his fawn. It starred David Wayne, Dolores Wilson, and Carmen Mathews.

It was the score of *The Yearling*, by Michael Leonard, that prompted Dolores Wilson to leave the opera house for Broadway.

DOLORES WILSON: "They tried to stay too close to the book and keep everything in. But it was a total downer, and you can't have that in a musical. Right from the beginning, I said, 'You have all these characters and they all have problems, but they're rustic types—don't they ever have a hoedown or something that's fun?' There was the boy and the fawn, and the husband with the snakebite. There was one disaster after another. It was just too heavy-handed."

The film version of *The Yearling* starred Jane Wyman, with Gregory Peck as her husband. David Wayne, like Wilson, had been attracted to the musical project because of the score: "It was amateurs from top to bottom. One of the faults, of course, was miscasting me. I should never have been in it— it needed somebody like Johnny Raitt, a big, bravura voice. I didn't have that. That was one of the big mistakes."

The show was directed by Lloyd Richards, who had a success with *A Raisin in the Sun*, but also was the director of *I Had a Ball*. The rest of the creative team had relatively little experience putting on a musical.

WAYNE: "I knew from the first day of rehearsal that the director didn't know what the hell he was doing. He didn't have the slightest idea of how to even block a scene. He later headed up the drama school at Yale; maybe he learned something from his students. *The Yearling* was really the only show I've done that had nothing but amateurs involved in it."

Then there was the set, with a mind of its own.

WILSON: "The set was gorgeous. But it was hard to manage and change. The house where all the main action takes place wasn't even on grooves. They were just rolling it on and off, and you never knew where it was going to go onstage; and all those pots and pans hanging there in the kitchen—the noise was terrible, and I kept trying to hold the pots down so you wouldn't hear it."

As things got worse, Wayne became more disgruntled. Eventually, Richards was replaced by Herbert Ross.

WILSON: "The direction was so heavy-handed, and they were shooting in all different directions, and David was getting more and more disgusted, and never really learned his part. He wouldn't learn the new music. Then, when Herb Ross was redirecting, he called me one night and said, 'Every time I make a change, I have to go into a dissertation for David on why it's going to help the show—and at this rate I'll never get through the show.'"

CARMEN MATHEWS: "There were a lot of differences, personality-wise. And I don't know that David was very at peace with the material. He was a

beautiful actor, and had had so many successes in the theatre and Hollywood. I think he came East thinking it was going to be another one for him.
David is a good guy, but it wasn't as smooth as I think he wanted it to be;
sometimes that happens."

The Yearling opened at the Alvin Theatre to scathing reviews. It closed
the next day. Later on, when Dolores Wilson went to audition for *Cry for
Us All*, it was again at the Alvin: "I had such bad feelings, it was like I was
looking at my own grave. I couldn't breathe." *Cry for Us All* was the musical
version of William Alfred's *Hogan's Goat*, the Irish–American drama about
New York City politics. Directed by Albert Marre, the cast included Joan
Diener, Robert Weede, Dolores Wilson, and Elaine Cancilla.

WILSON: "What a turkey! In the middle of winter we used to schlepp to
the scenic studio across from Yankee Stadium because the set was so huge,
and they wanted us to rehearse on a model of it. Well, I took one look at
that set, and I knew it wouldn't work. There was a huge staircase for Joan to
make her entrance and then to fall down and die. Everyone was raving about
this set, and I didn't say a word, and Albie finally said to me, 'What do you
think, Miss Wilson?' I said, 'You really want to know? I think it's a monu-
ment to the set designer's ego.' You knew for one thing, when you looked at
it, that Joan would never be able to fall down those stairs. The rake was all
wrong, and the thing was too big. I thought, she's going to kill herself. They
said not to worry. Then they had this stuntman come in from Hollywood.
He looked at the stairs, and examined them, and walked up and down; and
then he said 'It can't be done. The rake is all wrong and it's too narrow.
She'll kill herself.' He said there wasn't a stuntwoman in Hollywood who
would do a stunt like that."

ELAINE CANCILLA: "The show was geared mostly for Joan. The sets and
costumes were gorgeous. I remember we had this beautiful tree, which fell
one night, and we just said, 'A tree fell in Brooklyn.' We really sensed that
something was wrong with the show, but you couldn't put your finger on it."

Dolores Wilson was hit on the head by a falling sandbag and was out of
the show with a concussion, as Cancilla recalls. "She was literally knocked
out, and she had to be onstage in five minutes to do a couple of lines that
were important to the plot. I had a very small part, and since I was offstage,
they grabbed me and rehearsed me for all of five minutes to learn whatever
it was she had to do. That was fine until I got on the stage, and everything
went out of my mind. I couldn't ad lib, because I didn't even know what the
scene was really about. So I just pointed at someone and said in a brogue,
'I'll talk to you about it later,' and walked off the stage."

De Mille and De Lappe

EMZE De Lappe had already had a long association with Agnes De Mille, in such productions as *Paint Your Wagon*, by the time she was cast in *Juno*. The 1959 musical adaptation of Sean O'Casey's *Juno and the Paycock* had a first-rate team of talent behind it: music and lyrics by Marc Blitzstein, book by Joseph Stein, choreography by De Mille, scenery by Oliver Smith, costumes by Irene Sharaff, and stars Shirley Booth and Melvyn Douglas. Unfortunately, *Juno* also had more than its share of directors. Tony Richardson was replaced by Vincent J. Donehue, who was eventually replaced by José Ferrer.

"Agnes's work was wonderful, but we didn't have a good director—or the 'right' director. I really felt sorry for Vincent Donehue in a way, because that kind of direction . . . well, he used to get up close to an actor and just talk quietly to them—and it was all sort of strange. At the last minute they brought in José Ferrer—the last two or three weeks—but by then it was too late.

"I thought Ferrer was absolutely wonderful. If he had been brought in sooner, he could have saved that show. He was very good and very patient. I heard all these stories about his personal life and his relationships and all that, and I have no idea if any of that is true; but with us he was so patient and understanding. He understood what everyone had been going through, and he did his utmost to make it work.

"Then the producers—there was one producer who stayed with us to the bitter end, but the others all left and went to Florida, or wherever they go.

"The show was overproduced. There was too much scenery. It looked more like *Agamemnon*—Dublin wasn't like that at all, and the actors were dwarfed by it.

"But I still run into dancers and even some actors who remember the dances from that show. We only ran two weeks, and they're still remembered. A few years ago, for American Ballet Theatre, Agnes used some of the dances from *Juno* for her ballet based on the John Ford film *The Informer*."

While Wilson was recovering from her concussion, she told the producers she wasn't returning to the show.

WILSON: "I said to myself, this is a losing proposition. I'd had one song, 'The Verandah Waltz.' One day at rehearsal I was doing it, and I heard this chorus behind me—they were all humming. I couldn't even see what was going on. And all of a sudden I had the ballet and the choir behind me, and I just sat down on the set and watched it all. At that point they took away my song and gave it to Joan, with lyrics you wouldn't believe, like how when Matt became mayor, they were going to put garlands around the toilets in City Hall. I was backstage, rewriting my own dialogue, trying to make sense of things. It was so ludicrous, it was beyond the realm of sanity, and I was sweating bullets."

The producers begged Wilson to come back, offering to give back the song and anything else she wanted. "I finally told them I'd come back to the show, but I didn't want my name on the marquee. I didn't want anyone to know that I was connected with it. And that's what we did."

Cry for Us All closed after a week on Broadway.

CANCILLA: "I remember it had been pretty well sold out in Boston, and one matinee day we looked out and saw a sea of red chairs. We found out later from our box office person that it was a benefit for Hadassah or B'nai Brith ladies, and they all turned their tickets in when they realized it wasn't *Cry for Saul*. They didn't care to see *Cry for Us All*, a nice Irish Catholic show."

The ladies might have liked *I'm Solomon*, which was set in Israel. Karen Morrow co-starred with Carmen Mathews and Dick Shawn.

MORROW: "I was so wrong for the part. It had been written by Ernest Gold for his wife, Marni Nixon, and Alfred Drake. Of course, who did they get? Me and Dick Shawn. Isn't that silly? On our opening night, one of our producers gave us each a medallion—and the name of the show was spelled wrong on it—'Soloman.' And we all said, 'Is there any doubt the show went the way it did?' When things aren't right, they just aren't right, and it doesn't matter what you do."

This time, Morrow took the show for a reason that makes sense to any performer: she wanted the job. Besides, it had possibilities, including an enormous white set of the Israeli desert designed by Rouben Ter-Arutunian, and a troupe of Israeli musicians and ethnic dancers. But every facet of the production was working at cross-purposes. "We were dealing with bad material. And as is always the case, the director will say, 'It's not my fault, it's the scenery.' The scenic designer will say, 'It's not my fault, it's the costumes.' The costume guy will say, 'It's not my fault, it's the leading man,' and the leading man will blame it on the lyrics. Then the choreographer, Donny MacHale, had all his dancers. People wanted to see a lot of tits, and these people said, 'That's not what we're about. We're about Israel and North Africa.' I did have a good time because of the Israelis, though. I had never worked with anyone from a foreign country before, and the music was good. They had probably come here for a dollar and a half, because they were all living together in a basement apartment, and they would just play their music. They didn't know from making a show any better. They just knew from playing the bazouki, and they just sat there and played."

Morrow's job didn't last long. *I'm Solomon* ran seven performances at the Mark Hellinger Theatre and then closed. "It was so painful. These shows are all so painful. And the most painful thing is the day after the reviews come out, and then you have to go back and do it."

Carol Lawrence finds the same thing to be true: "You go to the theatre knowing that you have to work a hundred times harder to convince the audience that they've come to the right theatre that night."

Lawrence starred in *Saratoga* immediately following the success and organization of *West Side Story*. The musical version of Edna Ferber's *Saratoga Trunk* had a score by Harold Arlen, lyrics by Johnny Mercer, sets and costumes by Cecil Beaton, and was directed by Morton Da Costa. "I poured more blood, sweat, and tears into it than I did into Maria. It was called for, but I wasn't supported. The book wasn't there, and the score wasn't there, and everybody was sick who was creating it: Harold Arlen was in the hospital, and Morton Da Costa was in the hospital, and we were just flailing in the wind trying to make a 500-page book come to life—there were like 498 pages of dialogue—abadabadabadabadaba—musical comedy just can't do that. It was devastating after *West Side Story* because I thought that was the way it was done; I thought, now I have the key."

After a while, confusion gets to be a strain.

Minnie's Boys, about the Marx brothers' life at home, started out as a good idea with an amiable score and talented people involved, including Julie Kurnitz, who played the Margaret Dumont character: "I had a few scenes that were cut, and I ended up with only one scene, and the song 'You Remind Me of You'—I was probably very lucky to be cut down to this one infallible scene and song. But they were moving things from the first act to the second act, and during previews they had taken my one scene and song and moved it, figuring we needed it in the second act. And one day it wasn't in the show at all, because they hadn't had the time to put it into the second act. But I still had sixteen bars of music in the curtain call all to myself, even though I wasn't in the show, and I said, 'Don't make me go out there!' But they weren't going to rewrite the whole orchestral thing, so at the curtain call, they pushed me out there in my suit and my pearls and furs, and I came out and you could hear the applause kind of diminishing, and people turning to one another and saying, 'Hello? Who is she? Who is this woman?' I was so humiliated. I blocked out the whole experience for years because it was so frightening."

Something More was undergoing moment-to-moment surgery when Laurie Franks was thrown onstage out of town as Viveca Lindfors's understudy. "We had six different scripts. They were all completely different rewrites, and they were all on different color paper. First we had the white, and then the pink, and then the blue, then the green and the yellow, and then they started mixing them, and we didn't know where we were."

The story of a suburban American couple in Italy starred Barbara Cook and featured Peg Murray.

PEG MURRAY: "It was horrible. It just seemed to get worse as we went along, and the change didn't help. Barbara and I used to commiserate with each other all the time. I played the brassy next-door neighbor, and my part kept getting bigger and bigger. They even gave me the eleven o'clock spot. Then I knew the show was in real trouble, if they were giving it to me, because I was definitely a supporting player.

"Then, at one point, someone patted my fanny and I said, 'Grazie' and it got a big laugh; so they took the bit away from me and gave it to Barbara, and it didn't work. It just wasn't right for her character. Barbara was wonderful, though; she really worked hard."

Barbara Cook was talked into joining the cast of *Carrie* by its director, Terry Hands. "I turned it down several times, but I was won over by him. I think he could talk anyone into anything. But there was not one person involved who had done a show from scratch before; not the director, not the producer, or the writers or choreographer. They were so inexperienced that there were certain jobs that weren't even filled. They never did have a dance music arranger, and that's unheard of. Terry thought it wasn't necessary, so Debbie Allen [the choreographer] did her own arrangements. Well, you know, even Jerry Robbins doesn't do his own dance arrangements. He wasn't used to helping writers structure something. More than that, he wasn't used to laying down the law and setting rules: 'That number goes. I don't care whether you like it or not.' Or, 'We need a new song that will work better, so you have to write it, and fast.' It was difficult material, but I still think there is a way to present it in a way that wouldn't be ridiculous or laughable."

Despite the talent involved, Cook declined to continue with *Carrie* when it moved from England to Broadway, where it left its mark as one of the most appalling disasters in theatrical history.

It was when the experienced director came into A *Broadway Musical* that the trouble started. The show, about putting on a musical bomb, was originally a small production that had a short, successful run at New York's Riverside Church. In blowing it up to Broadway size, Gower Champion was called in. It starred Patti Karr, and Anne Francine as a Theatre Party Lady.

ANNE FRANCINE: "To my way of thinking, Gower ruined it. First of all, he was sick—he didn't pay too much attention. He tried, he did whatever he could physically, but he simply wasn't well enough. The show was changed drastically. They got stuck on the book, and couldn't get a proper ending, then there was in-fighting. His assistant, whose name thank God escapes me, ruined my number, which was the showstopping number of the show. It was fabulous, me and the ladies that helped me in the theatre parties, called 'Yenta Power'—this great Yenta and her little Yenta-ettes. He insisted on putting the men in it, and it just ruined the number. I was sick about it. It was too bad, because the show had promise, and a lot of people saw it who thought so and enjoyed it."

A *Broadway Musical* moved to the Lunt–Fontanne Theatre, and opened and closed on the same night.

PATTI KARR: "The opening number was dynamite. They were cheering and screaming, and I went to change, and I heard it again over the loudspeaker. Then it was like someone let the air out of a balloon; it never came back. They got hostile. They said, 'What is this?'"

Critic Clive Barnes called it "A grotesquely wrongheaded venture" though Francine's performance was called "wonderfully comic" by Christopher Sharp of *Women's Wear Daily*.

FRANCINE: "I went the next day to pick up some flowers that I'd left in the dressing room—I didn't want them to die. When I got there, they said, 'As quickly as you can, get everything out of your room.' I said, 'Why?' And they said, 'It's closed.' That's how I was told. It was as if I was hit by a two-by-four. It's just the most frustrating, horrible, empty feeling. And then the feeling of rage. I couldn't believe it."

A *Broadway Musical* never had the chance to be in trouble out of town and come back a hit. On the other hand, some shows are a hit out of town and come back in trouble. On the road, audiences loved *Jackpot*, a Vernon Duke/Howard Dietz project involving some sailors, some girls, and a lot of slapstick comedy. The show starred Allen Jones, comedian Jerry Lester, Nanette Fabray, and Betty Garrett.

NANETTE FABRAY: "On the road we were a very, very big hit. The plot was about three soldiers who bought a lottery ticket, and the winner got the opportunity to meet this girl, and if they got married, they got something like ten thousand dollars. I was the girl. The show was doing well, but Jerry

Lester kept putting jokes in, and it became like his nightclub act. Then they would take them out. We finally opened in New York, and Jerry just didn't have the courage to stick with what he'd been doing, so he threw in all these jokes—turning to the audience—and we were back in his nightclub act."

One critic referred to it as ". . . an unmitigated bore, an ocean-crossing of tedium."

BETTY GARRETT: "The New York critics not only gave us bad reviews, they wrote editorials about us for weeks afterward. It was so humiliating. It was one of those opening nights! Vinnie Freedley, the producer, was a very elegant, social man, and he filled that opening night audience with the cream of society. I guess they don't believe in laughing, but they sure didn't like all our slapstick shenanigans. And we had been getting all these glorious laughs on the road."

Jackpot disappeared after sixty-nine performances.

Susan Johnson left the success and security of *The Most Happy Fella* to go into *The Carefree Heart*, a musical adaptation of Molière's *The Doctor in Spite of Himself*: "When I'd signed on, Cyril Ritchard was going to direct it and be in it. But Lynn Loesser [the producer] really wanted to get the show on, and they had to wait six months for Cyril. So they went with Jack Carter [the nightclub comic]. But the audience didn't. Jack was a strong performer, but not a strong stage performer, and he didn't know how to build a character from scene to scene. So we were doing Molière, with a score by Forrest and Wright, and wonderful people, and I got to wear lovely clothes by Miles White, and I sang two great songs—and it was just a fiasco. They should have helped Jack; if they're going to hire him from a nightclub and stick him into this, they should have showed him how. I really thought I was going into something better than *Most Happy Fella*."

When Sally Ann Howes did *Kwamina*, she was married to its composer and lyricist, Richard Adler (half of the *Pajama Game/Damn Yankees* duo). Directed by Robert Lewis and choreographed by Agnes De Mille, the show was set in Africa, with Howes as a young doctor. It opened on Broadway in 1961.

SALLY ANN HOWES: "A lot of the problems came because there was a split about how far you could go with the black–white love story. If I remember, Robert Alan Aurthur [the librettist], Bobby Lewis, and Agnes De Mille wanted it to be basically a love story; and I think Alfred de Liagre [the producer] and Richard wanted something else, because it was too soon. Both sides were right. It should have been a love story, but it was too soon. I had my life threatened. My mail got so bad that I couldn't open it; it was taken and opened by somebody else. They said they were going to kill me, and that my career would be over. I even received used toilet paper in the mail. If it was done later, we could have gone full speed ahead with the love story. But back then, we never even touched. It lost its sincerity because of that. You can't have a love story without people touching. Terry Carter [the leading man] was dressed as a chieftain, and he had a gold bangle that he would slip up my arm. And I remember in Boston, when he slipped it up my arm and past the elbow, there was this gasp, and people got up and walked out. It was incredible. I'm still very proud I did the show. Even my mother said 'You mustn't do it. It will ruin your career.' That's all I ever heard."

About Howes, Richard Watts, Jr., of the *Post* wrote, "She sings beautifully, acts with skill, intelligence and emotional insight, and her clear enunciation of the lyrics of a song is a delight." Critics were not so enthusiastic about the book and the score, which they all found disappointing after a promising start. *Kwamina* closed after thirty-two performances.

HOWES: "There were so many rows with everyone, and cross arguments. Agnes didn't agree with Bobby on something, and Bobby didn't agree with Richard, and Richard and Agnes would go at it. There was a whole network of ideas about where we were going—so we didn't go anywhere. We stayed in a great spaghetti-pile of trying to work our way out of the mess and come up with what I still think could have been a marvelous show. It was never put on again because Richard Adler and Robert Alan Aurthur wouldn't speak to each other."

Karen Morrow was cast as the star of *The Selling of the President*, which had been a bestselling book: "I read the script, and said, 'At last, at last! Here is a substantial script. I am the part. The words come out of my mouth just great.' So I said, 'Let me hear the music,' and they said, 'You won't sing,' and I thought, 'Ah—my dramatic debut.' The script was so well written, and it was so interesting, so good. It turned out to be the ultimate nightmare, the definite low point in my career, the biggest nightmare I've ever had in my life."

In its review, WABC-TV said, "The best performance of the evening is Karen Morrow's as the cynical advertising agent whose philosophy is 'if you have a good advertising campaign, you don't need a product.'"

After reading the script, Morrow went home for Christmas: "They sent me the new script before I was supposed to report for rehearsals in January. I read it, and it was different. It was not the script I had read. Suddenly it was the same old thing. We started with a bad director, and we began getting into trouble. I had no way of knowing how to fix myself. I had the lead; I was the driving force in the show, and I just wasn't a substantial enough actress to know what to do."

In Philadelphia, the director was replaced by Jack O'Brien, who began rewriting the entire show.

MORROW: "I was getting twenty pages a day. I would memorize it, rehearse it, and put it in that night. People said to me, 'How are you doing this?' I said, 'I'll find out when my body tells me I can't do it anymore.' I was a Catholic-school girl, and you did everything the nuns told you to do. I had no way of knowing how to fix myself. Pat Hingle knew what he was doing, Barbara Barrie *indeed* knew how to protect herself. It was really the closest to a nervous breakdown I ever got."

Her hard work did not pay off. *The Selling of the President* opened at the Shubert Theatre and closed promptly.

The cast members of *Drat, the Cat!*, including Jane Connell, thought they were in a hit. During its week of previews at the Martin Beck Theatre, audiences loved the urbane musical comedy about a cat burglar: "Prell shampoo used to have an ad where they'd put a pearl in the Prell, and it would sink slowly down, and the shampoo would hold the pearl up, and that proved how thick it was. Well, honey, opening night at the Martin Beck was just like that. The house was full, but it was like there were dead bodies out there. And after we opened, it was straight downhill. I've never been able to figure it out. We were a big hit in previews. We were the toast of the town."

The show was confusing and the lighting was bad. Audiences hated it after the critics told them they should.

Every legendary creative genius has a flop at some time in his career. Rodgers and Hammerstein had *Oklahoma!*, but they also had *Allegro*, about the corruption of a small-town doctor, directed by Agnes De Mille and starring Lisa Kirk. "I'll never understand why we weren't a bigger success. I guess it was that Dick and Oscar had done *Carousel* and *Oklahoma!* and then they brought in *Allegro*, and it was just very good, and not brilliant. The critics, the audience wanted brilliance. I thought it was a great, great show, and I think if *Allegro* was produced now—not revived, because it has a stigma attached to it as Rodgers and Hammerstein's one flop—but produced as a new show, it would be a big hit."

Alan Jay Lerner had *My Fair Lady*, but (with Charles Strouse) he also had *Dance a Little Closer.*

ELIZABETH HUBBARD: "You mean *Close a Little Faster.*"

Hubbard stood by for Liz Robertson, who starred in the show based on Robert E. Sherwood's *Idiot's Delight*. Liz Robertson was also Mrs. Alan Jay Lerner.

HUBBARD: "It was a vanity piece for Liz Robertson. She wasn't really experienced enough to deal with all she had to deal with. I really thought that

The New Jule Styne Show

C ATHERINE Cox was excited to be cast in *One Night Stand*. After all, it was the new Jule Styne show—Jule Styne, who had written hits like *Gentlemen Prefer Blondes*, *Gypsy*, and *Funny Girl*. But this was 1980, and *One Night Stand* was about a composer who invites an audience to hear his songs before watching him commit suicide. With a book by Herb Gardner (*A Thousand Clowns*) and directed by John Dexter, *One Night Stand* closed after eight previews at the Nederlander Theatre, as co-producer Joseph Kipness cried.

"In my opinion—and it's truly just an insider's opinion—the big problem was that Herb Gardner and John Dexter just weren't simpatico. They didn't see eye-to-eye on anything, they were two totally different people. Jule is really a hoot. He treated you like a newcomer no matter how old you were, but I think he was my main champion in getting into the show.

"Another thing was that the salespeople described it as the 'New Jule Styne Show: the new Jule Styne show is coming.' And of course, all these people came to see the new *Gypsy* or *Funny Girl*, and this piece was about a man who had invited all these people to come and watch him commit suicide onstage—people weren't coming to see his plays and he thought he could get them there and fill the theatre if they were coming to see him kill himself. It was a black and very bizarre comedy.

"People left the theatre in droves. I had this wonderful two-page monologue in the second act, and I was supposed to walk through the audience. But by the time I got out there, most of the audience was gone.

"They really needed to work on it, but the writer and director didn't trust each other, so they didn't make any changes."

Dance a Little Closer was going to be it for me. An Alan Jay Lerner show! And I really thought that Liz Robertson was going to get tired, and that it was going to be my role.

"Alan was a charming man, but he was not well at that time. I remember we weren't paid well for the record, and I complained about it. I was told, 'Well, you'll never work again.' I thought that was really unfair. He had a lot of power, and we weren't being treated right."

Very often, when people are involved in an onstage disaster, one outstanding memory of the experience stays with them for the rest of their lives.

Constance Towers remembers working so hard to make *Ari*, based on Leon Uris's *Exodus*, into a successful show: "Once I was committed, I never would walk away. I broke out in hives from my shoulders to my toes, and I didn't even know that I was that upset, trying to give birth to something and having such problems."

Anita Gillette remembers *Kelly*, one of the most famous one-night bombs in history, about someone throwing himself off the Brooklyn Bridge: "When we opened at the Shubert in Philly, it was one of those freak, really hot December nights. There was no air conditioning. And the show didn't come down until midnight. A friend of mine was in the theatre, and as he was coming out he heard a man say, 'I thought that mother would never jump!' I thought that said it all."

Unfortunately, Karen Morrow doesn't like to work in New York anymore, which is not surprising. She has had great success and happiness doing shows and concerts everywhere else. "Broadway is just too goddamn critical. It's so scary. Every time I go back there people stop me on the street and ask 'When are you coming back to Broadway?' But it's too painful, with all you have to go through, and I don't want to subject myself to that rejection. I've had too much rejection. Sometimes I wake up and I can't believe I've been doing this for thirty years."

Morrow says she would come back to Broadway only if the role were right and the terms irresistible, or if they'd let her stay at the Regency. "When I saw Peter Allen's *Legs*, I walked into the Hellinger, where we did *I'm Solomon*, and the hair on the back of my neck went up. I immediately went, 'Ahh—,' and from the minute the show started, I had instant recall. I saw all the factions up there who hadn't talked to each other. And I thought, 'How does anyone come up with a hit?'"

9

Closing Too Soon

T HE closing notice for *Sadie Thompson* went up on New Year's Eve. The cast and creative team had poured blood into the Vernon Duke/ Howard Dietz musical. On closing night, leading lady June Havoc did what others only dream of: she beat up the producer, in this case, A. P. Waxman. "He was a little man; everyone loathed him. On closing night, he called the cast out onto the stage. I did not come out of my dressing room. Then the little man made the mistake of coming to my room. I don't know what it triggered in me, but he started toward me and I closed the door, locked it, and let him have it. I beat him unmercifully. I was taken to the hospital in my red shoes that Azadia Mamoulian had designed for me, in my full stage makeup. They gave me a sedative, and when I came to in the hospital, people from the company were sitting there waiting—they were taking shifts. They had *all* wanted to beat him up."

In a profession where so little is in a performer's control to begin with, there is nothing so heartbreaking, inspiring rage and helplessness, as a show closing long before it should. Who kills a show? The fate of a musical can be affected by anything as arbitrary as the wrong choice of theatre, or an inexperienced producer, or the competition from across the street.

107

The story of pen-pal shop clerks, *She Loves Me* was based on Miklos Laszlo's play *Parfumerie*—better known as the Jimmy Stewart/Margaret Sullavan movie *The Shop around the Corner*. With a score by Jerry Bock and Sheldon Harnick, it was director Hal Prince's first musical from scratch. The cast included Barbara Cook, Jack Cassidy, Barbara Baxley, and Ralph Williams.

Barbara Cook had already won a Tony for *The Music Man*. "I had some problems with Hal. I felt he was directing me too much in detail and not in fine strokes, and I felt confined. During the period of rehearsals where you would want to explore, I was not being allowed to explore. He had made up his mind about what he wanted to see and was fitting me into it, rather than letting me see what the other actors were doing, and all that. So there was sort of a hairy period there for a while."

Prince's vision, which is present for every show he works on, was there for *She Loves Me*, and he drove the cast during rehearsals, trying to get every detail just right.

Barbara Baxley, a stranger to the musical stage, went into the show with some trepidation. "I remember we did one little bit over and over again all morning—and then again after lunch. And at one point I noticed Hal looking over at me and he seemed to be thinking 'When is she going to blow up or get upset about doing this over and over?' But we were all very demanding people in our work. We wanted it right, not wrong, and were willing to work for that. No one in the cast was temperamental, or mean or stupid. And about every forty-five minutes Hal would make some crack that would make everyone fall on the floor, to relax you if you were getting uptight."

The score for *She Loves Me* contained twenty-three numbers, about ten more than was usual for a standard Broadway show. Ralph Williams played the delivery boy. To open the second act, "Try Me"—Williams's plea for a promotion—was the third song he was given. "I know I seemed like a real crybaby, but the first song just didn't support the show at all, and I was blaming myself. I remember Hal came in and said, 'You're absolutely right. The song doesn't work at all.' The second one didn't work either, and I got the third the day before we went to New Haven."

The show kept changing out of town, as numbers were thrown out and new ones added.

COOK: "I always felt the changes we were making were just moving us ahead. I felt that more than with any other show I ever worked on, with the possible exception of *Music Man*. In *Music Man*, I must have sung twelve different versions of 'My White Knight' before they came upon the one they thought was right. They kept rewriting it. That kind of stuff can drive you nuts. But that's the kind of courage it takes. You have to have someone in charge who knows what's important to the story, and then has the courage to say to the performer and writer, 'This has got to go.' No arguments. It's gone."

She Loves Me opened at the Eugene O'Neill Theatre on April 23, 1963, with a picture-postcard set costing a reported $67,000 (the most Prince had ever spent on a set). Everybody raved. "A bonbon of a musical," Howard Taubman of the *Times* called it, while Norman Nadel of the *World-Telegram & Sun* gushed that the show "is that rare theatrical jewel . . . dear, charming, and wholeheartedly romantic." Only Walter Kerr writing for the *Herald Tribune,* wasn't amused. Nadel went on to say that "The expression 'Sings her heart out' certainly applies to Miss Cook, who has both the heart and the voice to do it." Of Baxley's performance as Ilona, Taubman said she "proves that a fine actress can employ all her acting talents in a musical. When Jack Cassidy as a dashing playboy clerk seeks to reduce her defenses . . . Miss Baxley's wounded, melting looks and movements are irresistible." That was in April. By the following February it was closed. Everyone thought it would run forever.

Quality and long runs don't necessarily go together; neither do good reviews and long runs. Some shows, like *Something More,* get bad reviews and close right away. Others, like *Candide,* are greeted warmly by the critics and rejected by the public. *Abie's Irish Rose* was turned down by every producer in town before it opened on Broadway, financed by the playwright's life savings. Panned by the critics, it went on to run a record-breaking 2,327 performances.

Walter Kerr described *Gypsy* as the "Best Damn Musical I've Seen in Years!" The producers used the quote for the show's entire run. Kerr never objected or qualified the statement. The producers of *Cats* use the slogan "Now and Forever" in all their ads. Is that a promise or a threat? Why is there no critical superlative?

Possibly because the critics reacted as follows:

"*Cats* is an overblown piece of theater" (Douglas Watt, *Daily News*). "*Cats* . . . is a triumph of motion over emotion, of EQ over IQ. . . . The spectacle is the substance" (T. E. Kalem, *Time*). "A great show, in itself and by itself, it isn't, but see it" (Clive Barnes, *Post*). "The first act is flat and overlong" (Edwin Wilson, *Wall Street Journal*). "The profuse choreography, for all its quantity and exuberance, does not add up to quality" (Frank Rich, *Times*). Ten years after its 1982 opening, *Cats* was doing 86.5 percent capacity business.

Before the era of big ad campaigns, ushered in during the 1970s by *Pippin*'s one-minute television spot, selling a show was a different business.

Producers such as Mike Todd and David Merrick could keep their ventures running by pure showmanship. When his first show, *Fanny*, opened to mediocre reviews, Merrick erected a nude statue of the show's belly dancer in Central Park as a publicity stunt. The press loved it, and Merrick was able to push *Fanny* to an 888-performance run.

She Loves Me did not lend itself to publicity stunts.

COOK: "I was shocked when we got the closing notice; I had no idea we were in that kind of trouble."

The reasons *She Loves Me* closed were subtle and far-reaching.

BAXLEY: "The show was a gem. It was very delicate. They put the show in a small theatre because that's where it belonged. But because of that, the show didn't make money. So they made the right choices, but they just didn't pay off. We didn't have any chorus girls or any of that jazzy stuff. People came to New Haven and told Hal to add these things, but Hal stuck to his guns, and I respect him for that."

WILLIAMS: "It wasn't a bigger hit because the theatre party ladies wanted a chorus line. And Hal said, 'That's not what we're doing.' All the people who loved the show agreed with him. The show was what it was."

They have a point. The show was what it was, and *She Loves Me* was a hard sell. The theatre party ladies loved *How Now Dow Jones* because of the catchy title and the fact that it was a George Abbott musical. They stayed away from the intimate love story with songs. Hal Prince would have to wait a few years before having a megahit with *Cabaret*.

Some shows are such a hit out of town that nothing else is imaginable. When *Oh Captain!* opened in Philadelphia, the critics and the audiences went wild. The Jay Livingston/Ray Evans show, directed by José Ferrer (who co-wrote the book), was adapted from the Alec Guinness/Yvonne DeCarlo movie, *The Captain's Paradise*. Tony Randall headed a cast that included Susan Johnson and Alexandra Danilova.

RANDALL: "It was in 1958, and Joe Ferrer approached me about doing the show. I was under contract to Twentieth Century–Fox, and I had never done a musical comedy before. It was a wonderful score, the quality of the music was incredible."

SUSAN JOHNSON: "At the audition, José Ferrer had had me repeat a song. Then he came down to the edge of the stage and said, 'I wish there was a part for you.' Then I got a call to go over to his place at the Carnegie. I went over, and they had the script pasted all over the marble fireplace—the scenes, the songs, everything. The composers then said they'd written a song for me. Joe said Danilova and I were there for insurance."

RANDALL: "When we opened in Philadelphia, we were the biggest hit that ever landed there. One review said 'the greatest musical since *Show Boat*.' Tickets were going for $100 apiece. There were fistfights over tickets in the lobby. We were euphoric. On the basis of that opening we sold almost $3 million advance—almost unheard of! And we believed the notices; we believed we were the greatest musical that had ever been—and the audience believed it, too. They went insane."

"Then, when we moved to New York, we got a lukewarm reception; well, a little better than lukewarm, but nothing like Philadelphia. We came in expecting exactly the same reception."

Actually, most of the New York reviews for *Oh Captain!* weren't at all bad, especially for the cast. "Tony Randall does a lightly once-over pas de deux with that immortal of the classic ballet, the supreme, divine Danilova . . . Unbelievably entertaining," wrote Frank Aston of the *World-Telegram & Sun*. Walter Kerr added, in the *Herald Tribune*, "Susan Johnson, sporting purple hair and sequins on her eyelids, gives all she has (a very great deal) to 'Give It All You've Got.'"

The show closed in less than six months.

RANDALL: "It's one of the few cases in recent history where a show that should have run was closed. It was a very underrated show. But the competition in those days was tremendous. On the boards at the same time were *Music Man*, *West Side Story*, and *My Fair Lady*; and then Lena Horne opened in a big show and she was a major star. So there was terrific competition."

Kean was also a hit out of town. With an original score by Wright and Forrest (who had adapted others' music for shows like *Kismet*), *Kean* was based on the life of the eighteenth-century actor Edmund Kean. Alfred Drake led a cast that included Christopher Hewett.

ALFRED DRAKE: "That's a long, sad story. There was so much that was good about that show."

The show was both directed and choreographed by Jack Cole—his first time doing both.

CHRISTOPHER HEWETT: "I think if Jack Cole had been able to finish it, it would have been a big hit. But it was a clash of wills. Alfie [Drake] insisted on adding the soliloquy at the end, and it depressed everyone. You can't go out humming a depressing speech like that. Then I was in a number called 'The Fog in the Grog,' and Jack said, 'Do some of your terrible English steps for me, and put it together.' We stopped the show. Actually, we were a big hit in Boston. But by Philadelphia, somebody decided that Alfred Drake should be in the number, too. So instead of it being a lovely little thing, it became a production number."

DRAKE: "The rave reviews we got in Boston seemed to convince everyone that we didn't have to work that much. There was one critic at the *Christian Science Monitor*, and before we opened I said, 'Pay attention to that man. He knows a lot about the theatre,' and when he reviewed the show, it was the one poor review we got, and nobody listened to him. He pointed out things necessary to be done, and I thought his comments were brilliant. But everybody else raved about the show, and so we didn't do the work."

"Perhaps the expectations were too great," wrote John McClain of the *Journal-American* when it opened in New York, "but the sad fact remains that *Kean* emerged last night with more pretension than promise." The show ran ninety-two performances at the Broadway Theatre, and then closed.

The decision of at what point to close a show depends on the guts, faith, experience, bankroll, or ulterior motives of the producers. To this day, nobody (except maybe certain production people and their analysts) knows what happened to *It's a Bird, It's a Plane, It's Superman!* The Strouse/Adams musical, directed by Hal Prince, featured Bob Holiday in the title role and Jack Cassidy as the villain, and played to packed houses. For those who saw the show before it suddenly disappeared, Patricia Marand was Lois Lane. "There were mobs of people, and they said we could run forever," Marand recalls. "We had capacity standing room. They were hanging from the rafters. It was such a shame. I remember standing in the wings at the opening of the show every night. Superman used to dive down onto the stage—and watching these little kids in the first rows whose feet could barely touch the ground, looking at him with such awe in their eyes—I'll never forget that. Lois didn't fly in the show because of insurance reasons. Everybody has excuses for closing a show—we had a major airline strike that year, and it was one of the hottest summers New York has ever experienced. . . For some reason they just didn't think we were going to run, which was ridiculous, because we were doing great business."

John Raitt had been a major force in getting *A Joyful Noise*, the Oscar Brand/Paul Nassau musical, onstage. The show also featured Susan Watson, Karen Morrow, and Tommy Tune; it was directed by Dore Schary, the former head of MGM who had staged successes like *The Unsinkable Molly Brown*, and staged by first-time choreographer Michael Bennett.

RAITT: "It was a shame that didn't work. Gower Champion came, and said, 'Seventy-five percent of the show is good, it just needs a little bit of work, a little focus.' It didn't work. And we couldn't do anything about it. But people loved the show. We raised money from the audience. I used to say to the audience, 'You like this show as much as you do? See the guy in the back there with the beard? He'll take your money from you.' At Valley Forge we raised a thousand dollars. People still talk to me: 'Say, we enjoyed that show.'"

A *Joyful Noise* began in summer stock before heading for Broadway. Director Dore Schary left shortly before the show opened, and Karen Morrow and Susan Watson joined the Broadway company.

WATSON: "The show kept being rewritten. We started the rehearsals, and it went along fine, until Dore Schary just felt that he'd had enough. We were rewriting scenes each day, and Dore was helping with the writing. We were in trouble."

By Christmas, the show was closed.

RAITT: "It breaks your heart. It was the first time I ever cried at a curtain call. I'd worked so hard on that—I just knew it wasn't going to make it. The producer told me later, 'If I'd had $3,000 more, I'd have kept it open.' I said, 'Why didn't you ask me?' And the following week we were on the *Ed Sullivan Show*. It was just one of those things."

No one in the cast will ever forget the night the show closed.

MORROW: "We closed on Christmas Eve, in a blizzard, and the scenery was being packed out, and Bonnie Raitt and her little brother were backstage sobbing and weeping because it was over—they were just kids. It was quite a scene. And I remember thinking, 'All we need is a little match girl. . . .'"

A little musical revue, based on the offbeat stories by artist Edward Gorey, titled, appropriately, *Gorey Stories*, and directed by Tony Tanner, opened at the Booth Theatre in October 1979. Featured in the cast were Gemze De Lappe, Julie Kurnitz, Susan Marchand, Dennis McGovern, June Squibb, and Sel Vitella. The show had played off-Broadway the year before at the WPA Theatre and received a rave review from the *New York Times*. Its move to Broadway was inevitable. The show closed on its opening night on Broadway, the victim of a newspaper strike and perhaps its own uniqueness.

"I was the only one who wasn't there from the beginning," remembers Kurnitz, who replaced Liz Sheridan for the Broadway production. "I felt a little like an outsider, but I had always adored Gorey. I thought he was a wonderful, strange genius. The script had the possibilities of being a big hit, but it really should have moved to a smaller theatre, like the Lucille Lortel in the Village."

The rest of the cast had spent over a year working on the project, and believed in it completely.

GEMZE DE LAPPE: "The most wonderful thing about the experience was that it was a total ensemble. I still feel we all acted as one, and were totally committed. If we had gone to a small theatre instead of the Booth, I swear it would still be running."

SEL VITELLA: "What we had worked. But they brought in some hack friend of one of the producers, who rewrote the first act. We played it for one performance in previews and it died. It was discouraging. But then we went back to the original, and you had people like Agnes De Mille telling you how good it was. We felt pretty confident. I thought, 'This is it.'"

It wasn't. The producer with the money, Terry Allen Kramer, took her money and left the country the day before the opening.

SUSAN MARCHAND: "I remember the exhilaration of the opening night, and going to Sardi's, and everyone applauding. Then we all went to some townhouse for a party, and it was a disaster. Mrs. Kramer had gone to Paris, and there was no food. And then the reviews. Stewart Klein had given us a rave, and we all knew about it [the TV critic had filmed his review onstage with the cast four hours before opening night]. Then came Dennis Cunningham. He was vicious. It was devastating to watch him rip us apart, coming after the reaction we had gotten earlier in the night."

JUNE SQUIBB: "You could sort of tell by the look on the faces of John [Wulp] and Hale [Matthews], the two producers that were left, that we weren't going to make it—but none of us expected it to close so quickly."

VITELLA: "Closing so fast never let us get it out of our system. We never got to play it out."

KURNITZ: "I thought it was a joke the next morning when John Wulp called and said, 'Don't show up for work today.' I said, 'That's not funny, John.' I couldn't take it in. It seemed insane to close at that point."

DE LAPPE: "My sons couldn't believe something they loved could just be snuffed out like that. If the show had run, it would have changed the direction of my life. I would have gone into acting, and studied it seriously— which I always wanted to do—but I never had the time or money to do it."

Shortly afterward, Vitella ran into Dennis Cunningham.

VITELLA: "I saw him on the street before a performance of *Da*. I wanted to rush up and choke him, but I knew I couldn't kill him right there on 45th Street. He said to me, 'Well, I call them as I see them.' I couldn't say anything. I just turned around and started to cry."

The pain wasn't relieved by the fact that when the magazine reviews came out, they were positive. When the newspaper strike ended, Richard Eder of the *Times* gave *Gorey Stories* raves.

The first book musical by Richard Maltby and David Shire to open on Broadway was *Baby*, which debuted at the Ethel Barrymore Theatre in December 1983. It was a small, unpretentious show with minimal scenery

```
         GQA025(1217)(4-033672E304)PD 10/31/78 1217
ICS IPMMTZZ CSP
 2123541239 TDMT NEW YORK NY 47 10-31 1217P EST
PMS SUSAN MARCHAND, DELIVER, RPT DLY BY MGM, DLR
333 WEST 84 ST #1F
NEW YORK NY 10024
WE ARE TERRIBLY SORRY TO ADVISE YOU THAT GOREY STORIES WILL NOT
RESUME PERFORMANCES TONIGHT, AND THAT THE SHOW IS CONSIDERED CLOSED
AS OF LAST NIGHT'S PERFORMANCE. WE ARE DEEPLY APPRECIATIVE OF YOUR
HARD WORK AND PATIENCE AND WISH YOU ALL GOOD LUCK IN THE FUTURE.
SINCERELY,
   GOREY STORIES CO, TERRY ALLEN KRAMER, HARRY RIGBY, HALE MATTHEWS,
JOHN WULP, PRODUCERS (ALAN WASSER GOREY STORIES CO CARE SCHLISSEL
AND KINGWILL 226 WEST 47 ST NEW YORK NY 10036)
NNNN
SF-1201 (R5-69)
```

Telegram provided by Susan Marchand Madden

and a small cast, featuring Liz Callaway, Catherine Cox, Beth Fowler, and Martin Vidnovic. The album and CD are still bestsellers, and the show developed a cult following, but *Baby* never really caught on with the public.

"The show ran around seven months," says Vidnovic, "and there are different reasons for why it didn't run longer. I think a lot of people, especially tourists, just said they didn't want to go see a show named *Baby*—'What is that?'"

According to Beth Fowler, the competition also didn't help: "We were competing with *La Cage*. Now, that was one of those shows I went to see because I had a friend in it. Otherwise, I never would have gone. But the tourists loved it."

Baby's reviews were mixed to good, but they all emphasized the fact that there were no stars and no spectacle. It was just a show about three couples of various ages (one young, one in their thirties, and one older) who are all hoping to have a baby. The show had come from a workshop with very little advance publicity.

LIZ CALLAWAY: "Richard Maltby came to see a little revue I was doing at the St. Regis, and he asked if I'd like to come over and work on some material he was developing. So I said, 'Sure,' and I went over and learned 'The Ladies Singing Their Song' and 'The Story Goes On.' I'd go over there a couple of times a week, and one day there was a producer there, and I said, 'This is an audition?' and they said, 'You've been auditioning all along.' So I did the workshop."

In this way Callaway got her first Broadway leading role, and her first Tony nomination.

Catherine Cox knew exactly what she was getting into. "I did an early reading of the show when my character, Pam, was supposed to be a gymnast, tiny and compact, like Cathy Rigby." Miss Cox is statuesque. "I knew if they continued like that, they weren't going to consider me. So I said, half-jokingly, 'Why not change her to a basketball player'—and they did! They went that way—but I still had to come back a lot and audition. Then I did the backers' auditions and the workshop."

MARTIN VIDNOVIC: "Doing the show in workshop gave us a chance to work, really work, on the material. The show did change a lot. Also, the atmosphere was good because there wasn't anyone breathing down your back. Characters were cut; whole stories, songs were deleted and put in. Catherine and I had probably four different songs in the bedroom scene until we ended up with 'With You'—and frankly, all of them were pretty good. Musically and emotionally they were all beautiful—but they went with the one they thought was most in keeping with the play."

CATHERINE COX: "I was never athletic growing up, and I'd never played basketball. So when I knew I had the part, I got a ball and went down to this place in the Village where they play 'killer basketball,' and I got the kids to teach me some gimmicks."

LIZ CALLAWAY: "Fortunately, we went back into rehearsal before we went to Broadway, because I didn't have much acting experience, and that really was an overwhelming part. I did it when I was in my early twenties. I'm thirty now. I don't feel thirty—whatever that means—but I've had a baby myself. I still haven't had another role like that—I got to go through nine months of pregnancy every night onstage."

The song most people connect with the show is "Patterns," written for the character of Arlene (Beth Fowler), and cut before the Broadway opening, though it was included in the cast album. "*Baby* really got to me," says Susan Johnson, who had no connection with the production. "That song 'Patterns' just drove me out of my mind, it's so damn beautiful."

The decision to eliminate it was, naturally, very hard on Beth Fowler. "They cut it the night the critics came," Fowler remembers, "and I tried to be philosophical about it. They said it was for the good of the show. I remember calling my husband before the performance and telling him, 'Well, there goes my Tony nomination.' Everyone who had seen it during previews commented on the song, and I did it well, I guess—but they just didn't know where to put it in the show. Also, maybe, it was too negative for them. It showed the older woman having doubts about her pregnancy—and that was only part of what the show was about."

VIDNOVIC: "They didn't like what it did for the character. That was a real blow for Beth, but she accepted it."

FOWLER: "I trusted them, and it got recorded, which was good for me. I think the song has been in every production of *Baby* that has been done since ours. That hurts."

With a great score and a talented cast, why didn't the show run for years?

FOWLER: "Frank Rich's review in the *Times* really hurt us. He loved the show, and he was saying what he thought he should say. But there were no 'quotes' there. It was too ambiguous."

COX: "We were at Sardi's on opening night, and someone came up to me and gave me a copy of Rich's review and said, 'Catherine, it's great. Get up and read it.' I don't know why, but I did. I started to read it, and it was a decent review, but it was qualified. And all of a sudden I found myself doing this massive editing as I went along! I thought, 'I only want to read raves. Don't make me read this!'"

FOWLER: "The show wasn't sophisticated. It was about relationships and having babies—but not just about having babies. It was about the impact having them could have on a relationship, and what a gift it could be. The 'baby' was the catalyst in the show, but I don't think it was a good title. But what else could they have called it?"

VIDNOVIC: "Once people saw the show, they seemed to like it. But the problem was getting them in there."

CALLAWAY: "We had our closing notice up all the time, and we used to check the grosses in *Variety* and panic. If I had known we were going to run as long as we did, I probably would have relaxed and enjoyed it more."

FOWLER: "It was hard to sell, and they really didn't have the money to sell it. Also, it's funny—but people who saw it and loved it got so emotional about the show that when they'd talk about it, I think maybe it turned people off."

If a show can be judged by how the cast related to one another, *Baby* was definitely a hit.

COX: "With the three of us [the leading ladies], there wasn't one diva. We were all supportive of each other; and also we all had our own scenes, our own moments to shine. There was probably a twinge of jealousy when Liz was nominated for a Tony and I wasn't, but then Beth wasn't either. But that never affected us personally. You just do what you have to do, and we all had such different personalities."

CALLAWAY: "We all worked so hard on building and maintaining those relationships."

FOWLER: "In *Baby*, we were all very much of our own generations, and that was important to the show. I could never do what Catherine and Liz were doing, and they couldn't do what I was doing, and that worked so well for the show. We were all different."

Baby closed after a modest run of 241 performances.

CALLAWAY: "With the 'baby boom' going on now, it probably was ahead of its time. I think a lot of people would love to have that show running now. I know I would."

COX: "People don't come back and ask for your autograph and tell you how much they hated the show. They liked us."

VIDNOVIC: "A lot of people just didn't want to go to see a show about people having babies. I don't understand that."

FOWLER: "If the record had come out earlier, that might have helped. I can't tell you how many people told me they walked around all day listening to the cassette."

COX: "The thing about *Baby* that was most disappointing was that it only ran seven months. It should have gone nine, so that we'd have the full gestation period!"

Because of its small cast and modest production requirements, *Baby* has managed to have a longer life after Broadway than a lot of shows. *Plain and Fancy* was a bigger hit, but is rarely, if ever, revived. The same is true for the Gwen Verdon vehicles *New Girl in Town* and *Redhead*. Some shows whose lives were cut short on Broadway have gone on to future incarnations, thanks in large part to followings they developed through original cast albums. Two examples are *She Loves Me* and *It's a Bird, It's a Plane, It's Superman!* The pirated recordings of *Drat, the Cat!* and *A Joyful Noise* also are prized collector's items.

Robert Wright and George Forrest had worked for twenty-five years on the score of the failed *Anya*; it was produced and re-recorded as *The Anastasia Affaire*. Walter Willison, one of the recording's producers, feels the same thing could happen with *Kean*: "The whole score is good. 'Sweet Danger,' especially, is a wonderful song."

When director Tony Tanner revived his Broadway production of *Gorey Stories* in Los Angeles in 1992, it met with the same positive response most New York critics had given it. *Daily Variety* thought the macabre stories were "delightfully brought to life." Richard Scaffidi in *Drama-Logue* ended his review, "*Gorey Stories* is a grand romp in the park. It just happens to be a dark park."

But while it may be satisfying to know a show has been appreciated in the long run, it is small comfort to the performers who created it in the first place. The casts of a *She Loves Me* or a *Gorey Stories* are rewarded with unemployment—and as Gemze De Lappe observes, "If you're a star, or in the chorus, or somewhere in between, everyone feels that when a show closes, you'll never get another job."

10

Life with the Director/ Choreographers

W HAT the hell do we know?" says Chita Rivera. "I'm the girl that read the end of *West Side Story* and said, 'My Lord—a musical that ends with a dead body being carried over their heads? I mean, that's just not going to work.'"

West Side Story ended up working very well, thanks to Jerome Robbins. Successful shows are about vision and the power of the person in charge. Since the 1940s, dance has transformed musical theatre, becoming so integral to the fabric of the show that suddenly the director/choreographer reigned supreme. Performers were no longer as neatly compartmentalized as they had been in the early days. With Robbins at the helm (or Champion or Fosse or Bennett), actors became dancers, dancers became actors, and singers did some of each.

Agnes De Mille is credited with revolutionizing Broadway dance with her choreography for *Oklahoma!* She was not the very first to raise the caliber of Broadway dance by bringing in ballet dancers and giving them things to dance: George Balanchine had been doing that with shows like *On Your Toes*, which had featured ballerinas like Tamara Geva. Recalls De Mille dancer Gemze De Lappe, "At that time, there were a lot of good dancers in

American Ballet Theatre and the Ballets Russes, but they didn't have full contracts. They didn't work for a full year, so they had time available. They went between Broadway and serious ballet or modern dance, and you had this big pool of really good dancers available. Everyone was doing it—Nora Kaye, Alicia Alonso, Johnny Krisza. They were all great, famous dancers doing Broadway shows. Then we had Agnes, and Jerry Robbins, and later Michael Kidd, and they were not only doing real ballets on Broadway, but they were all very successful. The swinging back and forth was very advantageous for both Broadway and ballet. It developed dancers who could act."

De Mille brought a whole new kind of dance to the Broadway stage, with color and character. She had come to *Oklahoma!* after choreographing Aaron Copland's *Rodeo* for American Ballet Theatre. She was a formidable force to work with. Unlike many choreographers, she communicated clearly and was also very organized.

ALFRED DRAKE: "She was a very strong-minded lady, and she got her ideas across. And she was stern, especially in terms of her dances."

DE LAPPE: "Originally, at the end of the first act of *Oklahoma!*, Rouben Mamoulian [the director] did not want to give the end of the first act to the ballet. So he brought back the real Curley and Jud. It was really unnecessary because everything was clear. He added something that only worked when you had a star with the charisma of Alfred Drake: when he stood there and crossed his legs and crossed his arms, you believed it. It really meant something. But there aren't many others who could pull that off. That was a point of contention between Agnes and Rouben, that she couldn't have that first-act curtain."

Because of De Mille and *Oklahoma!*, suddenly every show (and movie musical) had to have a dream ballet. Gemze De Lappe had a ballet background in the Michael Fokine company, before she was cast in the national company of *Oklahoma!* as the Dream Laurey. "It was very clear to me when I was singled out by Agnes De Mille. She wasn't too keen on me, but time was running out and she finally accepted me. We went to Chicago and played for a year, and she came out and felt a little better about it. Then *The King and I* came along, and I got into it playing Simon Legree."

When De Mille was preparing to do Lerner and Loewe's *Paint Your Wagon*, De Lappe went to audition: "By this time I didn't really care whether she was liking me or not. My technique had improved and my ego had improved. I was very good as Simon of Legree [in the *Uncle Tom's Cabin* ballet], and Jerry Robbins liked me, and everybody liked me. So I went to audition for Agnes full of confidence."

She got the part, for which she won a Donaldson Award.

"Agnes used to have private rehearsals with us before the rest of the company: Agnes and Jimmy Mitchell and me. She would create all the pas de deux and solos for us before the day started. Agnes always knew what she wanted. She never picked people's brains. She knew what you had, and she used it. By the end of the run, I knew I was secure in her mind as an artist."

In what otherwise were a disappointing set of reviews for *Paint Your Wagon*, Walter Kerr wrote that "the most emotionally rewarding moments of the evening come from the dancers." De Lappe began an association with De Mille that has lasted for decades, and today she is the foremost guardian of De Mille's choreography, recreating it in theatre and ballet companies around the world. "Of course we had our ups and downs and problems, but the thing I really admire about Agnes is that you can have an argument with her and still remain friends. That's not always true of a lot of choreographers and directors."

One of the most influential and overlooked choreographers in musical theatre is Jack Cole. His hits include *Kismet* and *Man of La Mancha*. Though the latter has seen major revivals, the integrity of Cole's dances unfortunately has not been preserved.

From the beginning of her career, Gwen Verdon was acknowledged as the definitive Jack Cole dancer. "I'm so surprised when people remember Jack Cole. He had such an influence on musical theatre, and yet I teach students today who haven't heard of the man. But I think the two people who really changed Broadway musicals were Agnes De Mille and Jack Cole. Jerry Robbins, Alvin Ailey—they all learned from Jack."

Cole developed the jazzy style most people associate with Broadway. He was considered a terror to work for.

PATTI KARR: "Working with Jack Cole, which I did right after ballet school, solved my problems. Because after that, you could do anything. He was a maniac. He hired all ballet dancers, and we went through tortures you wouldn't believe. He picked on me because he liked me. But he used to scream at me, and yell at me and insult me. And my body was swollen and sore, and I could hardly get up the stairs. This lasted for about two months, and then one morning I woke up and it was gone. My body had adjusted. After turning out for all those years, and suddenly having to turn in and bend your knees and stomp on the floor and jump, without pliés—it was crazy, and it was total rehearsal."

VERDON: "Jack always operated on the theory that you couldn't do it, or weren't willing to do it—he was strange that way—and for me, the challenge was, 'Oh yeah? You just watch.' Even though I adored the man, there was always that 'I'm going to show you' attitude. He did it purposely. If you met his challenge, you learned not only an incredible amount about dance and how to dance, but you became quite expert at what you were doing."

CHITA RIVERA: "I think the dancers in those days had a lot more variety to their vocabulary: not just tap, but modern, jazz, East Indian. Jack Cole's work is mixed with a lot of things. Working with him was frightening—and so thrilling you could die. But it was scary, because he was the hardest of them all. He was brutal, and it wasn't terribly nice."

VERDON: "He was difficult, but working with him depended on your own point of view about work. If you were willing not just to learn, but to work very hard, and willing to accept the challenge, you were 'in.' Because if you did learn, he would be terrific with you. He loved to teach, and if you were willing, you didn't have to be wonderful or a skilled technician—the desire to learn was the most important factor. That was everything to him."

RIVERA: "If you've got great teachers, you're an idiot if you don't listen to them and do exactly what they tell you to do. Now I hear some dancers say, 'You can't talk to me like that.' I don't believe that attitude. You just do what you're told. If you do that, you've learned an awful lot, and you're much stronger for it. That's why people like Gwen Verdon and me have lasted as long as we have."

Nobody is more legendary for frightening performers than Jerome Robbins. As a director and choreographer, creating such shows as *West Side Story* and *Gypsy*, he was a genius. He could also be something of a bastard. Merle Louise remembers *Gypsy*: "Oh, Jesus, I've seen him make a grown man cry."

With a background in ballet, Robbins had been George Abbott's choreographer for a decade, choreographing and staging shows like *On the Town*, *Pajama Game*, and *High Button Shoes*.

Sondra Lee made her Broadway debut in *High Button Shoes*. "I found Jerry demanding because of his vision. He gave me a job and I would have done anything he told me. If you hooked into what he was doing and didn't interfere with his vision, or look for attention or special stroking, he really wasn't that different. When that magnetic mold is at work, it's incredible. I don't think he's cruel. He's a perfectionist. He had a common vocabulary with dancers, and that's why he's their champion."

The show starred Nanette Fabray: "He had a wonderful knack of not being locked into what he wanted you do do. He could look at you and see what you had to offer, and then help you to be the best that you could be. For instance, in 'Poppa Won't You Dance with Me,' it was originally a Castle

Maria Enraged

JEROME Robbins has been described as a genius and a monster. A young Carol Lawrence first worked with him in the original production of *West Side Story*, and she got the chance to see both sides of the director/choreographer.

"Jerry wanted to keep the show alive, and considering how young we all were, he didn't trust us to have the integrity to keep it fresh. One night in the last scene, which was my favorite moment, where I take the gun and go over to the other side and I say that there's another bullet here for you, Chino, and you and you and you.

"Then I was supposed to go up to Action, who was played by Eddie Roll. He was a terrific actor and a terrific person onstage, but deeply into his psychosis. In rehearsal I used a pencil for the gun. My bed was a piano bench. We had a ladder for the fire escape. We always just had the bare bones, but now I had a .45 in my hands and he looked into the barrel of the gun and he turned a color I've never seen before and his eyes rolled, and I burst into tears and fell to my knees.

"Well, that wasn't in the scene. It wasn't choreographed. But at the end of the rehearsal, Jerry said, 'I like what you did. Keep that in. That's frozen.' Then, about two months into the run, I walked over to Eddie and said 'And one for you!' and he looked at me and rolled his eyes and kicked the ground and said, 'Oh shit.'

"I wanted to kill him! He had taken away my moment of truth with the collapse, but I knew if I didn't collapse, the scene just wouldn't progress. So I fell to my knees and we finished the show.

"Then I immediately ran to his dressing room and asked him what happened, because he was supposed to look terrified, and he said that it just didn't scare him anymore! So I said, 'Well,' I said, 'It's supposed to,' and he just said, 'Well, it doesn't.'

"Now, by this time most of the guys in the show had become juvenile delinquents. They were doing bizarre things in their dressing room and they even brought real delinquents to see the show and challenged them to rumbles. It became unbelievable, the reality that show took on.

"The next night I got to that scene. The gun was loaded with blanks, and I put it right up to his face and I said, 'And one for you,' and I cocked the gun just as he was starting to smirk. The blood drained from his face. He never did that to me again. Sometimes you just have to take the law into your own hands and do what you have to do."

Walk. Everyone who did the show later did it as a polka. But it was a very exciting and stylized Castle Walk. Jerry went out and found three couples who were still alive and had done the original Castle Walk in vaudeville. He brought them in, and he learned everything there was to know about the dance. And at the very end of the dance we did a little polka. It stopped the show cold."

With *West Side Story*, his obsession with detail and quest for realism took on unnerving dimensions. During rehearsals he tried to recreate the tensions of gang life in the slums among the cast.

Carol Lawrence, who came to the role of Maria more as a singer than a dancer, wasn't ready for it. "Jerry called the stage a battleground. And in many cases, he was the enemy who beat us into submission, or towards perfection, or whatever he fantasized we should be. He approached the whole project from the choreographer-dancer's master-slave relationship which exists in ballet. He only dealt in humiliation and inciting to riot by degrading your talent—and that in front of the whole company. Now, for a dancer, that works. You get so much adrenaline rushing through your body that you jump higher, and you turn faster, and you're ready to kill him, but you can't. You rise to the occasion. But an actor can't be pushed into being more poignant. What you do is defeat their ego and sense of worth, and Jerry didn't realize this. Lenny Bernstein would always come to us and pick up the bleeding mass of our emotions that Jerry had left on the floor, and rekindle the strength and the reason why we would walk back out onstage. You would be completely destroyed by him."

Before inaugurating the trend of the almighty director/choreographer, Robbins had learned everything he knew about drama and staging from George Abbott.

CHITA RIVERA: "I considered that the greatest learning experience I had. They were great days. But this one is still feeding me. There were great moments when we confronted each other in the rehearsal hall. Peter Gennaro would choreograph the Latin stuff, and Jerry would do the other. We would be in different rooms, then we would surprise each other, like in the gym. Jerry really taught us how to act. Instead of dancing across the stage in one scene, he would say to me, 'Gee, look, you don't run to a window looking for a possible murderer by doing a grand jeté and two chaînés.' He really taught us how to think as people, not as highly energized dancers."

Robbins enjoyed manipulating his cast into the two warring camps that they represented onstage.

RIVERA: "He separated the Sharks and the Jets and told us all we were different. Knowing we were separated, and on different teams, consequently, we never went out to lunch together, we wouldn't spend any time with the other gang at all in rehearsal. We'd separate ourselves, and it made it very real. Every night, I'd watch the rumble, and watch Bernardo—Kenny LeRoy—get killed. Then the curtain would come down, and I would just step over Mickey Calin and go over and pick up Kenny and brush him off, and ask him if he was okay, and go to my dressing room. We didn't have to—it was just part of making it very real. It was exciting.

MARILYN COOPER: "The Sharks would wear red carnations and the Jets would wear pink carnations, so we could know who we were. I was a singer, and not a dancer, and in those days singers would kind of stand on the side with their hands at their sides, and we weren't that much involved in the challenge dances; so there wasn't anything negative about it. He was just trying to make us into two gangs."

Carol Lawrence remembers more than that: "There were moments of magical chemistry Jerry was responsible for. Just pairing off the people who played against each other. No Jet was allowed to talk to a Shark during rehearsal. He would pit people against one another and instigate feuds that were based on nothing but his imagination. He'd say things like, 'Oh, Jim told me your mother is a hooker. Is that true?' Things like that. And during the rumble, we had sixteen bars of free fight, and there were often teeth missing and bloody jaws. Someone out there wouldn't know why he was being attacked, but it was Jerry."

The famous story about Robbins is how during a rehearsal his entire company watched as he backed off the stage and fell into the orchestra pit. No one made a move to stop him.

Unlike De Mille or Robbins, Gower Champion had come to Broadway via clubs and Hollywood. With his wife, Marge, he had danced in such movies as the Kathryn Grayson/Howard Keel *Show Boat* before making his success as a director/choreographer with shows like *Bye Bye Birdie*, *Carnival*, and *Hello, Dolly!*

When David Merrick approached Carol Channing with *Dolly*, it was Champion she requested as director. "He was a showman," Channing insists, "and he *called* himself a showman—not a director, not a choreographer. He had the same quality that Bob Mackie has in clothes: he designs a great dress provided he has somebody in mind—for Cher, for Angela Lansbury.

"At first, he wanted *Dolly* to be an intimate musical. He said, 'You must start rehearsing with the "Hello, Dolly" number. If I were Josh Logan, we'd start with the dialogue, and we'd all be on our books for the first two weeks, until we had the lines learned. I can't do that. As soon as I know how you all sing and dance, then I know your characters.' It worked for him, and for all of us. What we say, how we walk, how we sit—these are just the facts. But the soul of the character is when you sing and dance it. Suddenly, the dream of you is what you become—you-without-flaws emerges, the essence of the person."

Harold Prince had been offered *Dolly* to direct. He turned it down because he thought the title number could never work.

CHANNING: "We spent the first two weeks on the "Dolly" number. He wanted it to be little. Then he moved the waiters in, and the cooks, and everybody in the Harmonia Gardens, and it got bigger and bigger. Then he said, 'I think we should make the steps higher.' And he would run around to the back of the theatre and say, 'Spread out more' and run back again. He would look and say, 'I can't get it big enough. These boys are too dinky—get bigger boys next to her.' Then he'd say, 'Gee, now we've got it.' It was getting mammoth, and he realized, 'I haven't got an intimate show here.' That's how Gower got his level."

Champion's first big hit was the revue *Lend an Ear*, in which the public and critics discovered the "unknown" Carol Channing. After fifteen years and stardom for both parties, Champion wasn't sure he wanted Channing for *Dolly*. "I had to audition for Gower. I had asked for Gower. But when Mr. Merrick brought Gower in, he said, 'I think the whole show is marvelous, but I don't think Carol can do Dolly.' So I said, 'Oh, come on, Gower, you did *Lend an Ear* with me, and I did twelve, fifteen different characters. I'll audition for you. Let me audition.' He was thinking of Nanny Fabray, which would have been another kind of Dolly. Mr. Merrick said, 'This is ridiculous.' But when I feel this way about a part . . . So we got the theatre where *Oliver!* was playing, and I got up on the stage and I had all the *Oliver!* sets in back of me, and I got the stage manager to play Vandergelder, and I started talking to him about Dolly. And Gower said, 'I'll buy that.' And once he said, 'I'll buy that,' we never disagreed. We stood right together."

Champion was a totally visual person, not a great communicator. Jerry Orbach first worked with him in *Carnival*, Bob Merrill's adaptation of the movie *Lili*; he would work with him again almost two decades later in *42nd Street*. "He was an imposing figure in the beginning. You were afraid to whisper in his presence. He had real control over everyone. I walked in to my first rehearsal for *Carnival*, and he had already been working with the dancers for a week. I came backstage and said something to Charlie Blackwell, and he said, 'Shhh—Mr. Champion's thinking.' So I thought, *oh*, he's *thinking*. He was always thinking in visual images. I remember I had this argument scene with Lili, and Gower said he wanted me to start the scene by walking around her, and just keep walking and make the circle tighter and tighter until you're face-to-face. And I said, 'You mean you want me to get angrier at her.' He said, 'Yeah, that's it.' He had a hard time, sometimes, verbalizing what he wanted out of us. He got better by the time of *42nd Street*."

Anna Maria Alberghetti won a Tony for her sensitive portrayal of the innocent waif, Lili.

ALBERGHETTI: "Gower understood about pacing, about setting something up so it would pay off. I was not crazy about the first song in *Carnival*. It was called 'What a Very Nice Man,' and it was just a song about a lot of props. It was the song that came before 'Mira'—which got a wonderful, wonderful reaction from the audience. Subconsciously, I really wanted that first song not to remain in the show. So one night in Washington we deleted the song, and made 'Mira' my first song. And as incredible a reaction as 'Mira' used to get, when we took the first song out, it just didn't work. And I learned one of my many lessons on what pacing was all about. Gower understood that so well.

"Gower never tried to carve a performance out of you. You brought in your performance. But he would go out into the audience every show and say, 'On a scale of ten, you have it at a nine now—bring the performance to an eight,' or 'bring it to an eleven.' He had a wonderful way of knowing where to push you and stretch you, even though he himself was not the kind of director who would sit down with you and talk about the character."

The year before *Carnival*, the Adams/Strouse musical *Bye Bye Birdie* sent Champion and all the show's creators to stardom. It starred Chita Rivera. "Gower was totally different from all the others. He was lighthearted. His work was very comedic, and very light, very colorful, very smooth—the Hollywood approach. He had done the whole framework of the Shriner's Ballet without me—and when he showed it to me, I looked at it and said, 'You don't even need me.' It was so wonderfully conceived. But Gower was a taskmaster. If he said he was going to rehearse something at 12:03, it was 12:03. Terribly organized."

Bye Bye Birdie was about the shakeup of a small, midwestern town when an Elvis Presley type named Conrad Birdie comes to visit. It made stars out of both its creators, Adams and Strouse, and Susan Watson, the ingenue, who remembers, "When I first read the script, I thought this was one of the most stupid things I'd ever read. But Gower had all these marvelous ideas. When we went to Philadelphia, he made a lot of really radical changes. Songs were shifted from the first to the second act, and he would have everyone up in his hotel room working on the show. But Gower always knew where he was going with it, and what he wanted."

High Spirits (the musical adaptation of Noël Coward's *Blithe Spirit*) was directed by its author and starred Beatrice Lillie, Tammy Grimes, and Edward Woodward. When it was in trouble out of town, Champion was called in to fix it.

TAMMY GRIMES: "He had all the blocking planned out in his head. If you said, 'What if I came on like this . . .,' he'd say, 'No, I've figured this all out' and he'd walk away. Then you'd say, 'Gower, Gower, never mind. I'll walk from here, I'll walk from anywhere you tell me.' Some directors will say, 'Sure, try it, let's see it.' But Gower knew the stage that way, and it all made sense when you saw the entire scene."

High Spirits turned out to be a disappointment in spite of Champion's help, Coward's play, and the sight of Grimes as the ghost Elvira flying around on a wire. "Gower was an indefatigable worker, and a perfectionist. But it was too late for Elvira and me. I think Noël wanted to hold on to his play. It worked; but I think it really could have been a great musical, and run and run and run."

Jeanne Arnold was in the cast of *The Happy Time,* which Champion wanted rehearsed in Los Angeles. "We had all these children in the cast, and they had to go to school. So David Merrick had to set up a school there in the Talmadge Studios. And I'll never forget the picture of one of those teachers going to Gower Champion and saying, 'I want so-and-so, and so-and-so, and so-and-so'; and Gower saying, 'Can't I please have them for ten more minutes?' and she said, 'No!' She didn't care if he was Gower Champion or not."

Mary Ann O'Reilly was a young dancer in the show. "He was very big on giving people their first break, also for hiring people for lead roles and then firing them before the opening night. I remember the auditions for that show. Gower was looking for acrobatics, and it seemed like there were a million people at the final call. There was a woman singing 'Take Back Your Mink' while walking in a handstand with her feet on her head. She didn't get the show."

Though *The Happy Time* went through many cast changes before it opened in New York, it didn't help, and it became the first in a string of failures for Champion. The last show he directed was *42nd Street*, with a cast that featured Lee Roy Reams: "He didn't work very well with dialogue. He was always saying, 'Too many words.' He also didn't like actors to stand still while they were singing a song. He always had to have something going on. It was all very cinematic: scenery just moved on and off, and there was never any real break in the action. There were a lot of fade-outs and fade-ins."

Joe Bova was also in the cast: "The book kept getting shaved. In fact, in the programs it says 'Crossovers by Michael Stewart.' Practically all our rehearsal time went to the chorus. We were out of town and Merrick was sitting there doing his crossword puzzle, and the principals were all lounging around outside the rehearsal room, and the stage manager was going back in. I was feeling kind of flip that day, and I said to him 'Ask Gower when he's going to rehearse the book.' It was a very saucy thing to say, and I could see David's pencil come down, and my face started to flush, and he sort of glared at me, and all the principals were staring. The next day, we were running through something, and I did some little thing that was different. And Gower jumped all over me. Later I found out that Merrick had gone to Gower and told him, 'Bova says you never rehearse the book.' Gower got angry about the fact that I had tattled on him. A few days later he came to rehearsal and said, 'I've left the next three afternoons just for book rehearsal.' We all arrived the next day and Gower wasn't there. He had gotten ill and gone into the hospital. At that time we joked that he just didn't want to rehearse the book."

It was no joke. Champion died in the hospital on *42nd Street's* opening night.

REAMS: "He was on medication, but it was never presented to us as anything serious. Then he would have blood transfusions, and come back feeling fine. But when the pressure out of town got so big, it was hard on him. When we got in town, David Merrick didn't think the show was ready, so we would run it every night to empty houses. It got so we were putting stuffed animals in the chairs so we would have someone to play to."

On opening night, Merrick announced Champion's death after the show.

REAMS: "David had a lot riding on the show, as did Gower's estate, and all of us. If he had to announce the death before the show it would have affected everything. It was a very smart business move on David's part. The papers got a better story, and we got a lot of publicity all over the world."

After six flops, Champion ended his career with the Broadway dream story of the hoofer who goes out a youngster but comes back a star.

REAMS: "I remember Gower telling me that he had finally realized that he was a song-and-dance man, and that's what he had to do. He said, 'That's the thing I do best.' He gave his life for that show; and he died doing what he did best."

Michael Bennett choreographed A *Joyful Noise*, *Henry, Sweet Henry, Promises, Promises, Company, Coco*, and *Follies*. He was director/choreographer for *Seesaw, Ballroom*, and *Dreamgirls*. He will always be remembered for A *Chorus Line*, an all-time Broadway attendance record-breaker.

Bennett's charismatic personality affected everyone who worked with him, including sixteen-year-old Neva Small, who was in the cast of *Henry, Sweet Henry*: "I was a teenager, and it was only his second show, and I had a crush on him. He couldn't do anything wrong, as far as I was concerned. I wasn't a great dancer, to say the least, and I remember he taught me the steps for 'I Wonder How It Is to Dance with a Boy" and I was very tentative, and he said, 'That's it! It's perfect! I want it just the way it is now.' I used to wander up West End Avenue and just stand outside his building and just look, because he lived there."

When Bennett choreographed *Coco*, Katharine Hepburn was also a novice to the musical stage. "What you have to remember here is that he was directing someone who had never done any musical work on the stage, had never done anything of that sort at all."

Hepburn played Coco Chanel in the Andre Previn/Alan Jay Lerner musical. "If you're any good—and he was very good, very smart—you always think you know everything, which is what he thought. I have the same problem. Then, inevitably, it turns out you *do* know everything. He had get-up-and-go, and imagination, and a pictorial eye. Energetic people get a lot done. He got a lot done."

John Cunningham was among the cast of Stephen Sondheim's *Company*, the small, "chorusless" show about marriage and relationships: "The fact that we were not dancers was a great credit to Michael—because he looked at us and said, 'How am I going to use these people?' The first thing he said in rehearsals was that he didn't want us to do dancing. Pretend we're in the PTA talent show. He said, 'Don't worry about it, I only want you to move the way the character would move, to make the person watching forget he's watching an actor.' That's when I began to realize how wonderfully talented Michael was."

Bennett was celebrated for experimenting (just as he developed *Chorus Line* with a workshop full of dancers).

JOHN CUNNINGHAM: "He had developed some whole routine where the guys were doing ballet—I thought it was funny. We worked for two weeks on it, and then we were going to really see what it would look like. So we did it to our best, and he looked at it. And he said, 'That's all shit. Forget it.' And he just dumped the whole thing. I've been through several musicals with people where they knew it was shit; we knew it was shit; but they were unable to just flush it from their consciousness, having spent that much time on it. They kept trying to fix it, fix it, fix it. Michael was able to look at it two weeks into the work and say, 'This is terrible—let's just dump it.' Remarkable."

After its development in workshop, *A Chorus Line* opened downtown at Joe Papp's Public Theatre before moving to Broadway. Carole Schweid was one of the dancers who helped to develop the piece but didn't get chosen for the original company: "I used to see Michael, especially during previews, standing there thinking—he was always working. You could tell his mind was racing about other things in the show. He was really inspiring, and he always made you want to do it better. It was almost like you were hypnotized by him, in a way. He would let you be creative, and make up steps, or do what you could do. Then he would just put it into the design of everything. In that opening number, you really knew everything about every character in the show.

"There was a different person picked every night down there. You never knew who was getting the job. It was all very up when we were down at the Public. You have to remember we were in the seventies and everyone was stoned half the time. Everyone was a hippie. Michael was a hippie and he was a mover. I remember one day when he came in and picked up his Marlboros and said, 'I'm going up to talk to Joe.' We had six- or seven-foot mirrors in the rehearsal room. He came back with the promise for those twenty-foot Mylar mirrors. He could do it."

After understudying in the Broadway company, Schweid was passed over the first time there was a vacancy as Morales. When the replacement didn't work out, she was finally hired. "When I found out I wasn't going to get the part, it hurt. He made us all audition—all the understudies had to audition, and that was really kind of shitty. Then I remember Michael telling me I wasn't perfect for the part, so they were hiring someone else. I adjusted to that. Then Barbara [Luna] got fired; she had played the part for two weeks and was out four times during that period. I got a call telling me they wanted me to take over Morales, and I was a wreck. It was all very, very weird. Michael came in and said, 'Okay, we're going to change this. You're going to say, "I have a Jewish mother and a Puerto Rican father and a lot of internal conflicts."' It was an attempt to fit the person."

After a while, the person didn't seem to matter as much as maintaining Bennett's vision of the show.

SCHWEID: "I was playing the part, and then I got fired. Nobody ever told me why. Years later I heard from an accompanist that the story going around about me was that Michael Bennett came backstage after the show and said to me, 'Carole, you're the best Morales I've ever seen. You're not Puerto Rican. You're fired.' That made me feel better. Maybe that's what he told other people. But he never said that to me. Jeffrey Hamlett was the production stage manager then, and he was the one who told me I was out. Michael never did."

After having already filled in for a month onstage in *A Chorus Line*, Mary Ann O'Reilly was made to audition by Bennett before she was allowed to go on the road. "I think he insisted that everyone audition so we could all go through the whole process again, and he could be 'Michael the Teacher.'"

When *A Chorus Line* became a Broadway hit, it dominated Bennett personally and professionally. When it wasn't filling his time with national and international productions, its success was haunting his future work.

Barbara Erwin joined the workshop of his next show, *Ballroom*, at the same time she was performing on Broadway in *Annie*. "I wasn't making a lot of money in *Annie*. I was probably making less than the dog, and I know I was making less than my understudy, and I had five kids, and I really thought I'd have to get a part-time job, maybe as a hatcheck girl or something, during the day. But the workshop was during the day, and it was perfect. I'd never auditioned for Michael Bennett before, and I was flattered when he picked me."

Bennett's production of *Ballroom* starred Dorothy Loudon. "I had been in *Annie* for nine months, and my husband had died during the run of the show, and just going to the theatre every night reminded me of his death constantly. Michael Bennett came backstage and we went next door to Gallagher's and talked at length about whether the role would be too difficult for me because of Norman's death. I went down to audition anyway, and I've never regretted it. *Ballroom* was one of my favorite shows."

The musical was based on a television movie about two lonely people who frequent a dance hall. Bennett assembled a company of middle-aged dancers to populate the ballroom. "All these wonderful people came out of retirement, and some of them were a little overweight, and as they started to dance they lost weight and began to look fabulous. Michael would run around saying, 'Go out and get a milkshake. Eat some french fries, get a pizza.' They were a marvelous group of people. There was a lot of love up there and we worked our fannies off. And all these dancers were working again after all these years. It was really like Michael's tribute and show of love to the older gypsies, that he had given to the younger gypsies in *Chorus Line*. People misunderstood all this. One review said it was like a slap in the face to older dancers, and that really hurt him. They missed the point."

Ballroom closed after 116 performances. Bennett would have success again with *Dreamgirls*, before his death from AIDS in 1987. But A *Chorus Line* became a kind of Frankenstein, and his later work, especially *Ballroom*, was victimized.

LOUDON: "Unfortunately for Michael—and for all of us—I don't think it would have mattered what he did after *Chorus Line*. Nothing would have pleased the critics. I don't say they were out to get us, but they got us."

Bob Fosse began as a vaudeville hoofer. He had danced in Hollywood, where his idol was Fred Astaire, in such films as *Kiss Me, Kate* and *My Sister Eileen*. On Broadway he apprenticed with George Abbott, starting his choreographic career as Jerome Robbins's assistant. His first big success (and a Tony) came with *Pajama Game*, which introduced the distinct Fosse style in numbers like "Steam Heat" and "Hernando's Hideaway."

Zoya Leporska was a ballerina with the New York City Opera when she was hired as Fosse's assistant and dance captain for *Pajama Game*. "Bobby was so precise. He taught me how to count. You always knew exactly where you were and what you were doing. And if you didn't know the count, forget it, Charlie. Every count was written down, every entrance—who came on from what side of the stage, everything."

Fosse's early hits included *Damn Yankees, Bells Are Ringing*, and *How to Succeed in Business without Really Trying*, which gave Elaine Cancilla her first job in a Broadway show. "Working with Bob Fosse was probably the thing I'm fondest of in my career. Back in those days you had three divisions: the dancing chorus, the singing chorus, and the actors. The dancers really worked their tushies off for the full eight hours of rehearsals. At five minutes before six o'clock you were told to do it again, from the top, full out. It was always 'one more time,' and you did it one more time, whether you got anything out of it or not. But there was never any time when I didn't enjoy it."

Cancilla went on to work in two more Fosse shows. "I think Bob liked my dancing, and that was all you could ask from a choreographer. The fact that he hires you again is the highest compliment he can pay you."

In *How to Succeed*, Fosse replaced choreographer Hugh Lambert during rehearsals, and restaged virtually all the numbers. Gene Foote was in the chorus and went on to become a mainstay Fosse dancer. "The way Bob reworked 'A Secretary Is Not a Toy' and 'Coffee Break' was wonderful. They were staged numbers. We all became characters; we had props—the girls had pencils and wrote little notes, and we all had briefcases. It was all character work. He had already done this in *Damn Yankees* with things like 'Shoeless Joe.' Even in *Pajama Game* there are a lot of numbers that are traditional, but then in the middle of it you have 'Steam Heat,' which is pure Fosse. In *Damn Yankees*, Gwen's numbers are always pure Fosse; and by the time we got to *Sweet Charity*, his style was all there. By that time he had begun to minimalize, and minimalize, and minimalize. There was less movement; and yet every moment was more full."

Annie McGreevey was in the cast of *Sweet Charity*. "He was demanding, and a perfectionist. When it comes to dancing, both in auditions and in rehearsals, I'm a klutz; I'm the worst. But I think he recognized my talent as a singer, and my enthusiasm for performing. I've worked with choreographers and directors who were cruel, and he wasn't."

Fosse's reputation was for being demanding and tough. He drove his companies, and himself, never slowing down. Eyde Byrde toured as the prison matron in *Chicago*. "When we went out on tour, the show was like it was still on Broadway. The show was that good, even though Jerry Orbach was the only one of the original stars who went out on the road."

GENE FOOTE: "In every show I was ever in, I had eyes that could see to the back of the house. In *Sweet Charity* at the Palace, it was my job to check for Bob. Many nights he would walk into the back of the theatre and stand there, and I'd just pass the word: 'He's here.' Then the performance would become very sharp and clean."

As the dance hall hostess in *Sweet Charity*, Gwen Verdon found her greatest vehicle. In Gwen Verdon, Fosse found his ideal. *Damn Yankees* began their lifetime association. They collaborated on *New Girl in Town* (a musical version of Eugene O'Neill's *Anna Christie*), *Redhead* (during which they were married), *Sweet Charity*, and *Chicago*. Between them they accumulated every award the theatre has to offer.

Fosse looked on his wife as his medium, and he was her best audience.

FOOTE: "When Gwen did the Milliken Show [an elaborate 'industrial' extravaganza that featured the most famous names on Broadway], Bob and I went. Gwen came out and did a kick and a little thing that she landed, and Bob turned to me and said, 'See—that's what I mean. A star. It's not what you do, and not how you do it, or how much. It's what you make out of what you do.'"

With *Chicago*, Verdon and Fosse went back to Fosse's vaudeville roots. The show also starred Chita Rivera and Jerry Orbach.

GWEN VERDON: "I had tried to get this property from the time I was in *Can-Can*. Everyone was saying to me, 'Whatever you want to do, darling, we'll do it.' And I'd say, 'I want to do *Chicago*.' For years, everyone turned it down. Then I got the project myself, quite by accident. I had tried to get to Maurine Watkins, who wrote the original play, for years, and I finally contacted her in Florida during the Cuban missile crisis. She said, 'How can we talk about that piece of fluff when I have guns aimed right at me?' I was pregnant at the time, and then my daughter was born, and when Nicole was about three years old I went back to work, on *Sweet Charity*. Maurine Watkins died, and from her attorney we learned that she had in her will that I had first refusal—so I got the rights. Bob and I took an option on it together."

With music and lyrics by Kander and Ebb, *Chicago* was the vaudeville-style tale of Roxie Hart, the chorus girl who shot her boyfriend.

JERRY ORBACH: "When I told Hal Prince that I was doing this show with Gwen and Bobby and Chita, he said to me, 'I'm going to make a prediction. There's going to come one moment out of town someplace where you're going to have to be the grown-up in the group.' I said, 'What are you talking about?' He said, 'These people are all gypsies who've never really grown up. Just remember I've said this. You're going to have to be in charge.'

"Well, it all came true in Philadelphia. The whole trial scene became such a mess—Bobby had people screwing on the stairs, and all these things were going on. I wanted it tightened up, because the material was really very funny. So I told Bobby I wanted to talk to him. I told him I knew he was going for this Brechtian effect—the alienation in the scene. He said he was. And I told him that even Brecht felt that first you had to get your audience hooked on a real level, and then you can hit them over the head with the message. I told him I thought everything on the set was distracting from the real scene. Well, he thanked me, and the next day he got rid of all that."

By the time Fosse did *Chicago*, he had already become fascinated with portraying decadence while directing the film version of *Cabaret*.

GENE FOOTE: "We were doing all these outrageous things [in *Chicago*] and he was encouraging us. In *Pippin*, he always said with the opening number, 'Make love to the audience.' With *Chicago*, it was 'Dare the audience to look at you, and look back at them with murder in your eyes.' An ensemble person has a more difficult time sometimes than a Charity or Roxie. But in *Pippin*, for the first time he said to us, 'You are one character for the entire evening.' At the time I had gotten to New York there were thousands of young boys coming here every day. So we were a dime a dozen. I had a gift for dance, but no great technique. I just could dance. Then when I discovered Fosse and found out that dance was about character, my life was changed. Bob changed my life."

Pippin and *Chicago* would turn out to be benchmarks in musical theatre, as Fosse steered Broadway's evolution away from the more structured, old-fashioned book musical into a kind of theatre where dance, instead of helping the story along, became the medium and the main event. With *Dancin'*, also a hit, the book disappeared completely.

FOOTE: *Pippin* was the beginning of the dancer being accepted in Broadway shows. When we opened the *New York Times* and saw the first ad for the show, we were all listed—all eighteen of us, not just the principals. We were all surprised and thrilled. But in that show we all had lines and identities. Bob loved his dancers, and performers of all kinds. He was impressed with anything you could do that was a little unique. He always used your energy. He'd say, 'Look, I know these steps aren't very good, but your energy is going to make this happen.' Of course, they were wonderful steps."

Fosse gained strength and power as he created on the bodies he knew.

FOOTE: "By the time he did *Pippin* and *Chicago*, Bob knew all of us. We had been around, or he had used us before. It did come out of us, but it was very improvisational. Once he had set up the skeleton, he got very specific about it. I remember there was one dance in *Pippin* I did with John Mineo, and it was basically a scene change. We did a cakewalk, and for four weeks we just improvised while they changed the scene behind us. And Bob watched it. Then, one day, he set the number in fifteen minutes, and I don't remember him ever touching the number after that. He made it exact; but he watched us to see what our fortes were, and how he was going to make us dance together."

Fosse had had his share of misses, particularly Frank Loesser's *Pleasures and Palaces*, which closed out of town. For his last show, 1987's *Big Deal*, he reached the pinnacle of the director/choreographer's total control by choosing not to work with a living composer or lyricist. He was tired of making compromises, and for the show about small-time hoods in Depression-era Chicago, he handpicked a score from old songs of the 1930s. The show starred Allan Weeks: "The producers requested a lot of things from Bob, but he didn't want to do it that way. He wanted to do it his way. There was a very daunting side to his personality. Bob was great to work with, but you had to work hard, and if you didn't, that was it. Precision was important to him, and he had no patience if he wasn't getting exactly what he wanted."

When it opened, *Big Deal* drew some raves for the dancing: ". . . whaddaya know? Broadway is Broadway again," wrote Watt of the *Daily News*, but unfortunately, the rest of the show was attacked by the critics for its weak book, and *Big Deal* didn't run.

Shortly afterward Fosse suffered a fatal heart attack in Washington, where he had been rehearsing a national tour of *Sweet Charity*. The company included Michael Cone: "The day he died he rehearsed us. He was different that day. I remember I had a line, and I was actually begging for a laugh on it, and he gave me a note, and told me 'You don't have to work that hard. The line's not that good, and you're better than that.' That's a great note to get from someone like Fosse, to know that he liked me—or at least liked my work. That night the line came up that I had been pushing so hard on, and I just said it—and it got a bigger reaction than it ever had before. I didn't think about it, I just did it his way. After the curtain came down, they called us all back on the stage, and told us that Bobby had died."

Fosse forever changed the face of the musical theatre, and left a legacy that is carried on by those he worked with and taught, like Gene Foote, who himself went on to direct and choreograph: "Bob always used to say he only had six steps; but what six steps! He never really trusted himself, or thought he was good enough. But for a generation or two of us, he was God. Michael Bennett was a great theatre man, but can you say what his style was? You can look at a piece of Bob's work, and there's no doubt that it's Fosse. What Martha Graham did for modern dance and Balanchine did for ballet, Fosse did for musical comedy. He would take a step and could distort it, and make it something wonderful and typical only of him. We had a step in *Sweet Charity* where we would sort of slide, taking little tiny steps. He told us it had been inspired by his seeing an old man run for a bus. He found things everywhere. He watched people all through his life, and he remembered and used everything."

11

Don't Call Him George

I N a musical," says Carol Channing, "you need a benevolent despot; a kind Hitler through whose eyes everyone sees the show." The American musical theatre was built on tyranny, not democracy. Getting a musical on may be a collaborative effort, but amid the turmoil of the composer, lyricist, librettist, director, choreographer, designers, and performers struggling to make a hit, one person's vision must overpower the others. Strength, not simply talent, is what counts.

Beginning in 1935, when he directed the Billy Rose production of Rodgers and Hart's *Jumbo*, starring Jimmy Durante, George Abbott directed twenty-six musicals in the next twenty-seven years, twenty-two of which were hits.

He discovered countless composers, writers, directors, and especially performers who among them built the entire framework of the American musical theatre. Nancy Walker came in to audition for his 1941 college musical *Best Foot Forward* with music, not comedy, on her mind: "There was an open call, and I just went down there and applied for it, and there were hundreds of people. I didn't think I was funny; he did. When I got through singing, he said, 'Well, there's nothing in the show for you, but

139

we're going to write something for you.' I almost fell off my seat. I never thought of comedy, just singing. It was a big shock."

Abbott was always interested in the nuts-and-bolts craft of engineering an entertaining hit.

The 1947 *High Button Shoes* was by first-time Broadway composer Jule Styne, with choreography by Jerome Robbins. Along with Phil Silvers, it starred Nanette Fabray.

FABRAY: "The whole show had no business being a big hit. On the first day of rehearsal, George Abbott said, 'I want you to all go home and write good parts for yourselves.' I had eight lines in the original script. They had called me in to meet with them, and they said I could either play the mother or the daughter. Mr. Abbott said to me, 'If you're smart, you'll play the mother, because it doesn't matter about your age. The mother has all the songs, and you're funny. Take the mother.'" She took the mother. "Then they made the part bigger, and he really gave me confidence that I could be funny. It should never have been a big hit." *High Button Shoes* ran 727 performances, Robbins won a Tony, and Abbott and Fabray captured two of the show's six Donaldson Awards.

Abbott spotted Willi Burke during an audition for *Tenderloin*, but had other ideas for her. "I went in to audition for a prostitute with a heart of gold. After I sang, Mr. Abbott came up onstage and asked me if I could belt, and I told him I couldn't. He said, 'Well, try,' and asked me to come back in a couple of days and belt something for him. He suggested 'Bye, Bye, Blackbird.' So I went home and tried to learn how to belt, and I came back and I was a nervous wreck, but I did it, and he came up onstage and said, 'You're right, you can't belt.' However, he did say he was interested in me for something else, and I had no idea what he was talking about."

Tenderloin, about sin in 1890s New York, was Bock and Harnick's 1960 follow-up to *Fiorello!*, which Abbott had also directed.

BURKE: "Right after that, my agent called, and I got the script for *Fiorello!*, and a few days later I came in and read for Mr. Abbott, and I got the job. I went into the show, but I never saw Mr. Abbott after that. I asked about it and said, 'Mr. Abbott cast me, and I haven't heard anything from him since,' and they said, 'Don't worry—you're doing all right. If he wasn't pleased, you'd hear from him, believe me.'"

Abbott had started out as a playwright, and he kept absolute control over his productions. In an Abbott show, there was never a question of who was in charge. Among his often-revived classics is *On Your Toes*, in which Abbott directed George S. Irving. "Abbott was a very careful director, and he knew exactly what he wanted. He wouldn't put up with any phoniness. He'd say,

'That's phony; it's phony, and I don't believe it.' And he'd make you say lines the way he wanted, and make them real."

Abbott discovered Joe Bova in an off-Broadway production of *On the Town*, and cast him in *Once Upon a Mattress*, the Mary Rodgers/Marshall Barer version of "The Princess and the Pea" that launched Carol Burnett to stardom.

JOE BOVA: "George Abbott worked on a musical as if it were a play. It wasn't just a question of putting a song here or there, with the right person to sing it. He really concentrated on the script; the reality of the script was what was important to him. He respected the character and the situation, and once he had those things established, the song and dance would grow out of that."

Working with his actors, he had no use for subtext or motivation; he wanted actors to say the lines, and very often he would give them a line reading to show them how. It infuriated some performers, but not Barnard Hughes, who was in the cast of one of Abbott's ill-fated projects, *How Now Dow Jones*.

HUGHES: "He'd give directions about words—which you rarely hear anymore. That used to be the only kind of direction you'd get: 'That's a period, isn't it?' or 'That's a comma there, it isn't a period.' 'There's a Z in that word—let me hear that Z.' I thought it was great direction."

WILLI BURKE: "He watched the show, and if he didn't like what you were doing, he'd let you know. He's not very verbal. The only direction I remember getting from him was, 'Make sure you get your voice up there to the back row of the theatre—you have to reach everyone.'"

Dorothy Loudon starred in the doomed *The Fig Leaves Are Falling* in 1969. "He would take notes down on yellow lined paper. And when he gave the notes he would tear off the paper, and crumble it up and throw it over his shoulder. And after the rehearsal, I would go over and pick up all these balls of paper, and take them home and iron them. I still have all those notes."

Gwen Verdon worked with Abbott on two shows, *Damn Yankees* and *New Girl in Town*. "He treated everyone the same way—the actors, Hal Prince, Bobby Griffith, all of us. Even if there was something wrong with the set or something, he would just say, 'Hal, Bobby, deal with it'—and he'd leave."

Even though performers often didn't understand his tactics, they understood that what he wanted were results.

Mary Louise Wilson was among the cast of Kander and Ebb's *Flora the Red Menace*. "He was always yelling at me, and at the time I didn't know why he was yelling. But you know, he never had any of that ego stuff. When

Nobody's Perfect

NOWN primarily as a dancer, Gwen Verdon was called on to create a real comic character for the first time in her career when she was cast as Lola in *Damn Yankees*.

"I didn't much care for working with Mr. Abbott because he could never find a way to make me understand what I was doing. He also didn't want to bother with a lot of things. You know, even when we did *Damn Yankees*, I thought he was really old then. He was seventy-something, and he'd tell you where to go like he was a traffic cop. But I was brand new and needed all the help I could get.

"If you asked questions, he'd say, 'Speak to Bobby Griffith or Hal Prince. They'll tell you what to do.' I was actually there when Stephen Douglas, the leading man, asked him what his motivation was, and Mr. Abbott said, 'Your paycheck.'

"I finally learned a trick from Bob Fosse, who had worked with Abbott before. We never got a full script—only what are called 'sides,' with your dialogue and the cues on them. So you didn't really know what you were saying or answering. Or sometimes the answers seemed to be coming out of left field. George would usually give you a line reading. I didn't mind, but most actors wanted to come up with their own creation. So Bob said to me, 'When he gives you a line, ask him what you would say as the character if you had more dialogue than was actually written.' So then he would talk more and more and you would find out what the scene was really about.

"He didn't want to push actors. Actually, all he wanted to do was to play golf or tennis every afternoon. It worked for him and it's still working. He's a great man. I love him, but working for him at that stage of my career wasn't easy."

---

he yelled, there was a reason. Looking back on it now, I realize that when he yelled at me, he was just trying to get me to do what he wanted. I've worked with so many directors, and they bring in a lot of personal stuff. He was just always trying to get the show right. There were just no neurotic things about him."

Abbott understood musical comedy shorthand.

M. L. WILSON: "We were out of town with *Flora*, and in the show there was a big scene in a park, with a rally going on. Liza Minnelli was downstage on a park bench, and there were various crossovers behind her, one of which was with me and the Cowboy. I'd had one scene with him earlier where nothing much happened. Well, in New Haven, Mr. Abbott came down the aisle and said, 'I've got a great idea. Now, this is really funny. The Cowboy crosses over this way, and then the Cowboy crosses again, and then Ada comes on again and Liza says to her "Hello Ada," and Ada says "Howdy."' And everyone just looked at him, and thought, what's so funny about that? Well, I said that line in the show, and the audience really blew up. The audience knew by that little thing that I was in love with the Cowboy."

The 1954 *Pajama Game*, with music and lyrics by Richard Adler and Jerry Ross, was about love and union disputes in a pajama factory. Based on a book by Richard Bissell, it is a typical "old-fashioned" Abbott musical. It starred John Raitt, Janis Paige, Eddie Foy, Jr., and Carol Haney.

JOHN RAITT: "With Abbott, by the tenth day we were on our feet doing the whole show. The only thing that changed in *Pajama Game* was that he tried putting '7½ Cents,' the labor song, into the end of the first act."

JANIS PAIGE: "He absolutely scared me to death, and I wasn't alone. He was—and still is—a very tall, immaculate, handsome, imposing man who used a minimum of words. He's all business. He had enormous control and exercised it. We did as we were told. I was terrified of him."

Also in the cast was comedienne Charlotte Rae, who lost her part.

RAITT: Charlotte played the boss's secretary—but she and Abbott didn't get along. So, ten days—and Charlotte was out. He *loved* Carol Haney, and he gave Carol two parts: her own, and Charlotte's singing role. Janis was all upset. She said, 'I'm no longer the star of the show.' She was ready to quit. I don't blame her. But Eddie Foy and I took her to dinner up in New Haven. We said, 'Hey, listen. We're all pros. We've got our names up there, we're expected to deliver. We're going to cry all the way to the bank.'"

The Pajama Game made a lot of people rich. Its chief ballad, "Hey There," was promptly made into a hit record by Rosemary Clooney, and the show went on to run 1,063 performances.

But Abbott's workmanlike approach and total lack of sympathy with artistic expression could make being a performer under his direction a strain.

When Gwen Verdon left *Damn Yankees*, Fosse, the show's choreographer, called in Gretchen Wyler to replace her. "Abbott did a terrible thing to me," Wyler remembers. "I went in for Gwen, and I got great reviews. And after about four or five months, I heard that George Abbott was out front. He had not put me in—Jimmy Hammerstein and Bobby and Zoya Leporska [Fosse's assistant] ran the rehearsals. Our director never even came to see me. Then all of a sudden he was there. Well, I was enormously excited, and I just couldn't believe he was there. After the show, we were all called out onstage, and they set up little chairs for everyone.

"Now, I had never met Mr. Abbott, and he didn't come over to greet me, and he was giving notes from one person to the next, going around the room, and all of a sudden he caught my eye, and I was really excited and happy. And he said, 'Gretchen Wyler, I have no idea what you were doing onstage tonight. I have no idea how you found this character you were playing tonight.' He was so horrendous to me, I left the stage in tears. I was not dismissed, I just left. I wouldn't come back.

"I went home that night and called my manager and said, 'You call Harold Prince tomorrow'—and he was just little Harold Prince then—not HAR-OLD PRINCE. I was so humiliated and hurt, and I thought, 'How can I ever face that company again?' I was the star of the show. And I said I would quit unless there was an apology from George Abbott. Can you believe it? But I did it, and I meant it. George Abbott called me and apologized. I don't think he meant it—I think Hal made him do it. I've never been humiliated like that, not before and not since. He has always been so extolled, but it's amazing how people get away with things like that."

Paige, a Warner Brothers contract player, came to *Pajama Game* from Hollywood. Her movie *stardom* followed this show, in such films as *Silk Stockings*. "There was one time during rehearsals when I didn't feel comfortable in a certain place in the show. I questioned something he was doing. So I asked to see him, and I went up to his office. There he was, sitting behind that huge desk, and he said, 'What is it, Janis?' and I said, 'Mr. Abbott, I'd like to talk to you about this scene. I don't feel good in it. I can do better.' He said, 'Janis, you have five minutes to make up your mind. That's the way it is. That's the way it's going to be. Now, you want to stay in the show, or you want to leave? You go outside and stand there for five minutes, and make up your mind.'

"Well, I burst into tears, which I'd had no intention of doing. Then I went outside, and my agent is standing there, and I'm sobbing. Then I dried my tears and said, 'He's not going to treat me this way.' And I walked back and said, 'Mr. Abbott, I'm staying.' He said, 'Good. Get back to work.' I was scared to death of him; but I did as I was told, and I got better. Closing night in Boston there was a note in my dressing room that said, 'Dear Janis, thank you for all the hard work. I'm proud of you. You've done a wonderful job. Good luck—George.' I have it to this day."

In *Flora the Red Menace*, Mary Louise Wilson shared a dressing room with legendary gypsy Cathryn "Skipper" Damon. "Mr. Abbott liked to go dancing at least once a week, and we'd hear him come down the hall humming. (We used to call him 'The Eagle'—he frightened us half to death.) He'd come in and get Skipper, and take her dancing to Roseland. And it was just dancing—no sitting down or anything. They just danced all night; nothing to drink—he didn't drink and didn't smoke. He just had her out to dance, and Skipper, of course, had been dancing all night in the show."

Flora the Red Menace was the second in Abbott's string of flops in the 1960s, and a signal that Abbott's brand of musical theatre was crumbling. A new breed of director/choreographer was coming into vogue. When Abbott took over from Arthur Penn on *How Now Dow Jones*, the show was unofficially co-directed by Michael Bennett, who was also replacing the original choreographer, Gillian Lynne. Musicals were now being treated as a totality. Production numbers were part of the whole, not a separate entity. Abbott was more comfortable with the standard musicals of the 1940s and 1950s.

Years before, Abbott had gone to New Haven to inspect *Oklahoma!* when it was shopping for a new director during its tryout.

ALFRED DRAKE: "The Theatre Guild was thinking of replacing Rouben Mamoulian. I had the habit of walking out onstage before a performance while the curtain was down, and one night I went out and George was there. I said, 'You saw the show last night?' He said, 'Yes,' and I said, 'What did you think of it?' and he said, 'I wish somebody had given it to me.'"

The impact that Rodgers and Hammerstein's *Oklahoma!* had on the musical theatre in some ways passed Abbott by completely. The director had worked with Richard Rodgers when Rodgers was still teamed with Lorenz Hart, on *The Boys from Syracuse* in 1938. Thirty years later, when the show was revived, time had left Abbott's libretto dated. The director, Christopher Hewett, was painfully aware of this. Mr. Abbott, unfortunately, was not.

CHRISTOPHER HEWETT: "The nicest thing about *Boys from Syracuse* was that I had Richard Rodgers right behind me. I said to him at the beginning, 'I've got to do something about this book,' and he wrote on a piece of paper, 'You have my permission to change this book—Richard Rodgers.' When Mr. Abbott complained—and he did, because someone had gone to a preview and told Abbott he didn't think it was very good—he called up Dick Rodgers and said nothing could be changed. But fortunately Dick had a contract that said nothing could be changed without the permission of George Abbott and/

or Richard Rodgers. So I was very lucky to have him on my side. I was also lucky that Fred Ebb came in and rewrote a couple of scenes."

In 1976, the idea of a new George Abbott musical based on a classic Shakespearean comedy intrigued everyone, including the cast. *Music Is*, an adaptation of *Twelfth Night*, had music and lyrics by Abbott's protegé Richard Adler, who had co-authored both *Pajama Game* and *Damn Yankees*. The company included Christopher Hewett, Catherine Cox, Joel Higgins, and David Holliday.

DAVID HOLLIDAY: "I don't think any of us were really prepared for the way he directed. Actually, he treated us like puppets."

Christopher Hewett auditioned for the part of Sir Toby Belch. "He said, 'Oh, no, that boy's not a Belch. He should play that other rotten part.' And that's the way he thought of it."

Hewett was cast as Malvolio.

The cast of *Music Is* thought that the mixed identity and farcical elements of the show would be a natural for Mr. Abbott. They were wrong.

HEWETT: "I remember one of the actors used to laugh when he was coming on in a scene, and Mr. A asked him why he did it, and he said, 'I thought it would be amusing.' And Abbott said, 'Well, it's not. Don't do it.' As Malvolio, I asked him if I couldn't have some more funny lines, and he said, 'What do you think I am, a gag writer?' He didn't adapt Shakespeare well. He eliminated all the fun, and tried to make *Twelfth Night* totally romantic. And you can't do that. The comics really are the play."

Abbott had built his reputation by directing classic American farces like *Room Service* and *Three Men on a Horse*. Comedy was his specialty.

CATHERINE COX: "The comedy in the show didn't work. That seems strange. From the body of Abbott's work you'd think he would be a shoo-in for directing all that lowbrow comedy in Shakespeare's play."

Also, there had already been a successful adaptation of *Twelfth Night*, called *Your Own Thing*, which had a successful run off-Broadway.

COX: "One day when we were out of town, I had the radio on and George Abbott was doing an interview, and they said, 'Mr. Abbott, why are you doing another version of *Twelfth Night*,' since they had done *Your Own Thing*. He took a pause and said, 'Well, if I had known that, we wouldn't be doing this one.' There was total reverence for the man. I'm sure they all knew there was *Your Own Thing*, but I'll bet they didn't even deign to say anything to him. He didn't know, and they weren't about to mention it."

Joel Higgins seemed to be able to get around Abbott better than any young actor ever had before.

HIGGINS: "I guess I was the only person who ever called him 'George.' He really didn't seem to mind at all, but it really freaked everyone else out."

HEWETT: "He always called Joel 'that Huggins boy.'"

HIGGINS: "He never could get my name right."

CATHERINE COX: "He kept calling me 'Patty,' and he called Pat Birch 'Cathy.'"

HIGGINS: "I had this one line, 'Antonio, why are you hiding?' Well, George didn't hear it like that, and wanted the upward inflection: 'Why are you hid*ing*.'"

COX: "It was all precision: you turn your head on this word, and all the sentences had to have an 'up' inflection."

HIGGINS: "So he'd say, 'Can't you hear that?' And I'd say, 'Yeah, I can hear it.' I knew what he was going for, but it seemed more natural the way I was doing it. So the next day at that point it would be, 'No, no—it's Antonio, *Why* are you hid*ing*.' About the fourth time he did it to me, he started 'No, no—' and I said, 'I *know*—it's "Antonio, why are you *hiding*."' and the whole place broke up."

COX: "I think part of the problem was that George Abbott was hard of hearing."

HIGGINS: "One time he wanted Sherry Mathis and me to go over this love scene we had, and we went out in the hall while they all were doing something else. And we were ready to go, and he was sitting there fooling around with his watch, and the stage manager was there, and we were all ready—and he wasn't paying any attention. So I said, 'George, are you going to watch this, or not?' And everybody sort of went white. But he just said, 'Oh, of course, go right ahead.' I really don't think he cared about all that standing on formality crap. You can't be tiptoeing around; hell, you have to work with the guy."

HOLLIDAY: "I think I had respect for him because of his history; and if there were frustrations, you just put up with them because you figured he knew what he was doing. I think this was easier for me because I had worked in London for ten years, and there you just did what the director told you to do."

A decade earlier Abbott had directed *Anya*, which had closed after sixteen performances.

CONSTANCE TOWERS: "The show was a disappointment. The subject matter of Anastasia was not really right for Mr. Abbott. On the second night he came to my dressing room to tell me that the critics had criticized his judgment in the way he had presented the show. He said to me that what he had thought would work really didn't, and he admitted he had been wrong. He not only admitted it to me, but to Wright and Forrest, who had adapted the score. That takes a lot of courage, a lot of integrity."

Abbott outlived his own obsolescence, and in 1982 he successfully revived *On Your Toes* for a new generation, with a cast that included Natalia Makarova and Lara Teeter as Junior. "Once you've worked with George Abbott," says Teeter, "you feel like you've worked with the entire history of the American musical theatre. At the age of ninety-five, which he was when we did *On Your Toes*, he had more energy than anyone in the room. He was the first one at rehearsal and the last one to leave. He didn't tolerate people being late. He gave line readings. He did not want the actor to become a parrot, but he wanted you to say the line in a certain way and make it work for you. It was a frustrating way to work in one way, but it was Mr. Abbott, and the show had a sense of pace. And there was one director—and only one director."

Early in her career, Abbott had cast Elaine Stritch in his revival of *Pal Joey*, and later in *On Your Toes*. "He was very practical," according to Stritch. "I'd played a lot of sophisticated women in summer stock: I wore hats, and came in and said, 'Hello, darling,' with fur stoles and gloves. That was my thing. So I said to him, 'I'm sick of coming in and taking off my gloves and saying, "Hello, darling."' He said, 'Get an umbrella.' It sounds funny, but I did. I went over to Saks on my lunch hour, and bought a nice, chic umbrella—and I've never had so much fun with a prop in my life."

EDDIE BRACKEN: "I saw somebody say to him on television, 'With all the shows you've done, a hundred years after you're gone, people will remember the name of George Abbott.' He said, 'They don't remember now.' In a way, that's true. All of us on Broadway love him and know him. But you say 'Mister Abbott' to a bunch of theatregoers today—a lot of them never heard of him."

During a Broadway career that spanned seven decades, George Abbott was a man of contradictions. He had enormous hits and total bombs. Many performers who worked for him found him cold and difficult.

After her *Damn Yankees* experience, Gretchen Wyler sums up her feelings: "I remember hating George Abbott."

Other performers developed friendships with him. Eddie Bracken met his wife while touring in an Abbott show: "I have five children and nine grandchildren—to this day my wife and I love the man."

Abbott's biggest success was *Fiorello!*, which won the Pulitzer Prize and beat out *Gypsy* to tie for the Tony with *The Sound of Music* as Best Musical of 1959.

Perhaps Abbott's softest spot was for talented young ingenues. He had cast Ellen Hanley in *Barefoot Boy with Cheek*, and used her again in *Fiorello!*, which starred Tom Bosley. As Thea, Fiorello's first wife, Hanley got the chance to see both George Abbotts—the stoic who shied away from emotion, and the closet sentimentalist.

ELLEN HANLEY: "In the scene before Thea sings 'When Did I Fall in Love,' Fiorello was going off on a laugh, and I felt I needed an emotional moment there. So I asked Mr. Abbott, and he said, 'Okay, I think it's all right, we can try it.' So he put in an embrace. But then when I gave Tom Bosley an embrace, George said, 'Okay, now Tom, tip your hat,' and he did something funny, and he got a laugh. So I got to embrace him, but I still didn't get my emotional moment.

"But then Jerry Weidman [the librettist] told me that one night in Philly, as I was starting to do 'When Did I Fall in Love,' Mr. Abbott was so moved by it that he said, 'Well, I have to go outside—I just can't deal with hearing Ellen do this song tonight.'"

Abbott was not infallible; the celebrated judgment was sometimes way off. *Flora the Red Menace* made Liza Minnelli a star, yet Abbott had wanted Eydie Gorme for the role. In the 1950 Cole Porter show *Out of This World*, he cut "From This Moment On."

In the end, practicality was the Abbott motto. When an actor tried to help a laugh line along, Abbott said, "Just deliver it. If it's funny, they'll laugh." When he was asked the secret of his success, he replied, "I make them say their final syllables."

12

Legendary Stars: The Women

T HANKS to Ethel Merman, they'll be calling *Call Me Madam* a smash hit."—Robert Coleman, *Daily Mirror.* October 13, 1950.

"The explosion in Forty-Fourth street last evening was nothing to be alarmed by. It was merely Ethel Merman returning to the New York theatre."—Brooks Atkinson, *New York Times.* December 7, 1956.

"What this town has needed is Ethel Merman. What Miss Merman has needed is a good show. We got her and she got it last evening, when *Gypsy* opened at the Broadway Theatre."—John Chapman, *Daily News.* May 22, 1959.

"Working in the theatre was the most natural thing in the world for Ethel Merman," says June Squibb, who played Electra the stripper in *Gypsy.* "It was like someone saying, 'Yeah, I dusted today.'"

Merman's reputation as a steamroller intimidated many fellow performers about to work with her, including Maria Karnilova: "When I got into *Gypsy,* people would say to me, 'Watch out. She's a bitch. If she doesn't like you, if you step on her lines, she'll have you fired.' But they were lying. That isn't how she worked at all. If she had people fired, it was because she was a

150

perfectionist and she wanted it right. Anyone on the stage who was silly or did something bad was cut out, and I can understand that. Why should she be out there eight times a week knocking herself out when everyone else wasn't?"

Merman never came up through the ranks, was never "one of the kids," which her friend Benay Venuta tried to remedy when they worked together in the Lincoln Center revival of *Annie Get Your Gun*: "She liked being called 'Miss Merman,' and she liked being respected. She was not chummy with the chorus. I think the first time she got to know chorus people was in the revival of *Annie Get Your Gun*, because I had some friends in the company who had been with me in *Carousel*, and I said, 'You've got to meet them.' And she said, 'But they're in the chorus.' And I said, 'Yes, but they're very nice people.' She really was in an ivory tower. I remember I said to her once, 'Do you realize you never went through a period where you had to audition or be turned down? You just became a star.'"

Venuta had replaced Merman in *Anything Goes* on Broadway in the 1930s, and they were lifelong friends. But until the *Annie Get Your Gun* revival, they had never worked together. "Working with her, I could see what a great pro she was. She was always on time, prepared. All big stars are always on time—they know their lines and they're never late. She was a great controller—and she knew how to do it. Like she was very strict about not changing material after a certain point. She would say, 'Call me Miss Birdseye—the show is frozen.' I was such a jerk that in one show they gave me a new song on opening night, and like a fool, I learned it and put it in on the same night. But Ethel knew what worked for her."

Jerry Orbach worked with Merman in the same *Annie Get Your Gun* revival. "She was tough, but in a way she had to be. She could look at a row of balcony lights in a dress rehearsal and tell you the third one on the right should be pink and not yellow—and the guy would say, 'Oh shit, you're right!' A lot of women in the theatre couldn't do that."

Merle Louise played Dainty June in *Gypsy*, both on Broadway and in the national tour. "I remember once, onstage, we were in the middle of the 'Mr. Goldstone' scene, and a couple of stagehands were listening to a ballgame on the radio—and you could hear it all onstage. And suddenly, Merman said, 'Excuse me.' And she goes off through the set and yells, '*Shut the fuck up!*' Then she comes back onstage and finishes the scene. She wasn't about to put up with that."

Sel Vitella was a member of a touring company of *Call Me Madam*. "I played the Court Chamberlain, and I had a stick that I pounded three times

Working with the Merm

FORTUNATELY, Betty Garrett had a good manager when she signed on to understudy Ethel Merman and play a small supporting role in Cole Porter's *Something for the Boys*. "I had a small part in the show, but my manager insisted that I have my own number and I did. It was called 'So Long, San Antonio.' It opened the second act and was probably the first bomb song Cole ever wrote.

"He came back to Boston, where we were trying out, and asked me what kind of song I liked to sing, as 'San Antonio' had to go. So I told him I liked the two things that were guaranteed to make him throw up—folk songs and boogie woogie.

"In one afternoon, he put the two together and came up with 'I'm in Love with a Soldier Boy,' and it stopped the show. Merman had to make an entrance right after the song, but the audience wouldn't stop clapping. So she stopped and made me come out for another bow.

"One night about a year after the show opened, they called me and said Merman had laryngitis and I was on. I knew the show completely, but I never really expected to go on. Also, I didn't have any costumes. Ethel had had a new set made. They took her old ones and pinned them on me. We were completely different shapes. I was big on the bottom and small on the top and she was the reverse.

"I played the role for a week and at every intermission, Ethel would call me and rasp, 'How ya doin', kid?' The first night I told her I was nervous, and she said, 'If they could do it better than you, they'd be up there and you'd be in the audience.' I know a lot of people take credit for that remark, but I think that's the first time she ever said it. And Merman said it to me!"

---

to make an announcement. There was a little head on the stick, and during one performance it fell off. Merman was offstage right, and she boomed, 'Oh, he's lost his thing!' And it echoed all over. God, I was embarrassed."

To the young members of a company, Merman was a formidable presence.

VITELLA: "If you talked to her, it took a lot of courage. And if she answered you, it was always like answering the group—she would include everyone.

It was always like she was being interviewed. She never said anything about my performance, but she would give me a few taps on the shoulder before I was ready to go on—and that was acceptance."

Russell Nype played Merman's Ivy League assistant in Irving Berlin's *Call me Madam* and stopped the show. By the time the show reached Boston, newspaper headlines read, 'A Star Is Born.' "The night after that 'Star Is Born' headline came out, Merman and Pat Harrington were standing onstage at the bottom of the staircase. And when I made my entrance, I heard her turn to Pat and say, 'Here comes the star.' So I just smiled and prayed I'd get to New York before she cut me out."

It never happened, even when Nype won a Tony for his efforts.

VENUTA: "I don't know where the legend comes from that Ethel wasn't good to her supporting players. She was very supportive. If you were talented, she was fine. If you weren't very good, then she wasn't thrilled."

Maria Karnilova played the stripper Tessie Tura in *Gypsy*. "All the scenes I had with her were my scenes—I had all the funny lines. Never once did she not play it full out with me—and I played it for two years with her."

VITELLA: "She knew everything that was going on, both offstage and on. Her antennae were always up."

KARNILOVA: "The first time we met, we were standing across from each other in the wings, and the big showgirls were going by with the tremendous knockers, and I made a gesture to her—and she shook her head and pointed to her own chest. And we roared. We were friends from that moment on."

VITELLA: "They'd had a collection taken up to get a cast picture taken to give her on closing night of *Call Me Madam*. I was one of the few people in the company who thought, 'Why bother?' But when the curtain came down and we gave it to her, she was genuinely moved. I felt awful then that I had thought she wouldn't care."

Seven-year-old Nita Novy was in *Gypsy* as the Balloon Girl, and wasn't really aware that she was working with a piece of history. "Miss Merman was just a nice lady to me. I had no idea she was this big, powerful Broadway star. What did I know? I remember she wore midnight-blue mascara, and on special occasions we would be trooped into her dressing room. And once, I think it was Christmas, I walked in and she was there bent over a candle, melting the mascara to bead her eyelashes. It was fascinating. At Christmastime, everyone would get a gift from her, from Tiffany's—all the cast, the orchestra—everyone would get a little blue box."

If colleagues could learn to support her, learning to take her place was something else. One of Elaine Stritch's early jobs was as Merman's standby for *Call Me Madam*. "It was a great honor to even be thought that you could go on for Ethel Merman—which you never could. You could forget about that—it was like working at home. You'd go to her dressing room and knock on her door and say, 'Are you okay?' and she'd say, 'Get out of here!'"

Every once in awhile Merman would take a dislike to someone mostly because she felt like it. Says Venuta: "She had terrible arguments with people. Ethel didn't get along with Stephen Sondheim. And to the very end of her life, she couldn't understand why he was such a great success."

If she liked you, though, there was no limit to her supportiveness, as Merle Louise found out the first time she went on as the understudy in *Gypsy*. "There was one line that got a big laugh that hadn't before, about how Mama makes up a story that two nuns went blind sewing the costumes. Merman was in the wings, and said to one of the showgirls, 'Hey, this kid gave the show a real kick in the ass.' When she came out for her solo call, she brought me two dozen roses that she had ordered in, and gave them to me. I remember it was a cold January night, and I walked home with these roses, and by the time I got home they were frozen. But I put them in a vase anyway and left them there for two weeks. The next day Merman was on the phone to David Merrick, and said, 'I want Merle in that part.' And I took over."

Merman was very particular about whom she was performing with, and wanted to make sure she kept the "right" people around her. June Squibb had already played the light-up stripper Electra on Broadway for a long time when it came time for the national tour. "The stage manager asked me if I wanted to go on the road, and I said yes. Then nothing else was ever said to me. You have to remember this was David Merrick's office, and at that time he had a hatchet man, and he was notorious for treating actors very poorly. So the weekend before the tour, they sent me a wire at my apartment offering me a ridiculous amount of money. So I went and told the stage manager I was furious and was not going on the tour. Then I told Merman. And she made a phone call. And I had the contract with money that was decent. She took that kind of responsibility, and she was being practical—she didn't want three new strippers."

When *Annie Get Your Gun* was to be revived at Lincoln Center, Merman and Benay Venuta, who was playing Dolly, wanted Jerry Orbach for the role of Charlie Davenport, the carnival manager.

ORBACH: "Benay said, 'Are you going to do *Annie*?' and I said 'I don't think so, the director thinks I'm too young for it.' Well, she called Merman, whom I'd never met, and Merman called the producer and said, 'Is Jerry Orbach going to play Charlie Davenport?' The producer said, 'I don't think so.' So she said, 'Well, then, get yourself another girl singer!' So I got the job."

NYPE: "She really was a very insecure woman, and this made it better for her. I was part of her contract for *Hello, Dolly!* I said if she did Dolly, which she had turned down originally, I'd play Cornelius. We eventually had a wonderful time doing the show. Ethel and I got along very well. I always treated her like a lady, never like a showbiz-y type."

For all her stage stardom, Merman never had any success in the movies. The greatest disappointment of her professional life was losing the film version of *Gypsy* to Rosalind Russell.

JUNE SQUIBB: "We were all very upset for her when she didn't get the movie. It was very painful for her."

MERLE LOUISE: "She really wanted to do that film. I remember we were in Los Angeles and she'd gotten a call from her agent. Somehow they had screwed up and she was on the phone this one matinee, saying to her agent, 'Yeah? Go fuck yourself!'"

BENAY VENUTA: "She really wanted to make it in films, but never did. That's when she married Ernie Borgnine."

The disastrous marriage rated a blank page in Merman's autobiography.

Merman won a Tony, but not for her greatest triumph. Her Mama Rose lost the 1959 award to Mary Martin's Maria von Trapp, while *The Sound of Music* robbed *Gypsy* of the Tony for Best Musical.

In her later years, Merman limited herself to concerts. While retaining her older fans, she also attracted a large and loyal gay following. It didn't matter who or what they were—the audience was the thing most important to Merman.

MERLE LOUISE: "They used to say Merman never liked gays. But we went to this club once in Detroit, and it was a gay club—and everyone was surprised she went in the first place. One of the men asked her if she would please sing a song. And I thought, 'Oh, Jesus.' But she said, 'Sure.' They had this piano that wasn't in the greatest tune, and she sat on top of that piano and sang 'There's No Business Like Show Business.' And those guys wept. We all did. She just liked people. If you were nice *people*, she liked you."

"Merman was something that was so special in a real sort of way," says Farley Granger, "like Mount Rushmore."

* * *

"Not that there's ever been the slightest doubt, but Beatrice Lillie's performance as Madame Arcati, the happy medium in *High Spirits*, re-affirms her place in the recorded history of the 20th century, along with the Battle of

Jutland and the Salk vaccine."—Norman Nadel, *World-Telegram & Sun*.
April 8, 1964.

Beatrice Lillie gained fame as the funniest revue comedienne of the twentieth century. When she opened at the Alvin Theatre in *High Spirits*, it was
the fortieth anniversary of her Broadway debut in *Charlot's Revue of 1924*.
A Noël Coward star who performed in his *This Year of Grace* and *Tonight at
8:30* among others, Lillie had had a string of Broadway successes, all with
rave personal notices, and all revues.

High Spirits was based on Coward's *Blithe Spirit*, and co-starring with
Lillie were Tammy Grimes, Edward Woodward, and Louise Troy.

TAMMY GRIMES: "My daughter [Amanda Plummer], who was about nine,
used to come to the theatre, and she'd always call for 'Bealillie. Mom, can
I go downstairs and play with Bealillie?' She never saw the veins in Bealillie's
hands, never saw the lines in Bealillie's neck. Bealillie was like her—a contemporary."

Grimes and Troy played respectively the dead and living wives of a writer.
Whenever Lillie missed a performance, Beulah Garrick went on as her
standby.

GARRICK: "I adored Bea Lillie; I kissed her feet in adoration of her talent.
However, to work with her was something else. I was not allowed in the
rehearsal hall; I was not allowed in the theatre to watch her in the show. I
guess I was such a threat to Bea that she was terrified. I said to Noël, 'Why
am I here?' She was one of the most insecure people I've ever worked with—
and this was one of the great geniuses of all time."

TROY: "Beatrice Lillie was really off the wall. She would do the oddest
things, and you never really knew why. She was used to working 'in one,'
and she really didn't like other people around."

GARRICK: "I used to send her flowers and little cheer-up notes because I
heard she was having a terrible time with some of the dances—she wasn't
very young when she did *High Spirits*, and it was hard for her. She was
having trouble with people. Noël said he had never seen her so badly
behaved, never seen her act so dreadful. She had this terrible man, John
Philip, who was like her confidant and manager, and he'd go tell the stage
manager I was sitting out front, and make him get rid of me. When she
opened in New York she was quite confident, and then I was at least allowed
to watch the show. Understudy rehearsals really don't prepare you; and the
fear and pressure when you're going on for a star is really awful. I thought,
I'm going to leave the theatre and become a manicurist."

High Spirits had a score and lyrics by Hugh Martin and Timothy Gray, and was directed by Coward, with the last-minute assistance of Gower Champion. Despite rave notices for Lillie and the rest of the cast, the show was a disappointment. It was Lillie who kept it running almost a year.

TROY: "She did this thing with her beads—and years later I was in Los Angeles having a drink with Hermione Baddeley, and I told her about the beads, and how they would break and there would be beads all over the stage. Hermione said, 'Oh my God, she forgot the trick!' I said, 'What are you talking about?' She said, 'The bead trick was mine—but they have to be on an elastic to make the trick work.' But Bea didn't think about that, and three or four times a week we'd have beads all over the stage, and the dancers would be tripping over them."

GRIMES: "She was remarkable in terms of inventing business. She wasn't really an actress. She didn't spend her life doing plays with other people—she did musical revues, and mostly her own act. Just like Judy Garland would get up and do her own act. I doubt very much that Bea Lillie played other characters. She was really Bea . . . all the way."

*   *   *

"Vivien Leigh is incredibly beautiful, incredibly graceful and incredibly charming, and would make any musical in which she appears distinguished."—John Chapman, *Daily News*. March 19, 1963.

Scarlett O'Hara had made Vivien Leigh a legend. The British star had won Academy Awards for *Gone With the Wind* and *A Streetcar Named Desire*. Yet when she arrived on Broadway in *Tovarich*, she was a novice, never having done a musical.

The cast of the David Shaw/Lee Pockriss/Ann Choswell show included Jean Pierre Aumont, Louise Troy, George S. Irving, Michael Kermoyan, and Maggie Task.

MAGGIE TASK: "The first day of rehearsal, Vivien took Jean Pierre by the hand and went up to every one of us and said, 'My name is Vivien Leigh, and this is Jean Pierre Aumont, and what's your name?' Then, the next day, she knew us all."

LOUISE TROY: "It didn't matter that she couldn't sing. She danced like a dream. She was a very hard worker, and she'd do those dances until she got them right. Every night it was like clockwork."

TASK: "She would do all the rehearsals in high heels, and I remember asking her why she didn't get some ballet slippers or something; but she said she'd have to perform in heels, so she might as well rehearse in them. I think maybe she was self-conscious about being so petite. She also used to hold her hands straight up when she wasn't working, so the veins in her hands wouldn't show."

Tovarich was based on Robert E. Sherwood's 1930s comedy about a royal Russian couple forced to take up new lives as house servants in Paris. The American musical had a British star, a French star, and a totally American supporting cast.

TASK: "Vivien gave a party for the Fourth of July, and she invited us all. I said to her, 'Why are you celebrating the Fourth? That's when you Brits lost us. You should be in mourning.' We laughed a lot about that. That evening at the party, she had a little black handkerchief on, and I said, 'What did you do, cut yourself?' She said, 'No, darling, I'm in mourning.'"

On the road, Leigh had director Delbert Mann replaced with Peter Glenville, and cast changes included the replacement of Taina Elg with Louise Troy, and John Emery with Alexander Scourby.

GEORGE S. IRVING: "It was tough on her. She was ill and not strong. Business was up and down, and at one point, when it was building, she felt she needed a vacation. She told them, and they pleaded with her to stay, and she did. And eventually, she had a breakdown."

Michael Kermoyan had a featured role in the show, and he also understudied Jean Pierre Aumont. "I did Jean Pierre's role in Boston, when he started to lose his voice. I found out later that Vivien held a meeting after the first show I did, and Jean Pierre's agent was there, and Vivien said she wanted him bought off and out. He was getting a considerable amount of money, and they would have had to pay him for as long as the show ran. But Vivien said she didn't care; they could take some of the money out of her salary. She just wanted him out, and I still really don't know why."

With her deteriorating mental condition, Leigh probably didn't know why herself. Richard Burton, a mutual friend of Leigh's and Kermoyan's, tried to explain it.

KERMOYAN: "Richard Burton told me later that she had tried to get me to take over because she felt more free with me—but I don't know about that, it was a very difficult time."

Leigh began to miss performances on and off, and when she did, her standby, Joan Copeland, went on. Almost six months into the run, after winning a Tony for her role, Leigh finally snapped during a performance.

KERMOYAN: "I remember it was a Saturday matinee, and in one scene she and Jean Pierre were having an argument. And she looked out at the audience and started talking to them and said, 'What does the Frenchman know'—or something like that. To Jean Pierre's credit, he tried to keep the story line going. She was just a shambles, and she came off and came running up to me and said, 'Michael, you must go on. I won't work with that Frenchman anymore.' I didn't know what the hell was going on. Then the stage manager came over and told me that Vivien wanted me to take over. I asked if there was anything wrong with Jean Pierre; he said no, she just wanted me to take over. Then they decided Joan should go on for her, and Joan got dressed. But Vivien didn't want that. And if you didn't know her, from the way she was speaking, you would have thought she was just pissed off. But later we found out something more was wrong. Our producers were all in her dressing room, and she was dancing for them."

Leigh was taken back to England and hospitalized. Four years later, she would die of tuberculosis. Michael Kermoyan had stopped off to see her sometime after the incident. "She seemed normal, but she didn't want to talk about the whole experience."

When Leigh left the show, Eva Gabor was brought in to replace her, but *Tovarich* closed two months later.

TROY: "When Eva Gabor replaced her, it just wasn't the same show. It didn't have the same magic. When Vivien came out on the stage, she looked like she was twenty-eight years old; and she was around fifty at the time. She was graceful, and unique. And when you see someone like that in a role, that's the only person you can see doing it for the rest of your life. She was like that."

* * *

"Miss Holliday is only sensational."—John McClain, *Journal-American*. November 30, 1956.

"Miss Holliday is immense. The outstanding virtue of both *Bells Are Ringing* and its star is a warm-hearted friendliness that is wonderfully endearing."—Richard Watts, Jr., *Post*. November 30, 1956.

Judy Holliday's beginnings were in a club act that teamed Betty Comden and Adolph Green—*The Revuers*. In 1946, she became an instant star when she replaced Jean Arthur out of town in Garson Kanin's *Born Yesterday*, later winning an Academy Award for the film. Ten years later she starred in her first musical, *Bells Are Ringing*, tailored just for her by Comden and Green and composer Jule Styne. The show was directed and choreographed by Jerome Robbins with Bob Fosse, and as Ella Peterson, the Susanswerphone telephone operator, Holliday won a Tony.

Bells Are Ringing had been running for awhile when Phyllis Newman was hired to stand by for Holliday: "The most valuable thing for me was being able to watch her perform every night. There still is no one quite like her.

She would give the same performance consistently—and yet she was able to make it look even more fresh every night. That's very hard to do."

Adrienne Angel and Laurie Franks also went into the show late in the run.

LAURIE FRANKS: "I remember one night she hurt her finger on the switch-board, and you could tell that she was in pain. She was really in pain. Her eyes kept getting bigger—and she had big eyes anyway. She went on perform-ing as if nothing had happened."

ADRIENNE ANGEL: "The night before I went in, they told me I had to go to Judy's dressing room. She really wanted to look me over because she was concerned that I looked very much like her—big smile and brown eyes—and she didn't want someone out there in the chorus who looked like her. So they put glasses and babushkas and hats on me, and I was terrified going in there; but she gave me the okay."

NEWMAN: "Off the stage Judy was very quiet, very intelligent, very non-show business."

ANGEL: "She was incredibly shy, and totally different from this warm, open person you saw onstage."

The dark side of Holliday's personality came to the surface during her next musical comedy vehicle, *Hot Spot*. *Hot Spot* was a sure-fire formula its creators thought couldn't miss. Holliday played a Peace Corps volunteer, and the supporting cast included Joe Bova, George Furth, Sheila Smith, and Mary Louise Wilson.

It became one of the greatest nightmares in Broadway history. From the start, it was a mess.

JOE BOVA: "You knew from the third day of rehearsal it wasn't going to work. It felt phony—and I don't know if it was me, or the writing, or what."

SHEILA SMITH: "We only had the first act, and it was 107 pages long, and nobody knew how the show was going to turn out. It was all very distressing. We needed a good editor and some good jokes."

BOVA: "They sent me the script, and I feel the weight of it, and I remem-ber turning to the messenger and saying, 'Oh boy, are we in trouble.' I could tell from the weight that we shouldn't be rehearsing until they cleaned it up and we had it down to a proper size."

SMITH: "I did like nine auditions for it, singing vocal scales, and I ended up with a nonsinging role, playing Joe Campanella's wife. I had the one really funny line in the show."

Holliday was not in good health. She would eventually die of cancer.

MARY LOUISE WILSON: "There was a guy in the show close to her who swore that she'd had an operation but as far as she knew she was fine; but then Jack Weinstock, the co-author, said she was very sick at that time. She had to work, though; she really needed the money."

SMITH: "At that time, Judy had been given a clean bill of health, but I don't think she was well. She really couldn't learn the scenes, and everybody was babysitting her. Stephen Sondheim wrote some of the songs—I don't think that was any great secret—and Judy couldn't learn the lyrics. So they'd post them in the orchestra pit and she would move from stage left to stage right and read them."

After a grisly pre–Broadway tour with a revolving stream of directors and daily script overhauls, *Hot Spot* limped to New York. Whatever there was of the show was carried by Holliday.

WILSON: "She would sort of struggle through the week rehearsing, and then opening night in any city, she just came to life. She just rose above herself—it was unbelievable."

Walter Kerr wrote in the *Herald Tribune*, "She is expected to take care of everything; I'll bet they've got her down in wardrobe between acts, sewing costumes. Again and again she comes on to go it alone, standing in a spotlight and piping her heart out. . . ."

WILSON: "Judy Holliday was wonderful. But one of the things she was best at was interaction. She made the other performers look great. To be onstage with Judy Holliday was just unbelievable. I felt I was funny because of her. And she could make the most awful material good."

*   *   *

"I don't know what all the fuss is about. I always knew Mary Martin could fly. She's always bounced along as though the earth were made of innerspring mattresses, and that piping, rollicking voice of hers would carry anyone aloft, wires or no wires, any old time."—Walter Kerr, *Herald Tribune*. October 21, 1954.

"If Mary Martin is satisfied, so are the folks out front. A lot of the exuberance of Texas has stolen into the legend now. Peter Pan may have been a proper Victorian original. He is a healthy, fun-loving American now."—Brooks Atkinson, *New York Times*. October 21, 1954.

She was Venus in *One Touch of Venus*, introducing the Kurt Weill classics "Speak Low" and "That's Him." She was Nellie Forbush, the "Cockeyed Optimist" "in love with a wonderful guy," in *South Pacific*. As Maria in *The Sound of Music*, she taught the world to sing with "Do Re Mi." She won the Tony for Maria in 1960, beating out Ethel Merman, nominated the same year for *Gypsy*. Merman understood: "How do you buck a nun?" she retorted.

Mary Martin was as different as one could possibly be from the brash, game-girl image Merman projected. Ethel was raucous and liked a good time; Mary was a lady. Susan Watson recalls how her brother-in-law, Tom Jones, the composer of *I Do, I Do*, Martin's last Broadway musical, described rehearsal lunch break. "Her husband, Richard Halliday, would come with a picnic basket lunch and they would set it up very formally in her dressing room."

The image she projected to her public was that of a lady—sweet, gentle, and feminine. But she will always be best remembered for her performance as Peter Pan, the embodiment of James Barrie's "little boy who never grew up."

As a child actress, Nita Novy would eventually work with Martin as one of the von Trapps in *The Sound of Music*. Before that, she was the Balloon Girl in *Gypsy*, with Merman. "All the time I was in *Gypsy*, I really wanted to be in *The Sound of Music*, and that was because I knew who Mary Martin was. And she was Peter Pan!"

If Martin is Peter, then Kathleen Nolan is Wendy—the first actress to play the role in that production.

KATHLEEN NOLAN: "She really *was* Peter. She identified with the role, and I think it's the part she'll be best remembered for. She used to tell the story about being asleep, and her grandchildren bringing their friends into her room so they could see Peter Pan sleeping. She was the ultimate professional, always prepared, with no star quirks or outrageous demands—except that it be professional."

The production's original Tiger Lily, Sondra Lee, agrees with her. "Mary was a very focused person, and she just got on with it."

Peter Pan's journey from San Francisco to Broadway was not an easy one.

LEE: "We made so many changes on the show, and Mary rolled with them. We originally had one number where she played the violin and I played the frying pan. I loved it, but it was cut."

NOLAN: "The first writers on the show were Moose Charlap and Carolyn Leigh. Mary and Richard Halliday were driving home one night and they heard Frank Sinatra singing 'Young at Heart' on the radio, and they decided right then that Moose and Carolyn were the ones to do *Peter Pan*; they thought the two of them would be perfect for the material. Then later, in San Francisco, they brought in Betty Comden and Adolph Green. They wrote some great stuff, but we still missed a lot of the old material."

The release of *Peter Pan* on videotape ensures that children for a thousand generations will think of Peter Pan and see Mary Martin.

LEE: "Frankly, I'm tired of being associated with Tiger Lily. But the attention to that production is unwavering, unflagging. People still recognize me and stop me on the street. I finally changed my hair from blonde to red."

Richard Halliday, Martin's husband, was totally devoted to his wife and her career.

NOLAN: "Richard was very protective of her and took care of all the business things so that she could give all her attention to the show. They made quite a team."

LEE: "She was isolated—no, not isolated, *insulated*. She had her people around her all the time."

NOLAN: "Mary wouldn't even leave the dressing room or the theatre between shows. It was never, 'Oh, I'll meet you for dinner at six,' or anything. She just rested up and gave her all to each audience."

Legends are legends because they live on long after the originals are gone. Vivien Leigh, Judy Holliday, and Beatrice Lillie are all remembered for their work in other media, in many cases preserved on film for future generations. Ethel Merman and Mary Martin were creatures totally of and about the Broadway musical stage. Between them they embodied American musical comedy.

Forbidden Broadway, the ongoing musical revue, has been satirizing the Broadway theatre since the 1970s. The Merman/Martin material is a continuous staple of the show. Says *Forbidden Broadway*'s creator, Gerard Alessandrini, "They are absolute icons. Merman and Martin were what Broadway was all about. Mary Martin was the flip side of Ethel Merman: she was the Richard Rodgers side, and Merman was Berlin and Gershwin and Jule Styne."

Except for original cast albums, the performers who parody the stars (with lyrics like "Everything's comin' up Merman for me and for me") have relatively little to go on. Roxie Lucas found an affinity for Mary Martin thanks to the television version of *Peter Pan*: "After seeing her on TV in 1953, I ended up in the hospital with an almost broken collarbone and a bad whiplash when I tried to fly. But Mary Martin was one of my early idols. I became a musical comedy performer because of her."

Merman, whose best work was never captured on film, posed a bigger problem for Toni DiBuono: "The only way I had known her was from a dishwashing liquid commercial she did, and I thought she was terrible. But my mother told me she was a famous musical comedy performer. I had to do a lot of research on her."

In musical theatre, where everything is transitory, only the strongest personalities survive, staying alive for the generations who never had the opportunity to see them onstage.

DiBuono: "A star could keep a show running for years back then. A book may not have been great, but it was tailored for a Merman or a Martin. That was enough. They were real stars."

As Alessandrini observes, "When you think of a star vehicle, you think of women. Maybe it goes back to Ziegfeld. But there is something about a female star. . . ."

13

N EVER does Mr. Brynner fall into the facile way of being a dashing leading man. . . . He gets depth, honesty and complete credibility into an authentic characterization of a man whose awakening mind and emotions are at work."—Richard Watts, Jr., *New York Post*. March 30, 1951.

When Rodgers and Hammerstein's *The King and I* opened at the St. James Theatre on March 29, 1951, the "I" was Gertrude Lawrence. The role of the King had been rejected by both Rex Harrison (he played the part in the film *Anna and the King of Siam* with Irene Dunne) and Alfred Drake. Mary Martin suggested her co-star in *Lute Song*, Yul Brynner, for the role. He auditioned and got it.

On March 30, 1951, Brynner was a full-fledged Broadway star. Anna would be played by many actresses—Lawrence, Deborah Kerr (in the film), Sally Ann Howes, Patricia Marand, Constance Towers, Mary Beth Piel, and many others—but for most people the "King" would always be Yul Brynner. He won a Tony for the role and later an Oscar for his performance in the film.

When he performed the King for the last time on Broadway, his Anna was Mary Beth Piel, who was nominated for a Tony for the role and went into the project with some trepidation. "When I first started rehearsing the role in Los Angeles, the stage manager said to me, 'Everything will be fine with Yul, but there are two things that you have to remember: never look him in the eye, and never touch him.' I thought, 'Oh great, now they tell me!' The day before he arrived everybody was very nervous. I was sitting off in the corner and he came running over to me, looked me right in the eyes, embraced me, and said, 'Welcome to the family.' So much for that myth. I don't know where that one came from. Maybe somewhere along the line he laid down the law to someone about not making eye contact, but it didn't apply to me. Yet there were a lot of people who were afraid of him."

Yul Brynner *was* the King, and he was demanding—a perfectionist. His return to *The King and I*, which kept him employed up until his death, came after a major theatrical disaster, *Home Sweet Homer*, which opened and closed at the Palace after a single performance, a Sunday matinee on January 4, 1976. The show was a retelling of the *Odyssey*, with book and lyrics by Erich Segal (the author of *Love Story* and a professor of classics at Harvard), and it had started touring the country in December of 1974.

The star was playing Odysseus, but he was still the King, with well-reported demands about accommodations—in hotels and in the theatres where his dressing room always had to be painted a certain shade of brown. Appearing with him in the show, which was definitely a star vehicle, were Russ Thacker and Martin Vidnovic.

It was Vidnovic's Broadway debut. "We were on the road for eleven months. Unfortunately the show was horrible and it kept getting worse and worse. A lot of the book was cut in Cleveland, and that was the beginning of the end. It wasn't even *The Odyssey* anymore. It was something totally different. In San Francisco, we got a new choreographer, who couldn't figure out how to solve the problem either. By the time we got to Broadway, there were seven dancers just standing around with nothing to dance. All of their stuff had been cut."

And no matter what name the character was given, audiences still came expecting to see Brynner as the King of Siam.

VIDNOVIC: "In the second act he had a beard and long hair and he looked just like some old man. People paid good money to go and see *him*, and they saw a very good performance, but it was different."

For Russ Thacker, the tour was the beginning of a lasting relationship. "Other people might knock him, and there were a lot of bad stories going around about his temperament, but I saw none of that. I'm a good supporting player, and I cater to stars. I love them. So when I first met him, I was sort of crunched down, trying to make myself shorter. He got out of the limousine and I was introduced to him and he said, 'Oh yes, Hank Fonda said to say hello.' Then later we went out to lunch and I'd loosened up a little bit, and I said to him, 'Did you say Hank Fonda? Henry Fonda? I've never met him,' and he said, 'Well, Hank saw you in *Take Me Along*, with Gene Kelly, thought you were really great, and sends regards.'

"I thought that was so sweet. Then he asked me why I was standing all scrunched up, and I told him it was because he was so short. He really loved that. I think he really liked it when people stood up to him."

Michael Kermoyan was in the cast of *The King and I* and also stood by for Brynner for years. "A lot of people are intimidated by working with big stars, but I never found Yul to be that way. I always thought of him as a friend and colleague. He and I always got along very well. He was almost like a child at times. A lot of stars keep their guard up and Yul would do that too, but once you got to know him, that guard would go by the wayside."

Home Sweet Homer opened to devastating reviews. Douglas Watt of the *New York Daily News* described the show as "close to two interminable hours, with uninteresting tunes equipped with uninteresting words." The *New York Post's* Martin Gottfried observed: "*Home Sweet Homer* demonstrates the monstrous capacities of the musical theater when its forces are placed in the hands of the ill-equipped, and in the pursuit of the ill-conceived."

Despite the negative press, Brynner always seemed to believe in the value of the show.

VIDNOVIC: "We got some good responses during previews, standing ovations. But the critics were lying in wait for us. The opening performance— it was a matinee—was like a morgue. The only real response we got was when we were lifting a rock to prove our worthiness to Penelope, Odysseus's wife, and her son said, 'This is ridiculous!' There was a roar of laughter and applause. A good comment on the show. And still there was Yul saying, 'We're going to run for two years.' I don't know if he believed in it or if it was just his ego."

It was his ego that brought him back to his single triumph, *The King and I*, which he continued to perform until shortly before his death. The first of his many Mrs. Annas in the ongoing farewell tour and Broadway runs was Constance Towers.

TOWERS: "We had a very special relationship. Our opening night in Indianapolis was the first moment of my understanding of what it was exactly that Yul Brynner had. That first night he had profound laryngitis. He couldn't even whisper. No sound at all came out. So he went away with a Tibetan lama for two days while we were in the last days of rehearsal. He did send me a note saying, 'Don't worry. I'll be there opening night.'

"His son, Roc, came in, and he was wonderful. He read the lines and he had the same timbre in his voice as his father, and that was important to us. On opening night Mr. Brynner arrived and he still couldn't speak. So Roc went into the orchestra pit and read the part and Mr. Brynner came out onstage and all he could do was gesture and pose it. I told him that all the audience wanted was for him to come out there and be there and that I'd support him in any way I could. And that really was true. The audience just wanted to see him. He had such incredible presence it didn't matter whether he could speak or not.

"By the second act his voice started to come back and by the death scene he was totally back into the show and Roc stopped speaking for him. It was then I realized what a powerful presence he was. He walked out onstage and he *was* the King!"

During his final triumphant tour the King was dying of lung cancer, and his leading ladies changed frequently.

MARY BETH PIEL: "The Mrs. Annas came and went with some regularity. I'm probably very fortunate that I met him when I did. I had no idea really at that time that he was sick or just how sick he was. Most of the time I was working with him, he was very ill, and he was aware of it. When you're in touch with your own mortality, you look at your life and the people around you in a different way. He had just entered into his final marriage and he was very happy in both his personal and his professional life."

Patricia Marand worked with Brynner in the second-to-last company before he died.

MARAND: "The part of Anna calls on every emotion you have as an actress in addition to the vocal demands. She's onstage for the entire show, except for 'Is a Puzzlement' and the ballet.

"I think a lot of the good things I did in the show were due to Yul. He took over the directing and really helped me. Of course, I was in love with the character, and that's the first step to being good in a role. Just before opening he said to me, 'Just think that every night you have this jewel box and you're handing it over to all these people in the audience.' I loved every minute of the show."

TOWERS: "After working with him for a few months, I realized one reason he was so special and people reacted to him the way they did. I suddenly understood that he really liked women, and I don't mean that in a patronizing way. He really appreciated women and was sympathetic and sensitive to them. This communicated to the audience.

"He wanted you to come out onstage and be as beautiful and talented and brilliant as you could possibly be. That's what he encouraged you to be. He created an atmosphere where we weren't competing and I wasn't threatened by him and he wasn't threatened by me. I was just encouraged to go out and do the role and be the best I could possibly be, and it was a wonderful experience."

PIEL: "While the ballet was going on, we would sit in his dressing room and talk. He would tell me about things he had done with Gertrude Lawrence, and the way it worked then and some of the outrageous things she had done or they had done together. And he'd tell me about all the ways the different Mrs. Annas had played a particular moment and which way he thought it had worked best. I learned a lot."

Martin Vidnovic resumed his working relationship with Brynner, playing the role of Lun Tha in *The King and I*.

VIDNOVIC: "He would have Connie Towers in his dressing room every night during the *Uncle Tom's Cabin* ballet, and I thought it was like a nightly get-together, chatting and a nice kind of thing. Then I found out from Connie's dresser that he was in there giving her notes all the time. The Mrs. Annas had the hardest time with him because they had the most to do with him."

MARAND: "He really thought he was the King, offstage and on, and once you understood that, your life was a little bit easier. You have to take a stand, though, and even though he really taught me everything I knew about the part and he was a very giving actor onstage, he did do a few things that weren't very nice."

As the tour continued, Brynner's control over the show and the other actors grew stronger and could be seen in the tiniest details of the production.

MARAND: "There was one moment where Anna was preparing for the British Ambassador to come to the court and the King is giving her all these instructions. I had a pad and a pencil and I was taking notes, not just scribbling. I was writing down everything he said. Then one night I got a pad and the pencil was just a stick. There was no longer a pencil here. Now, why did he do that? There were other little things that happened, too, that I'd rather forget about. It was sad."

VIDNOVIC: "As great as he was in that part—and it was his part—it really isn't a one man show. It was written for Mrs. Anna, after all, wasn't it?"

TOWERS: "He did give me notes, but if I had something I wanted to tell him, I felt perfectly comfortable about doing it. I did find that if I posed my comments in a certain way it would make them a little more successful. If I would say, 'Remember that wonderful idea you had in rehearsal? Why don't you try that now? Try it again,' that would make it a little more palatable."

KERMOYAN: "A lot of actors just walk through it night after night. Not Yul. And he used to yell at the stagehands a lot if they did something he didn't like."

In one famous instance, he also yelled at Gertrude Lawrence.

MARAND: "He said she used to tie bells to her shoes and one night she was onstage and the bells were ringing away. Well, he got furious and he slapped her when she came offstage. The man hit Gertrude Lawrence! And he said, 'She never did that again. There were no more bells.'"

In the midst of the temperament, there were also moments of consideration.

TOWERS: "He helped me, and if he saw something that could be improved upon, he was delicate and sensitive about presenting it to me. If he saw me doing something that he thought was wonderful, he complimented me on it. There was one point in the run where he thought that I was gesturing too much and he caught himself onstage letting me know during a performance. Well, he was so afraid that he had offended me that the next day a whole blooming quince tree arrived at my dressing room door. I was so grateful for the help. It never occurred to me to be offended."

VIDNOVIC: "I went to him a couple of times because I was having trouble with the director. And he said, 'You think you're having problems with him! In the important scenes, that's where we're really having problems!' And he meant, of course, all of the scenes that he was in."

He wanted the production to be loved, but by this point, he was more interested in making sure that the audience loved him.

For better or worse, a piece on *60 Minutes* during the last *King and I* tour glorified his reputation as an overbearing star.

PIEL: "I never saw his demands so much as a sign of temperament as of practicality. This man was spending ten years of his life on the road! He was never home. It was two weeks here and two weeks there. The theatre was virtually his home, and the only way he could create any kind of stable ground was if he painted the walls in all these drecky dressing rooms. He had his furniture and art works and mementoes, and he found a warm chocolate brown color for the walls that was very soothing. Everything in the room fit with the basic color and it gave him a feeling of stability as he went from dressing room to dressing room. Something he could count on.

"I remember people like Lena Horne and Carol Channing saying to me, 'Thank God for Yul Brynner. He cleaned up every star dressing room in the country.' It wasn't outrageous, believe me. They still weren't all that glamorous."

THACKER: "They had a whole list of demands that he made that were published in *Variety*. But he looked on it as a joke. He was just pushing management to see how much he could get. He'd say, 'Okay, I have the brown walls and the brown rugs. Now, what else can I ask for?'"

PIEL: "Some nights he worked harder than others, but he was always there. He adored the part and he was criticized by friends or ex-friends for *becoming* the King. They thought he had crossed over the line. Maybe they were right.

"Power does something to you, whether you're a politician or an actor . . . I think when I was working with him near the end, that sense of power was tempered by his sense of his own mortality."

THACKER: "When he was doing *The King and I* at the Uris and I was out of work, he used to invite me to come down and visit with him while he got made up. He loved to have people watch him make up. It was like a Kabuki sort of thing, a whole ritual with him. So I'd go down and talk. He knew I was out of work and he'd give me a thousand dollars and say, 'Just keep it. Spend it.'

"He did a lot of good things for charities and Vietnamese Children's Adoption Service and things like that, but people never heard about it. I think he didn't want things like that publicized a lot because of the image."

His public saw him as brooding, intense, and slightly dangerous. Russ Thacker remembers him as a man who "giggled a lot."

The one major revival of *The King and I*, since Brynner's death, starred Rudolf Nureyev, and was a colossal failure. In all likelihood, future productions will focus on the character of Mrs. Anna. The King is dead.

* * *

"Danny Kaye is so warm and lovable an entertainer . . . that for me at least he can do no wrong."—Clive Barnes, *New York Times*. November 11, 1970.

Let's Face It and *Lady in the Dark*, both produced in 1941, made Danny Kaye a major Broadway star. He then left for Hollywood, where his work in films and later on television made him a superstar. He returned to Broadway in 1970 in the Richard Rodgers musical *Two by Two*, based on *The Flowering Peach*, the Clifford Odets play about Noah. Prominently featured in the cast were Joan Copeland, Walter Willison, and Marilyn Cooper.

COPELAND: "They wrote the show for Danny and he was, of course, a force to be reckoned with. He felt that he knew what was right for him, and when you're a big star, like he was, you're surrounded by a coterie of people who are there to protect you. In my opinion, he tried very hard to play the role legitimately. He respected the piece, his character, and his colleagues for a long time."

Problems with his fellow actors began when he tore a ligament in his leg and was forced to perform in a wheelchair. The situation worsened when Kaye did not receive a nomination for a Tony Award.

COPELAND: "Harry Goz was Danny's understudy and he went on for four or five performances and he was very, very good, but people had come to see Danny, who did come back to the show, but with his leg in a cast. Of course he was triumphant, because the audience had come expressly to see him, and there he was, being so brave."

COOPER: "Danny was wonderful to me. You know it's a very professional thing. You go in to do your work. That's what you're there for. Anything else that happens—well it happens. As long as people do their work, nothing else affects me. I just go out onstage and do my work."

Meanwhile, Kaye's behavior both on- and offstage became the talk of the theatrical community.

WILLISON: "The night I was nominated for the Tony, I was a little late getting to the theatre, but I had my roommate call to tell them. I got there around nine minutes late. The night before, Harry Goz was about fifteen minutes late and there wasn't any problem.

"Part of the reason I think I got the nomination was that I was maintaining a performance and Danny was screwing around. If he had done the show every night the way he did it on opening night, he would have won the award. Well, I got to the theater and my understudy was there in my costume. Danny walked out and put his hands on his shoulders and said, 'You'll be fine. You'll listen to me. You'll do what I want.'

"I was destroyed. Tears were rolling down my face. I had just been nominated for a Tony Award and now I couldn't go on."

COPELAND: "It was hard to rein him in. He wasn't being very respectful to the material or to his colleagues. He started having difficulties with the cast, and I think I was probably the last holdout, but . . . ."

WILLISON: "I was playing the defiant kid onstage and I acted like that offstage. I really wouldn't put up with any of his shit and I stood up to him. Then, every night after the show, I'd go over to Joe Layton's [the director] and he'd give me lessons in how to deal with Danny Kaye. I was just a kid."

Problems like these had cropped up earlier in Kaye's career. During the run of *Let's Face It* (1941), his co-star, Eve Arden, was sick and her understudy, Carol Channing, went on. The audience loved her. Kaye was not impressed. Channing was soon without a job.

Two by Two was Danny Kaye's last appearance on Broadway. The show closed when the star's contract expired. He was mentioned as a possibility for the lead in *On the Twentieth Century*, but John Cullum got the job. Broadway could no longer afford to deal with Danny Kaye either financially or artistically.

The public could see Brynner only as the King, and Kaye would always be the lovable boy next door. They were adored by the public, even though their colleagues found them difficult. The same could be said for Ray Bolger, who will always be remembered as the Scarecrow in *The Wizard of Oz*.

"Ray Bolger is not the greatest man in the world. But why quibble? In *Where's Charley?*, he is great enough to make a mediocre musical show seem thoroughly enjoyable." Brooks Atkinson, *New York Times*. October 12, 1948.

Bolger's show received mixed reviews, but critics and audiences always loved him. He knew how to play to the crowd. According to Benay Venuta, his co-star in the last Rodgers and Hart musical, *By Jupiter*, "He could be very difficult!" They introduced the song "Everything I've Got Belongs to You." But Bolger wasn't very giving when it came to his colleagues.

"It was difficult working with Ray," recounts Nanette Fabray, who replaced Constance Moore in *By Jupiter*. "He never really looked at you. He was sort of off on his own. He wasn't mean or anything. He just had no contact and never paid any attention to you. And that was my first lead and I really needed support."

VENUTA: "Ray Bolger was a very sweet man, but he was very one-directional. He was interested in Ray."

Frank Loesser's *Where's Charley?*, the musical version of the classic farce *Charley's Aunt*, opened to definitely mixed reviews, but the critics raved about its star, Bolger, who managed to keep the show running for 792 performances and made the song "Once in Love with Amy" a huge popular hit. The song became his trademark, and he would coax audiences into singing a reprise of it with him after every performance.

A young dancer who had been performing on Kate Smith's television show made her Broadway debut in *Charley*.

GRETCHEN WYLER: "I was the baby in that show, and I loved Ray Bolger intensely. I used to stand in the wings every night and watch him. I would go to the theatre every night early to work out and so would Mr. Bolger. He even gave me my name. He said if I was going to stay in the theater—and I was—I needed to have a name for the marquee. My original last name was Wienecke. So one night he said to me, 'What do you think about Gretchen Wyler?' I would have settled for Schwartz! I couldn't believe it. The great Ray Bolger giving me a name!"

The dancer/comedian toured for years in *Where's Charley?* and made the film version but never had a success to equal it. His last two appearances on Broadway were in *All American* (1962), which ran for a disappointing eighty performances, and *Come Summer* (1969), which lasted for seven performances.

All American had a lot going for it. It was directed by Joshua Logan, with a score by Adams and Strouse, who were fresh from the success of *Bye Bye Birdie*. The book was by Mel Brooks.

The show's ingenue, Anita Gillette, had a huge part, and one Philadelphia critic compared her impact on the audience to the one made by Mary Martin singing "My Heart Belongs to Daddy." Ingenues often suffer for being too good.

GILLETTE: "A lot of my stuff was cut after Philly. I really had a lot to do, but by the time we got to New York, it had all been cut. I'm not saying the book was great, but if we had played it the way Mel had written it—off the wall—it could have worked.

"Ray didn't want to play the crazy professor Mel had written. He wanted the man to be real and down-to-earth so that he could get to the people."

Protecting the star became a matter of family business in the Bolger household.

GILLETTE: "His wife was finally banned from the theatre. He'd be in rehearsal and he'd be fine, but then his wife would tell him about the other performers and performances and, well, his wife was real trouble. I had to rehearse my one remaining number, 'Nightlife' [which stopped the show at each of its eighty performances], in one of the bathrooms, with Josh sitting on the sink and me standing in front of the johns, because they were afraid to let Ray see it."

The girl who had been his protegée worked with Bolger again in 1960 in Las Vegas.

WYLER: "I was the opening act for Donald O'Connor and I did a takeoff on and tribute to Ray. Well, they held me over and the new headliner was going to be Ray Bolger. I was so thrilled. The night before Donald closed, they told me that Ray and Gwen, his wife, were in the audience, and I was really excited. The stage manager came back after the first show and said

The entire cast of *Applause* was gathered together by assistant choreographer Tom Rolla for this photo, given to director/choreographer Ron Field as an opening-night present. The company is draped in tablecloths from Joe Allen's restaurant, the setting for the title song in the musical.

(Photo courtesy of Mr. Rolla and Laurie Franks)

Rehearsing for *Wonderful Town*: George Abbott (standing) with Rosalind Russell and George Gaynes.
(Photo from the authors' collection)

George Abbott's discovery Ellen Hanley as Thea in the director's production of *Fiorello!*
(Photo courtesy of Ms. Hanley)

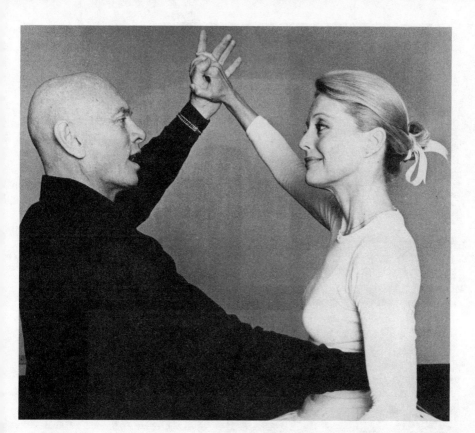

Yul Brynner and Constance Towers rehearse
"Shall We Dance" for the revival of *The King
and I*.

(Photo from the authors' collection)

Hot Spot was Judy Holliday's second and
last appearance in a Broadway musical.
The show, a colossal failure, closed after
43 performances, despite the star's
popularity.

(PLAYBILL is a registered trademark of Playbill,
Incorporated, New York City. Used by permission)

Career beginnings: Dorothy Loudon (l.) and Sheila Smith in a 1959 Tamiment revue number, "How Do You Like Us—So Far?" Woody Allen wrote some of the sketches for the show.
(Photo courtesy of Ms. Smith)

"Through this portal walks the greatest musical cast ever!" Producer David Merrick had the sign put up outside the stage door at *42nd Street*. In front of it are Sheila Smith (l.), who was playing Dorothy, and the film's original Peggy Sawyer, Ruby Keeler.
(Photo by David Gould, courtesy of Ms. Smith)

Zoya Leporska and Bob Fosse (in front) perform for the cast during a break in rehearsals for *Damn Yankees*.
(Photo courtesy of Ms. Leporska)

Eyde Byrde, James Randolph and Ernestine Jackson
(l. to r.) in the 1976 revival of *Guys and Dolls*.
(Billy Rose Theatre Collection. The New York Public Library
for the Performing Arts, Astor, Lenox and Tilden Foundations)

Constance Towers, Michael Kermoyan, Irra
Petina (l. to r.), and Lillian Gish (seated) starred in
Anya, the musical version of *Anastasia*, for 16
performances at the Ziegfeld Theatre.
(PLAYBILL is a registered trademark of Playbill, Incorporated,
New York City. Used by permission)

Michael Kermoyan and Constance
Towers, the King and Mrs. Anna, in a
City Center revival of *The King and I*.
(Photo courtesy of Mr. Kermoyan)

Sally Ann Howes: "I was always very fortunate and got to work with the most wonderful conductors—Franz Allers, Hal Hastings, Lehman Engel, Paul Gemignani. Nothing but the very best!"

Anita Gillette (on *Kelly*): "When we got to Boston, Eddie Lawrence and Moose Charlap [the show's creators] were dressing up in wigs and moustaches. They had to come in disguise to get into the theatr to see what was being done to their show."

Laurie Franks (on her Broadway debut in *Copper and Brass*): "I got to see the whole work process of a Broadway show and that was really very special for me. But then, I've always been lucky."

Julie Kurnitz: "I was taken to the theatre a lot when I was a little girl. My sister and I would sit there in the dark with a bunch of strangers letting magic happen. Audiences aren't like that anymore."

the national magazine for theatregoers

I'm Solomon starred Dick Shawn (top), Karen Morrow, Carmen Mathews (r. to l., row 2), Salome Jens (bottom), a cast of 60, and an entire dance company. The show closed after 7 performances.

(PLAYBILL is a registered trademark of Playbill, Incorporated, New York City. Used by permission)

John Schneider as the Baron and Zina Bethune as the ballerina Grushnishkaya in the Tommy Tune–Wright/ Forrest musical *Grand Hotel*.

(Photo by Carmine Schivone)

Beatrice Lillie (l.) and Tammy Grimes as Madame Arcati and Elvira in *High Spirits*.

(Billy Rose Theatre Collection. The New York Public Library for the Performing Arts, Astor, Lenox and Tilden Foundations)

Robert Preston (r.) and Iggie Wolfington as Professor Harold Hill and Marcellus in the original production of *The Music Man*.

(Billy Rose Theatre Collection. The New York Public Library for the Performing Arts, Astor, Lenox and Tilden Foundations)

Mary Martin (r.) shows Kathleen Nolan the way to Never Never Land in *Peter Pan*.

(Billy Rose Theatre Collection. The New York Public Library for the Performing Arts, Astor, Lenox and Tilden Foundations)

that Mr. Bolger insisted I cut the section about him. He didn't want me doing it.

"I was devastated that he didn't really love it. After that he never really spoke to me. It was just a cordial 'Hello' and 'Goodbye.' I never knew why he didn't like me, but I ended up loathing him. He's dead now, so I can say that."

Where's Charley? made Bolger a star and his trademark song was always a part of his performances.

GILLETTE: "His big thing during *All American* was to sing 'Once in Love with Amy' after the curtain call while we all stood onstage watching. We finally had to get up a petition that said if he wanted to do his nightclub act that was fine, but we wouldn't have to stand there every night for his number and curtain speech."

Ray Bolger's last curtain speech on Broadway followed the final performance of *Come Summer*. It was a blistering attack on the critics who had panned the show and on the whole Broadway system. The press had been savage, and the economic climate of the time had no room for an old-fashioned musical with nothing going for it but a star whose time had passed. Bolger was no longer the critics' darling and left Broadway a bitter man.

*   *   *

"Zero Mostel offers a brilliantly resourceful and intelligent performance in the central role."—Richard Watts, *New York Post*. September 23, 1964.

For the final years of his career, the critics always endorsed the work of Zero Mostel. His first major Broadway musical, *A Funny Thing Happened on the Way to the Forum* (1962) was a surprise smash hit and ran for 964 performances, in large part due to Mostel's ability to make the audience accept the musical's makeshift plot devices and corny jokes.

Mostel's performance as Tevye in *Fiddler on the Roof* (1964) gave him superstar status and secured for him a high ranking in theatrical history.

The performer's generosity to friends and even to strangers was well known. His close friend Jack Gilford created the role of the nervous slave, Hysterium, in the original company of *Forum*. The job revitalized Gilford's career, which had been all but destroyed by the blacklisting of the fifties. "I won't say that Zero got me the job, but he certainly helped. There's not a word I would say against him. Onstage he was magic."

However, many of his colleagues found him to be extremely difficult. Maria Karnilova played Golde, Mostel's wife in the original production of *Fiddler*, and her husband in real life, George S. Irving, also performed with Zero.

IRVING: "I worked on a film with him once, and he was so mean to all the little gofers. It was really terrible."

KARNILOVA: "He was a very great artist and a very disturbed man."

IRVING: "He fancied himself a painter and thought the theatre was his avocation. I went to his studio one day and it was huge. There were paintings all over the place."

KARNILOVA: "They weren't very good. It was all late Picasso. I guess I shouldn't say they weren't good. Good and bad is all in the eye of the beholder."

Whatever the quality of his paintings, as Tevye in *Fiddler*, Mostel was hailed as a genius. His co-workers found him to be, at best, an erratic genius.

KARNILOVA: "Zero was a crazy man. He played the role straight for three weeks and then he went bananas! You never could find him on the stage and you never knew what he was going to say. He was always talking to the audience and he really messed up the show."

Actress Barbara Colton toured with Mostel and agrees with Karnilova. "It was absolutely incredible. I think Zero was one of the most talented and tormented people I've ever met or worked with. He was totally undisciplined."

KARNILOVA: "He was actually a comic. He liked nightclub comedy and he wanted *Fiddler* to be a one-man show. He never played with you directly and he and Jerry Robbins had terrible battles. That's why they let Zero go so quickly. Jerry just couldn't stand what he was doing to the show. He was just clowning around."

When Mostel's contract expired, it was not renewed, even though the star had won a Tony for his performance. He was replaced by Luther Adler, Herschel Bernardi, Paul Lipson, and Harry Goz, among others. The show survived without Zero and ran for 3,242 performances. But up until a year before his death, whenever Mostel revived the show, people flocked to see him as the dairyman Tevye. Still, members of every *Fiddler* company found him treacherous to work with.

COLTON: "He was constantly doing schtick at the expense of the company, the play, the music, and the audience. However, I must admit that the audience seemed to love it. Zero also used to do physical things that were wrong, too, especially grabbing people."

KARNILOVA: "Any delicate little girl and anyone who was vulnerable, he would go after. One day we were sitting on a bench learning lyrics to a song and I had to hit him really hard in his stomach with my elbow. He'd put his hands anywhere and he put his hands on my boob and I bopped him. He never touched me again. But he did that to all the girls and it would upset them. If they were inexperienced, they didn't know how to react."

When another actor in the company was having trouble with Mostel, he went to Barbara Colton, who was at that time vice-president of Actor's Equity, to find out what could be done about Zero's outrageous behavior.

COLTON: "I explained it to the actor as best I could. I very honestly said to him, 'You're right and you're wrong. The world is not made so that everything and everyone is equal. Positions are not equal. There are "us" and there are "stars." So you can bring him up on charges, but even if they are sustained, you have to think about what this is going to do to your career. Whatever the outcome, the audience isn't paying to see you or me or even the show. They're paying to see Zero Mostel. That's a fact of life and you have to live with it.'"

Veteran character actress Beulah Garrick worked with Mostel in *Ulysses in Nighttown* and agrees with her colleagues. "Zero was very, very creative, but for me it was not very easy working with him. There was a lot of it that was not very joyful. The star system is really funny because it always depends on who the star is. People may disagree with me but I think we have to have the star system in the commercial theatre; but there are stars and then there are stars!"

No one can disagree with the fact that Zero Mostel sold tickets. That alone made him a star. Garrick played Nora Muldoon in the original production of *Auntie Mame* with Rosalind Russell, who also sold tickets. Russell treated her fellow actors with respect and maintained a good working atmosphere backstage. Stardom has its perks but also its responsibilities.

*   *   *

"A triumphant performance in a triumphant musical!"—Robert Coleman, *New York Daily Mirror.* December 20, 1957.

A true star respects the play, the supporting company, and the audience. Robert Preston did all of these. He could play comedy and tragedy; his peers referred to him as an "actor's actor." Typed as a villain or second leading man in countless films, he returned to Broadway and supported such superstars as Gloria Swanson, Margaret Sullavan, and Claudette Colbert. Then when he was cast in Meredith Willson's *The Music Man*, the journeyman actor became a megastar. Audiences and his colleagues loved him.

Preston was also a very private person. "He was a very good actor but, you know, in all the time I worked with him, I never really got to know him," recalls Barbara Cook, the Marian to Preston's Harold Hill in *The Music*

Man. "He was a very, very private man in spite of all of his affability and social things."

During the run of *Music Man*, Preston and Richard Burton (who was appearing in *Camelot*) formed a Shakespearean workshop for other actors on Broadway so they could refine their technique. Burton's relationships with his leading ladies (Julie Andrews excepted) were one of the theatre's worst-kept secrets. Preston was much more discreet, and selective.

COOK: "He never made a pass at me. I was very happily married at the time and there was none of that."

Called in to replace Jacqueline Mayro as the young girl in Preston's second big musical, *Ben Franklin in Paris* (1964), the newly married Susan Watson also was not subjected to any romantic advances. "Of course, he always fell in love with his leading ladies, and he did in that show, but he was such a nice man."

Ulla Sallert obviously also thought he was a nice man. She had played Eliza in the Swedish production of *My Fair Lady*, and was imported to star opposite Preston in *Ben Franklin* and the two co-stars became close. If there was an affair it ended when the show closed.

One of the show's ingenues, Rita Gardner, points out another problem the Scandinavian actress faced in her American debut. "You couldn't understand a word she said. She had never been on the Broadway stage either and I guess she just went back to Sweden or Norway or wherever she was from." Audiences were baffled, and she's unintelligible on the original cast album. In all probability, her friendship with the star allowed her to keep her job.

The vehicle was weak, but Preston did his job.

WATSON: "He would just *become* Ben Franklin. He would slip into that character so easily."

GARDNER: "Some of the speeches that he had as Franklin were so moving. The audience would applaud and bravo."

He also knew how to treat his fellow actors.

GARDNER: "He'd never go to the stage manager like a lot of stars would, but he'd come right up to you and say, 'Rita, you know at this moment, I think we should try this,' or 'Would you like to try this,' or 'I love what you're doing there, but do you think we could try something else?'"

Unfortunately, after *The Music Man* he found only one vehicle worthy of his talents, *I Do, I Do*, with Mary Martin. *We Take the Town* (1962), in which he played Pancho Villa, closed out of town. Jerry Herman's *Mack and Mabel* (1974), based on the lives of silent film director Mack Sennett and comedienne Mabel Normand, garnered great reviews for Preston and has achieved cult status but ran for a mere sixty-six performances.

The latter was another Gower Champion extravaganza that rehearsed and opened in Los Angeles before limping to Broadway. The production dwarfed the characters, and intimate moments were lost. One of Preston's co-stars in that production, Lisa Kirk, vouched for his professionalism on the job: "He never let up for a moment, and there were some pretty rough times with that show. He was always in there working, and he was a leader. He was everything that the star of a big musical has to be."

The company of *The Music Man* found that Preston possessed all the qualities of a real star. "As a show goes on, morale can get low," claims Iggie Wolfington, the original Marcellus, sidekick to Preston's Harold Hill, "and it's really up to the star—the one at the top—to keep things up and going, and Bob was always there. He'd say, 'Let's get the company together. We need a party to pick things up.' And it worked."

The monotony of repeating the same words over and over every night is enough to drive anyone crazy, and in a long run, tensions tend to crop up regularly. They didn't last long within the *Music Man* company.

COOK: "He absolutely sparked the company. His energy was always up. I never remember him letting down, and he had a wonderful sense of humor."

Cook also remembers a nightly ritual she shared with Preston that made the show special for her. "He was always ready about fifteen minutes before the show and I didn't go on until fifteen minutes into the show, so every night he'd come to my dressing room and we'd talk about the day and who was out front that night.

"He'd often make little announcements before the show over the PA system, little jokes, and he kept people in a good mood. There was always an airiness, a lightness about him."

WOLFINGTON: "Eddie Hodges, the little boy in the show, was replaced by Paul O'Keefe, who was this cute, tough little kid from Boston, and he adored Preston. Whenever I would change costumes, I would move my rosary from one costume to the next because I always carried it with me, and Paul would watch me do this. One night he said to me, 'You Cat'lic?' and I said 'Yes,' and he said, 'Is Preston Cat'lic?' and I said, 'I don't know,' and this little kid who idolized Bob said, 'I think he is.'"

Robert Preston's last show, *The Prince of Grand Street*, with a Robert Merrill score, closed in Boston in 1978. The show dealt with stars of the Yiddish theatre, and former child star Neva Small was cast as Preston's young wife.

NEVA SMALL: "It was always like a party, working with Robert Preston. He also had a brilliant mind. Bob Merrill makes a lot of changes and Preston seemed to get them right away.

"I also remember him telling stories about Hollywood. He thought Gary Cooper was the best actor he ever knew. He said that when Cooper died in his arms in *Beau Geste*, you thought he was really dead. Stuff like that was just so much fun."

Grand Street unfortunately had a book that was deemed unfixable, and a cast that was too large to be kept on the payroll while extensive changes were made.

SMALL: "It was hard for him when the show closed. You usually tend to blame the star. He was miscast or whatever, but it really wasn't his fault. I think it was that they just didn't have the money, so they threw in the towel."

Preston didn't need to worry about his reputation or standing in the theatrical community. The role of Harold Hill became so identified with him that to this day few stars are willing to tackle the part. The last major Broadway revival starred Dick Van Dyke, who would have seemed a natural for Harold Hill. The director/choreographer was Michael Kidd and the cast included Meg Bussert as Marian and Christian Slater in his Broadway debut as Winthrop. It was a disaster and closed quickly.

The material was the same and *Music Man* had won the Tony for Best Musical in a year that included the original production of *West Side Story*. Another revival by the New York City Opera starred Bob Gunton. The critics admired his acting, but all said he was no Robert Preston.

WOLFINGTON: "How good was Bob Preston? I'll tell you. He wasn't out often and his understudy was good, but whenever Bob was out, I would walk around the stage and I felt like I was following a suitcase. It just was never the same."

COOK: "I got pregnant during the show and he was so happy, but he was also afraid. We had little lifts when we danced, and after a month or so he said he wasn't going to do them. So we sat out the dance a little longer than the other couples.

"Every time he'd see my son, Adam, he'd say Adam had kicked him. I was five months pregnant when I left the show and he was convinced that Adam had kicked him several times."

WOLFINGTON: "Bob Preston *was* Harold Hill. I feel sorry for anyone else who has to play that part."

14

The Second Team

Replacing in the Theatre

I DON'T really admit to this," says Gretchen Wyler, "but other people say, 'Poor Gretchen. It never really happened.'"

Since her star debut in *Silk Stockings*, Wyler has had a very successful Broadway career in the greatest "star" roles of musical comedy. But, with one exception, she has never originated a role, always stepping into the star part as a replacement. "You see, I had been trained as a dancer, and I was a very good dancer. So when Bob Fosse called me to ask me to replace the great Gwen Verdon in *Damn Yankees*, I agreed, because I wanted to be seen as a dancer. I lost my manager over it. He said, 'You can't replace somebody because you're very hot right now.' As a result I've spent almost an entire career replacing people. It was okay. I got to do some great shows."

She also got star billing, but she never became a real "star": "I also came to learn that it's never easy for a cast to accept a replacement. I know when George Scott left *Sly Fox* and Robert Preston came in, we were all just devastated. We thought that Bob Preston was just the worst actor who ever was, just because he was different from George. I learned that all those years I had been replacing Gwen and Chita, everyone must have hated me."

Going into the cast of a show that's already running, to replace someone whom everybody likes, is one of the hardest things a performer can do. There is not only the pressure of doing a good job, but the pressure of living up to the memory of the person before, as well as trying to fit into a group that is already used to being together. It's a cross between arriving at a new kindergarten in the middle of the year and subbing for everyone's favorite first baseman.

John Cunningham has taken over roles in such shows as *Cabaret* and *1776*; and while replacing can be exciting and good for an actor's career, as it was for Cunningham's, it can also be frightening: "It's like somebody coming up to you and saying, 'You're going to be in the rodeo.' 'Fine.' 'We're going to have you do the Brahma bull.' 'Okay.' Now, I'd like to be able to look at the bull awhile, off in the chute, get him tied down, let me get on him, get all settled and comfortable—then you release the bull into the arena. But they say, 'No, that's not how you do it. See, the bull is bouncing around, and with a skyhook, we drop you onto the bull—and you have to hold on for the next five minutes.' That's what it's like, you're dropped onto a gyrating Brahma bull. And good luck to you."

Replacements are not afforded a lot of rehearsals, especially with the rest of the cast already in place. Both Penny Fuller and Anita Gillette went into *Cabaret*, which had been directed by Hal Prince.

PENNY FULLER: "I worked with Hal a little bit, but then went on after four rehearsals. It was very strange. I always seemed to have my rehearsals on my feet in front of 1,500 people. I never have the actor's nightmare of having to go on when you're not prepared because I was always thrown on."

ANITA GILLETTE: "I went into *Cabaret*, and I really didn't want to do it, but they assured me that Ron Field [the choreographer] and Hal Prince would work with me. So I did it. Well, we rehearsed for a few days, just with the stage manager, and then Hal came in to see what we'd done. His only comment was 'You're too good.' Then he turned around to walk out, and it was like, 'Well, help me to be bad.' I know he really didn't want me to be *bad* bad, but the role was very difficult, and I don't think I really got the help I needed."

Sometimes people get a second chance to do something they'd missed out on the first time around. Carol Lawrence joined *I Do, I Do* when she and Gordon McRae went on to play matinees for Mary Martin and Robert Preston before they took over the roles permanently. Lawrence later found out that fate had kept her from the original company: "The show was offered to my ex-husband, Robert Goulet, and myself at the very beginning, and I didn't know about it. That's a little bit criminal. But I'd seen the show in the first week, and I was in love with it. Everyone was. Then I found myself on a plane, sitting next to David Merrick, and I congratulated him and told him I couldn't wait to do it in summer stock. He said to me, 'Well, then, why didn't you play it originally?' And I said, 'I beg your pardon?' Then he told me that it had been offered to me. I wanted to put on a parachute then and there and kill that person—who shall remain nameless—who hadn't told me about it."

By the time Lawrence went into the show, its director, Gower Champion, was nowhere in sight. "Lucia Victor, Gower's assistant, put me in. As often happens after a show is a hit, once the baby has been born and is a success as *I Do, I Do* was, the director is off to do other projects."

Anne Jeffreys had originally turned down Cole Porter's personal request to do *Kiss Me, Kate*, but she later joined the Broadway company. "Cole would just turn the show over to you. When I first went in, Pembroke Davenport was the conductor, and he had his tempos all set. I had been doing the show on tour for two years, and my tempos were a lot different. My whole interpretation was different. He didn't want to change anything, and he gave me a fit. He would criticize what I was doing, and it got so bad that I had to call Cole one day after the matinee, and I told him I couldn't do the show the other way. I said, 'You liked the way I was doing it, and John Wilson, the director, had given thumbs-up on everything we were doing.' So Cole called Pembroke and told him he was to play the score with my tempos. Cole was very liberal in that way, unlike someone like Richard Rodgers, who wanted every quarter note dotted."

Julie Wilson had initially turned down *Pajama Game*, and two years later she was offered another chance after Janis Paige had finished her run. "It's scary. You kind of go in on a wing and a prayer, because you know that the cast is totally devoted to the person they've been with. And everything's set, and they're comfortable. So when you come in, you're the odd man out. It's difficult. But Zoya Leporska, Bob Fosse's assistant, put me in. She treated me with kid gloves—she couldn't have been dearer or more supportive. She stayed longer at rehearsals, and would make it as easy as possible."

Janis Paige, in turn, was in the same position some years later when she replaced Angela Lansbury in *Mame*. Paige not only had to make the regular adjustments to the role and company, but since she was much more petite than her predecessor, she had to adapt to staging that was not designed for her comfort. "I was pretty terrified, not wanting to be compared, and holding my own. My husband pointed out, 'You're not as tall as she is, you have a shorter stride—so watch those things. Let them adjust to you.' Which they did. The first time I ever rehearsed with Anne Francine, she said, 'Jan, you're not keeping up!' I said, 'Annie, you're almost six feet tall, I can't do it.' She turned around and started to laugh and said, 'Oh, I never thought of that.'"

Anne Francine had gone through her own adjustment torment when she came into the show as Vera. "Right away you're compared. I remember that Angie was upset. Extremely. And I don't blame her, but it was awful for me, because I was so nervous. And then she was not pleased that Bea Arthur left. So here it was a big hit show, and one of the stars makes waves and goes away and then is replaced by somebody she never knew—a perfectly strange woman coming into the show. You get used to doing a duet with somebody, and here comes this stranger, and it was hell. It was hell. I looked tortured. Of course, it worked itself out, after about six weeks. Then we got locked, and we played happily together for over a year. Then, when there were other Mames, it was trouble for me. It works both ways."

Here's Love, Meredith Willson's adaptation of *Miracle on 34th Street*, was not a hit show, but Lisa Kirk took over the starring role from Janis Paige anyway. "I came into the show near the end of its run, and then took it on tour with John Payne. I had been away from Broadway for a few years, so it was a good way of getting my feet wet again, even though the show wasn't . . . well, it was a good idea, but it really didn't work."

Being forced by the director to replicate someone else's performance is one of the most constricting aspects of being a replacement. Chris Sarandon took over from Raul Julia in the rock musical *Two Gentlemen of Verona*. "Basically, I was expected to do everything that Raul did. Personally, I think that was a mistake. Raul and all those people created those characters. They wanted me to do everything down to the smallest detail that Raul had done. Even down to timing, and turning this way or that. I was being poured into somebody else's costume; even Raul's ad libs were given to me as being scripted. I wouldn't call it exactly a horror experience, but it was not a hell of a lot of fun."

Michael Kermoyan was already in the cast of *Anya*, standing by for George London, when the singer became ill. "They had been rehearsing for at least two weeks, and George Abbott asked us all to come onstage. And he said, 'I have a card here for George. He's ill, and we all want you to sign it. He won't be with us anymore. Of course, Michael is taking over.' That was the first I had heard of it. I couldn't believe it, and then I felt terrible. I knew I could do the role, but I felt so sorry for George; he was such a sweet person. So I called him, and he said, 'Don't worry, Mike, you're the one who's going to do it, and I wish you the best of luck.' I'm sure the show would have run longer if he had been in it."

A dramatic musical about White Russians was obviously not George Abbott's milieu. *Anya* closed after sixteen performances and probably wouldn't have run that much longer even with George London in the cast. The critics hated the show—the book, music, and staging were working in different directions, and it was generally considered to be too heavy-handed.

Eddie Bracken has created a number of roles on Broadway and replaced other people countless times, in over 14,000 career performances. He played opposite Carol Channing in *Hello, Dolly!* for four years running. "I've replaced everybody. In *Dolly*, Walter Kerr said he couldn't understand how I got to sound and do the part as David Burns had. But the matter is that Davey and I were very, very close. So I could impersonate him, and I had fun doing it. I put in my own stuff, and I have no ego trip as to whether I'm better than this or that."

Actors have nightmares about replacing stars who have put their indelible stamp on a role. Picture going on for Ethel Merman. She almost never missed a performance. Her understudies rarely had the chance to go on. But her standby in *Call Me Madam*, who had never gotten to go on for her, was chosen to replace her for *Madam's* national tour—effective at the last matinee during the company's second week in Washington. It was Elaine Stritch. And Merman stayed to watch.

STRITCH: "Having Merman watch me was almost too much to bear. Before the performance, I went to my dressing room, said two decades of the rosary, and had a brandy. I thought, 'One of these has got to work.' I was standing out on the stage, scared shitless, and Merman was backstage on her way down to her seat, and she looked at me onstage and said, 'Goodbye!'"

Giving a "command performance" for Merman could have been an unnerving experience for her replacement, but it turned out to be a blessing. According to Stritch, "Sometimes little things like that 'Goodbye!' really help."

Revivals can be easier on a performer. When a show has become a classic and the memory of original performances begin to fade from public memory, recreating a role can allow more freedom.

Mary Beth Piel would be the last Mrs. Anna to play opposite Yul Brynner in *The King and I* on Broadway. "When Risë Stevens had been doing *The King and I* at Lincoln Center, it was right after I'd signed a contract with the Met National Company, and I was sort of her baby. I was thrilled, and awed, and impressed. So my mother and I went to see the show, and we went backstage afterwards, and there were these incredible gowns in the room, and she saw me looking at them, and she said, 'You know Mary Beth, someday you'll probably wear those costumes.' About twenty years later, when I went for my costume fittings, there in the ballgown was Risë Stevens's name."

Performers in revivals are inevitably compared to those who created the roles. If the show's original creators (or their representatives) are still around, it isn't always easy. The Rodgers and Hammerstein office—with or without Rodgers and Hammerstein—has always been notoriously exacting about what goes on in its productions. Barbara Cook found this out the first time she did a Rodgers and Hammerstein show, the national tour of *Oklahoma!* "There was a man named Jerry White from their office who rehearsed all those productions—and I did not like working with him. With all the best intentions, he insisted that each person do the role exactly as it had been done by the original person, down to the gestures. It was a really destructive thing to do.

"Dick wouldn't have been quite that way. When I did *Carousel* that first time at City Center, I did Carrie, and I remember Dick saw a couple of rehearsals. Jean Darling had played the role originally, and there was one exit where she did this funny little walk, and flounced off, and her bustle moved. And she got a big laugh. Dick wanted me to do this little walk. Well, it worked perfectly for her, I'm sure, but I didn't have any idea what it came out of. I said, 'You know, I don't understand why she's doing that—she never walks that way any other time. And I don't want to do it.' It was not easy to say no to Dick Rodgers. But I did, and I showed him what I wanted to do— and he laughed, and said, 'That's fine,' and made a little joke. He was perfectly amenable to things, as long as they worked."

In the 1960 City Center revival, Cook played Anna in *The King and I* opposite Farley Granger. If there is ever a time an actor worries about comparisons, it's when playing the King.

GRANGER: "I did everything differently than Yul. I didn't shave my head or any of that. I tried to create a completely different character. You can do that, you know. I was so thrilled when I found out Barbara was going to do Anna, and it all just worked brilliantly. Rodgers and Hammerstein were going to transfer the show to Broadway; but then the Actors strike happened, and it went on and on, and everything fell to pieces."

Show Boat has become one of the most classic of American musicals. It is performed regularly in revivals in New York and regionally, and is now a standard part of the repertory of opera houses.

BARBARA COOK: "Most of the things I did didn't have a long history. When I did *Show Boat*, it had been done so long ago that I didn't have some great performance icon to be measured up against."

Cook played the show's heroine, Magnolia, who has all the soaring soprano music. She found interpretive freedom, but also a few surprises: "A rather strange thing occurs in that show. Magnolia's the main, running character—the whole show is hung on her story. Yet she never has a scene or a song that she 'buttons up,' where she carries the moment. It's so obvious, when you're in it. You sing like crazy, you do a whole scene, you're doing it fine, you think—and then one character comes in and buttons up the scene. Or you're singing a song, and Ravenal comes on and ends the song. You don't get your moments—again, and again, and again, those moments where you could get the applause, or really do that last, final moment to clinch the scene or the song—it's taken away from Magnolia. Constantly. It's so arbitrary, it's insane. And there's nothing you can do except think, 'How in the hell did I get myself into this?' It really upset me at the time."

Constance Towers played Julie in the same Lincoln Center production. Julie has only two songs: "Can't Help Lovin' Dat Man" and "Bill."

TOWERS: "Opening night, when I stopped the show, was one of the great moments of my life. It had never occurred to me beforehand to be nervous. Fortunately, all the critics were positive, and I was lucky. It was one of those moments in my life that I will never forget."

BARBARA COOK: "Then, of course, what the hell's her name—Julie comes out, sits on the piano, and pulls the show apart. It was very frustrating."

Helen Morgan originated the role of the tragic half-caste, which she recreated on film (Ava Gardner played Julie in the 1951 version). Towers was not the only performer to find Julie a satisfying role.

BETH FOWLER: "My husband proposed to me on Jones Beach after seeing me sit on that piano and sing 'Bill' under that full moon. I think it helped put him over the edge."

Adrienne Angel played Julie in a bus-and-truck tour of the show, playing one-night stands all over the country: "The cast was very good. Then there was Butterfly McQueen, but we won't talk about her. [Ms. McQueen had obviously been hired for her name more than her suitability.] The show does hold up. You can't be revisionist about it, because it was true to the period. I've done *I Do, I Do*, and people say, 'How can she say, "I'm only a woman when I'm really in love"?' Well, I'm a feminist, but that's the way it was. I can't revise history."

Whether *Show Boat* is dated comes up more often than with such other classics as *Oklahoma!* because of the racial aspects of the plot. Rosetta Le Noire co-starred in the Lincoln Center production, which also included William Warfield singing "Old Man River."

LE NOIRE: "People complain about the stereotypes, but you can't worry about that. It was true to the period. As long as you're playing the truth, it doesn't bother me."

TOWERS: "To be honest, I had never seen *Show Boat*. The first time the whole cast was together and we went through the score, I cried. I had no idea how those songs flowed from one into another. It was overwhelming."

The Lincoln Center production was directed by William Hammerstein and produced by Richard Rodgers.

COOK: "There was one point in the script when Magnolia is auditioning for the job at the music hall after Ravenal has left, and it says, 'Magnolia picks up her guitar, moves downstage, and accompanies herself singing "Fish gotta swim, birds gotta fly. . . ."' So I kept looking at that and thinking, 'They don't really mean that. I'm going to fake it or something.' Finally I went to Billy and said, 'Does this script mean what it says, 'cause I don't play the guitar.' I'd never picked up a guitar in my life. And the musical director said, 'Forget it, she'll never be able to do it.' Of course, that was all I had to hear. They taught me some simple fingerings, and I did it. I nearly drove myself crazy, but I did it. I'd wake up at four o'clock in the morning and do the song and go back to sleep."

Sally Ann Howes became a star after replacing Julie Andrews in *My Fair Lady*. By the time she did a City Center revival of *Brigadoon* (for which she received a Tony nomination), Lerner and Loewe had dissolved their partnership: "They hadn't spoken to each other for a long time. They'd had a terrible row, and they were going around backstage congratulating everyone, and ended up together in my dressing room. And after ignoring each other, they had to talk, and that got them back together again. That was sort of nice to know."

Sometimes the passing years make a show's creator take a new look at the original work. Martin Vidnovic, Meg Bussert, and Michael Cone were in a revival of *Brigadoon* directed by Vivian Matalon, with the show's original choreographer, Agnes De Mille.

VIDNOVIC: "I liked what Vivian Matalon tried to do with it, trying to bring something new to it, not just recreating the original."

BUSSERT: "When I started doing revivals, people felt that just because they were written twenty or thirty years ago they were old fashioned; and that's not true. They're classics. They only get better. Vivian said he was so thrilled with my audition because I showed him the way to do 'Waiting for My Dearie,' something that was palatable that he could work with—a lot of passion and confusion. The lyric is there, and the music is there, but you never take anything at face value—you always have to dig deeper."

The Domino Principle

S OMETIMES a performer gets a coveted role for reasons that wouldn't seem to make sense in the real world.

"I had auditioned for *Bloomer Girl*, but I was at the bottom of their list," remembers Nanette Fabray. "They were doing a musical version of *Rain*, *Sadie Thompson*, at the same time. They wanted Ethel Merman for it, and Celeste Holm was going to do *Bloomer Girl*. If Ethel didn't do *Rain*, then Celeste would do it and I'd do *Bloomer Girl*. Well, Merman took Sadie; Celeste was the 'bloomer girl,' and I was back on unemployment.

"After a few weeks Merman left her show and June Havoc replaced her, but the show still didn't work. Then they let Celeste go about three months into the run of *Bloomer Girl*.

"The producer, John C. Wilson, came in one night and saw that Celeste had changed her hair and her whole look because she was doing a nightclub act at the Plaza. Well, *Bloomer Girl* was about the Civil War, and it did need a certain look.

"So he went across the street to Sardi's. My agent was there and John said to him, 'Is Nanette available?' My agent told him I was and John sat down right there and wrote out a notice for Celeste, and I got the show. That was a great part for me."

The critics agreed and Fabray went on to take the show on a successful tour after the Broadway run.

CONE: "Jamie Jamison assisted De Mille. The first time we put the McConechie Square number on its feet, she kept looking at it and saying, 'This is terrible!' She was looking at us through these thick glasses, and she leaned over to Jamie and said, 'Did I do this?' He said, 'Yes, this is what you did in the original.' And she said, 'Well, it stinks!' Then she apologized to us and told us it wasn't our fault, it was hers—and she restaged the whole thing."

Once a show has been around long enough, characters like Laurey in *Oklahoma!*, Julie in *Carousel*, and Fiona in *Brigadoon* stop being identified with individual people and take on a life all their own. When Meg Bussert played Laurey in a production of *Oklahoma!*, she was being watched by the show's original Ado Annie, Celeste Holm.

HOLM: "She played her wonderfully. She made her a girl who was so much in love but didn't want anyone to know it. She made her tough and defensive. It's not an easy part because people tend to think of her as a conventional ingenue, and she's not."

Bussert has played all the great musical theatre ingenues, which are sometimes considered thankless roles. "I approached Laurey the same way I approach all of those so-called boring, straitlaced musical comedy ladies. I love those roles. There is a lot going on inside, emotionally. Those characters are not much different from the ladies today. They want very much to be partners with their men, and they're not going to settle for anything less."

In the City Center revival, Susan Watson was the first performer both to play Laurey and to dance her in the dream ballet. "I was doing Carrie in *Carousel* at Lincoln Center, and Mr. Rodgers, who was producing, came back one night and said, 'How would you like to do *Oklahoma!*?' Well, I can't tell you how my heart was beating. Agnes De Mille was going to do the choreography, with Gemze De Lappe starting it. So I told him I'd really like to dance the 'Out of My Dreams' because I had been trained as a dancer, too. So they checked it out with Agnes, and we did all the original choreography, and damn, it was hard. I wasn't sure I'd really be able to do it, but I worked my little tail off."

Rodgers also knew that by having one performer both sing and dance the role, he wouldn't have to pay two salaries.

Oklahoma!, considered by most people to be a landmark in the evolution of the modern American musical, was a landmark in the life of Susan Watson: "My first Broadway show. We were on a trip to New York, and my parents took me to see it. And I remember sitting in the balcony of the St. James and being absolutely floored. I knew then that was what I wanted to do. I said, 'Yeah, that's for me. That's how I want to spend my life.'"

Joel Higgins and Martin Vidnovic played Curley and Jud, respectively, in *Oklahoma!*'s 1979 Broadway revival.

HIGGINS: "With me being from the Midwest and all, it was natural for me to be a rural sort of guy. How does it get any better than walking out onstage in chaps singing 'Oh, What a Beautiful Morning' a cappella? There's nothing quite like that."

VIDNOVIC: "I love the feeling of the show, and what it represents—the change it made in American theatre."

HIGGINS: "One night in our scene together, a piece of cheesecloth or something caught on fire. So I tried to put it out with my hand; I patted it and tried to go on with the scene. Well, the damn thing was still burning, and Marty, staying right in character, spit on his hand and rubbed the fire out. Didn't miss a beat."

Occasionally in reviving a classic, a whole different concept is given to the piece. All-black versions of shows were nothing new when *Guys and Dolls* was revived with an all-black cast.

ALLAN WEEKS: "We have to get to the point where the best talent gets the role, like they have in high schools and colleges. Unless it's something really specific. Like Ernestine Jackson can do Sarah Brown, but she can't do Fanny Brice. And by the same token, there's no reason why Bette Midler shouldn't do *Ain't Misbehavin'*. People think of that as a 'black' show, but it's really just a celebration of somebody's music."

Ernestine Jackson had played Irene Malloy in David Merrick's black version of *Hello, Dolly!* "I was lucky that I came to New York during the period they were going into all those black versions of musicals, like *Dolly*, and I got to do a lot at that time. The wonderful thing about *Dolly* was that we were doing the original production with all the orchestrations, and everything that had always been done."

The *Guys and Dolls* revival was directed by Abe Burrows, who had staged it originally, with a cast including Ernestine Jackson, Ken Page, and Eyde Byrde. Jackson thought the experience would be similar to the one she had with *Hello, Dolly!*

JACKSON: "When we started to do the show, we had all the original orchestrations, and it was really just an all-black reproduction of the original. Then when we were in Philly, I think, someone suggested that the show be 'niggered up.' That's what I heard. So they came in with a lot of different arrangements. I sort of liked what they did with 'If I Were a Bell,' but I don't know whether that helped or hurt. It really didn't need that. The show stands as it is. If a Japanese company came in and did that show the way it was written, it would run."

EYDE BYRDE: "I loved working with Abe Burrows, and I loved what he wanted to do with the show. There were some other people who wanted to make it really ethnic. I just thought it should be *Guys and Dolls*. What else do you need? We had a bunch of black people just doing what a bunch of white people had been doing. You're just seeing a little more color, a different shade. I thought the black people brought a warmth in the dances and singing, a sort of soulful thing that you don't often get, especially in 'Sit Down, You're Rockin' the Boat.' But actors are actors, and a piece is a piece. They've had white women singing Madame Butterfly forever; black women, too. It really shouldn't matter. It's a piece of entertainment."

When a show is revived, the creators naturally want to protect the essence of the original, but certain changes are bound to occur. They are usually made to accommodate the talents of the new cast. With *Guys and Dolls*, the changes were made gradually and grudgingly.

KEN PAGE: "They were very adamant about the show's score being done exactly as written, which posed some interesting problems, or questions, with a black company. We had something to bring to it musically which wasn't in the original score. Everyone—except Ernestine with 'If I Were a Bell'— had to stick right with the original. Then they got kind of lenient with me, too. After all, 'Sit Down, You're Rockin' the Boat' is Loesser's attempt at a gospel number. Jo Sullivan [Loesser] was around all the time. She and a man from the Loesser office sat there in front of us during rehearsals with the score and checked it note for note."

The bottom line with any revival is that the creators—the composer, lyricist, and librettist—wrote what they wanted to see on the stage, and it is important that their wishes be respected. As musical comedies become part of the universal repertory, guarding the creators' original intentions becomes more difficult.

BARBARA COOK: "I've heard productions of Rodgers and Hammerstein shows where the singers don't really sing the songs giving the notes the proper values. Dick was very much a stickler for giving the notes the proper value. I believe he was quite right in this. What happens is that sometimes it really detracts from the music. The way he wrote it gives it a certain weight— otherwise it can get poppy and frivolous, and just not have the right weight. If you were doing his songs outside the show, he appreciated jazz versions and all kinds of other versions. But in the show, as the character, he really wanted them to be sung as he had written them. And I think he's absolutely right."

When the intention of a show, or a part, is not clear, it can be hard on the performer. When people go in as replacements, the original director is usually not around and it can make for a lot of confusion and insecurity.

Elaine Cancilla had stood by for Chita Rivera in *Chicago* before she took over the role. "I was certainly different than Chita; and I wasn't there originally, so I never heard the original direction—which with Fosse, at that point, was very much involved with images. Getting images thirdhand is hard: when you're doing a happy number, to be thinking about dead babies in Vietnam. . . . I would say, 'Excuse me? I don't know what that is.' I made it mine at the end of the run, but it was very hard."

Carole Schweid had been with *A Chorus Line* in its workshop phase, and she understudied when the show moved to Broadway. When she was called in to replace the role of Morales, Michael Bennett was not there. "I got a call on Monday morning telling me they wanted me to take over. I was a wreck. I worked with the stage manager, who really hadn't been there from the beginning—and it was all very, very weird. We had a new cast. The national tour had just gone out, and we had a whole new staff and stage managers who hadn't been around. The worst thing was that I didn't have an understudy. So if I caught a cold I was up the creek. The pressure was incredible. I did play the part for awhile, before I got fired."

Stephen Sondheim's *Sweeney Todd* moved from Broadway into the standard repertory very quickly. After some major productions in opera houses, the show returned successfully to Broadway in a scaled-down version with a cast that included Bob Gunton, Beth Fowler, and Annie McGreevey.

BETH FOWLER: "It was marvelous when the people who had adored the first production adored us, too."

Even in revivals, there are replacements. One of them in *Sweeney* was Annie McGreevey (Mrs. Bob Gunton), who eventually played the Beggar Woman.

BOB GUNTON: "It was very difficult for me as Sweeney, in the first few performances, to look down and see Annie as the Beggar Woman. I was seeing my wife."

His wife's interpretation was another example of the changes every actor brings to a role.

ANNIE McGREEVEY: "At first I had been standing by for Mrs. Lovett and the Beggar Woman, and then I got to go on. I don't really have the temperament to be a good standby and do the same performance that someone else has done. The director came in and saw what I was doing, and she made some changes—but generally approved."

GUNTON: "Annie played her as a crazed, happy woman begging to survive. Her vulnerability made it easier to understand what Sweeney was mourning for when the audience discovers after her murder that she was his first wife.

"When I went into *Sweeney*, I had no preconceived notions about it. I think because of the scale of our production, we were able to focus on the individual stories, and people got more of a message about the inequities of the class system at the time than they did from Hal Prince's production, where the scale was so much bigger."

Mrs. Lovett, who baked meat pies filled with the remains of Sweeney Todd's murder victims, has fast become one of the classic women's roles— like Salome—that everyone wants to interpret her own way.

Dorothy Loudon went into the second cast in the original production, and recalls one of the show's most memorable scenes: "I think Mrs. Lovett's best spot in the show is 'By the Sea.' It was my favorite moment. There's such a sweetness about that song. I think maybe I was thinking about the seventeen years I waited to get married. I was going with someone who really wasn't free, and seventeen years is a very long time. But that's what the song is about: how wonderful it would be when they were together by the sea; all the high hopes she had in that song were heartbreaking."

FOWLER: "For me, 'By the Sea' was my big pitch for respectability. I was seducing him into wanting it as much as I did. I had problems with the character in finding evil in me. Bob Gunton tended to dig very deeply, and things would change. And I like to change."

GUNTON: "I had originally been doing the 'By the Sea' scene almost zombie-like. But Steve told me I couldn't be so detached. So I tried to connect with her. In the midst of all this blood, lust, and violence, what has he won? This maniac next to him who wants to be down by the sea. This is a man who was shipwrecked and was on an island for fifteen years, and the last thing he wants is to be by the f–g sea with her or anyone else."

Especially when performers stay in a long-running show, making a good salary, the change that comes about when new people come into the cast can keep the show fresh. Lee Roy Reams played in *42nd Street* for eight years. "I played the show with thirteen or fourteen Peggy Sawyers. Some of them were okay, and a few of them were great. I never mind when a new actor comes into a show. I like change. I always like to see what they have to offer, and never try to force them to give a carbon copy of the person who was playing the part before. Sometimes an actor's not good, and then it's frustrating. But when Anne Baxter went into *Applause* and did things differently, I got two new laughs."

Louise Troy came into *42nd Street* late. "The girl who was playing Peggy Sawyer, the ingenue, was very different from the original, and it was impossible to believe that she would ever replace me in a show—which is what the character does. For example, you wouldn't have Carol Burnett understudying Lynn Fontanne. So as things went on, I started to change my character and make her something of a nut, really. Then we matched. I had to work hard to have it make sense."

It's not always enough to be right for a role; a performer has to be aware of what roles are opening up and when. Zina Bethune was in California and had been tipped off by a fan when she auditioned for Tommy Tune to replace the role of the ballerina in *Grand Hotel*. "You dream about people coming up to you and saying, 'You've got to do this part!' "—which was exactly what happened to Bethune.

A show that is heavy on props or details complicates a smooth transition, as Joel Higgins found when he went into *City of Angels*: "It's a very picky show, so much happens. There's all that forties dialogue you have to spit out, and then there's the cigarette to deal with, a lot of props, and the fight that's choreographed. There are a lot of little details—it's not a leisurely show like *Oklahoma!*"

John Schneider found preparations for replacing the Baron in *Grand Hotel* more than adequate, having come to Broadway from television and film. "There, everybody is just thrown in. So having two whole weeks to prepare was a luxury. I never had the luxury of working in a feature where there was any rehearsal time. So sometimes you'd meet your leading lady at breakfast at six o'clock, and an hour later you're into a clinch. In those two weeks, I saw the show fourteen times, from all over—the balcony, the orchestra backstage, everywhere—so I could get the feel of how the show looked. By the time I came on the stage, it was just like watching it from a little closer."

Nevertheless, stepping into unfamiliar material in strange territory is an experience that most performers find, at the least, disorienting.

JOHN CUNNINGHAM: "When I took over as John Adams in *1776*, I had never seen some of these guys. The only time I saw them was when they were onstage in their eighteenth-century costumes. I had never seen them before in civilian dress. I actually ran into a couple of them on the street. They thought I snubbed them. But I didn't even know who they were."

15

Ready, Willing, and Able

As the dance captain in *Pajama Game*, Zoya Leporska had the job of choosing a new understudy for Carol Haney. She picked a girl named Shirley MacLaine out of the chorus: "I said, 'Shirley, learn it.' So in New Haven I took her down to the basement and taught her everything. Lo and behold, poor Carol hurts her foot during the 'Jealousy' ballet, and Shirley went on. And Hal Wallis, the big producer from Paramount Pictures, was in the audience, and there you are."

Shirley MacLaine was cast in the movie *The Trouble with Harry*, and became a star.

That's the way all understudy stories are supposed to end. Actually, it's the exception. In fact, understudying is just a job. Sometimes there is a payoff, but often there's not.

The difference between an understudy and a standby is that an understudy is someone already in the show employed to know a part in case something happens; a standby is simply a performer who is paid to come in once a week and rehearse—and always be ready to go on.

Elaine Cancilla has stood by for many leading ladies, including Chita Rivera in *Chicago*. "I think being a standby or an understudy is the hardest thing you can do in the theatre. After standing by for Velma in *Chicago*, I told myself, 'Never again.' I was trained to perform in my own way; they want you to stay as close to the body language of the performer you replace as possible. And it's hard to be thrown on at the spur of the moment and do whatever you have to do just to keep the curtain up."

Allen Weeks stood by in *The Wiz*: "It was rough for me—unless the star is going on vacation and you know you're going to go on. But that calling in every night gets rough: 'Can I go to the bathroom? Can I go on with my life? Or do I have to come in to the theatre?'"

Walter Willison stood by in *Pippin*. "In some ways being a standby is easier. You didn't have to be there. You'd just call and tell them where you'd be, and that was it. It was a great job; you'd come in once a week and run through the show, and get your paycheck."

Michael Kermoyan, who understudied Jean Pierre Aumont in *Tovarich*, went on when Aumont lost his voice. "They had never given me a revised version of the play—it was very different from the original. The stage manager called me and said, 'Mike, get your ass down here. You're going on tonight.' This was the first preview or something. So I took a shower and got there, and everybody was waiting. So we started through the show from the beginning, and it was the two of us in bed. Vivien said her first line, and I had to answer. And I couldn't remember the line. And I'm sure everybody's thinking, 'Who's this jackass who's going to have to go on tonight?' I felt really sorry for Vivien. So I barked out, 'What's the goddam line?' And I got it, and I went right on through. No mistakes or anything. I guess I just had to get mad enough at myself to be able to do it."

Vivien Leigh's standby was Joan Copeland. "Vivien called me to her dressing room one matinee day and said, 'I need a little rest and my doctor has urged me to take the night off. So I won't be here tonight.' We found out later she was in a very bad emotional state. At the rehearsals, they would play the songs in my key, because Vivien was a whiskey baritone, and I am a high soprano.

"So I was getting ready to go on that night and Stan Lubovsky, the musical director, came over to wish me good luck, and he said, I have to tell you that although we had been doing the songs in my key during the understudy rehearsals, he had never gotten the money for the transpositions. They would all have to be played in Vivien's keys. I had been with the show for ten or eleven months, and they'd never prepared for this! He said he could play my songs solo in my key and cut the orchestra—or I could sing in her key. I thought, 'My God, you're going to have a sixty-piece orchestra pull out every time the star for the evening appears? What is the audience going to think?' So I decided to try to sing down there. My first solo was a very beautiful

Who Needs Costumes?

C ASTING for the Circle in the Square's Broadway revival of *Pal Joey* was definitely subject to change. The original Joey (in the revival), ballet superstar Edward Villella, was replaced by Christopher Chadman, and the original Vera Simpson, the leading female role, was scheduled to be played by a "movie star." On opening night the critics raved about Joan Copeland, who had been standing by for the "Lady from Hollywood," whom Copeland—who is also a lady—declined to mention by name.

Villella left the show due to "artistic differences." Anyone who has read John Willis's *Theatre World* knows that the "Lady" in question was the fine actress and multiple Oscar nominee, Eleanor Parker.

JOAN COPELAND: "They had started the first week of previews when I joined the show. On my third day of rehearsals, the 'Star' was off for a costume fitting and the director asked me to fill in for a scene. I was still carrying the book, but I did the scene.

"You know, I was the new girl in town. So *everyone* in the cast was sitting around watching me. And I was good! I was very funny also, and for some reason the lady who was playing the part hadn't realized that these lines were funny. But that was that. She came back from her fitting and I disappeared into the woodwork again.

"I was very unlike her physically, temperamentally, and vocally, but they didn't want me to do what she was doing. They said I could do anything I wanted—within reason, of course. So I learned the movement and words and worked on the music at home.

"Well, after about ten days I got to the theatre at about five minutes to eight and the stage manager asked me if I knew the part and could play it and I said, 'Well I guess so. When are you planning on me doing it?' and he said, 'In ten minutes.'

"The day before, I had spoken to the musical director on the lunch break to talk about the songs because I knew I couldn't sing it in the keys this woman used. Her voice was deep, and I'm sure people thought it was perfect for Vera, but it was nothing like mine.

"So he said he'd get the transpositions done, but this was the day after we talked! Then I also thought, 'What do I wear?' It was summer and I was in jeans and a tee shirt, and Vera Simpson is the most gorgeous creature you can imagine, a designer's dream. A few days earlier it had occurred to me that they weren't coming to me about costumes. So I got together eight or nine things I had and put them in my front closet and told my husband they'd be there in case he ever had to bring them to me in a hurry.

"I asked the stage manager to call him and they told the conductor I was going on. It was too late to change anything. So I was going to have to sing the score in her keys. At that time, I didn't even know how to get around backstage. The stage manager said he'd have someone there to lead me around.

"The lady who had been playing the part was still in her dressing room and she refused either to leave or to go on stage. I never knew why and I didn't want to get into the politics of the thing. So I never did find out why she didn't go on. Anyway, they took me to the chorus dressing room and I borrowed some makeup and eyelashes. I guess the star thought they wouldn't go on without her, but that's what I was being paid for.

"When they made the announcement that I was going on, they also announced that my costumes hadn't arrived yet and out there I went in my jeans and tee shirt and I felt like I had been catapulted out of a cannon. The first entrance Vera makes is smashing, but fortunately she doesn't say anything for the first few minutes. She takes in the totality of the whole situation and gazes at various parts of Joey's body, and if the audience is with you, it really doesn't matter what you are wearing. They know exactly what is on that woman's mind. They were with me.

"By the time I got to singing 'Bewitched, Bothered, and Bewildered,' I got an ovation. They went wild and we couldn't go on with the scene. It was amazing. Maybe they were surprised, or maybe they just liked what they heard.

"During the first act, our 'Hollywood Lady' had left the theatre and my clothes had arrived, but I decided not to wear them because the audience had already accepted me in the clothes I'd been wearing. In their minds they had me clothed in the most gorgeous clothes in the world."

---

ballad, 'The Only One,' and I started singing and I didn't know from note to note what was going to happen. I didn't know where these sounds were coming from that seemed to be coming out of my throat. But they were there. And at the end of the song, the audience stood up and cheered, and the orchestra was applauding. When you have no other recourse, you discover what resources you have. It costs a lot, and sometimes it's painful, but you do what you have to do."

For seasoned performers, standing by is a part of the business, and it can often be a lucrative part. It's not always the starry-eyed youngster waiting for her big chance. Many times people do it for the security and would prefer not to go on at all.

Sheila Smith was a Broadway veteran when David Merrick asked her to stand by in *42nd Street*: "He offered me a lot of money, and it was just to cover. It turned out to be one of those things where six weeks later I was on. I was thinking of sitting around for two years and collecting the money and enjoying being at home."

Understudying a star in a show where the audience is coming for only one reason is the hardest job of all. Marilyn Cooper understudied Eydie Gorme in *Golden Rainbow*, which also starred Steve Lawrence. "The anticipation was worse than actually having to go on. The first time I went on was in previews, and I was really nervous. That evening it was Steve and Marilyn, and not Steve and Eydie, which was what people were coming to see."

Annie McGreevey stood by for a production of *Call Me Madam*. She never went on, but she was intimidated by the whole prospect. "Do you believe I stood by for Ethel Merman? She could walk into a room, and the electricity was incredible. Elaine Stritch has that same kind of quality. When she walks out onstage, you know she's there."

Adrienne Angel understudied Judy Holliday in *Bells Are Ringing*. "I had to go on without any rehearsal. She was there in the theatre, and I got called to her dressing room to go over the first scene. I knew she was upset because I was too green, and I was terrified—this was my first Broadway show. She looked at me and said, 'Could you play it older?' I walked out of there and I was sweating. But I went out there and did the first scene, and I got a laugh that had never been there before. And the scene played well. After the scene, the set revolved and Judy was there. She said to me, 'What did you do? You were wonderful!' She was great to me after that."

When *Applause* was out of town, the producers needed to find someone to carry the show if something happened to Lauren Bacall. It's not unusual to ask other stars to stand by, and in this case they asked Julie Wilson: "I was flown to Detroit. And I said to myself, 'I don't want to be her understudy.' I'd been starring in shows. I'd been a solo lady for many years! So I told them 'I really don't want to.'"

Gretchen Wyler took the assignment. "I went to the opening of *Applause*, and at the party, I ran into Larry Kasha, whose very first job was stage managing *Silk Stockings*, and now he was producing *Applause*. I told him I wanted to get into producing, and I was looking for properties. So he called me the next morning and said, 'Look, if you want to be a producer, wouldn't it be a great idea to have a big income? Why don't you stand by for Bacall? We'll give you a lot of money, and you'll probably never have to go on.' So that's what I did for a year. I stood by for her and made the money, and produced a couple of flop shows."

In *Applause*, Gene Foote understudied the role of the hairdresser. "Gretchen Wyler was wonderful as Margo. She was my Margo, because I got to do the rehearsals with Gretchen. We developed many moments in our rehearsals. There was one where he asks her if anything's wrong, and she says no, and he puts his arm around her shoulder and they walk off. The first time I had to go on, Betty [Bacall] wouldn't rehearse with me. Well, I did this with Bacall the way I had done it with Gretchen. And I got off the stage and she started screaming at me, 'Must you hang all over me onstage?' Now, she hated changes of any kind, but it was just the natural thing for me to do. I was so scared, and it was my very first night."

Barbara Colton was an understudy in a show with Katharine Hepburn. "Hepburn is the only star who regularly rehearses with the understudies, just in case she has to go on with them. That's almost unheard of. The first time I rehearsed with her she stopped after three minutes and said, 'Upstage me, upstage me. You're the new girl on the stage, and the audience has been listening to my voice for five thousand years—and if they want me, they know where to find me!'"

When Marilyn Cooper was in *Gypsy*, she understudied the role of Louise. "I had been in the show a long time doing Agnes, and I asked if I could audition when an understudy left, and I got it. It's incredible what understudies and standbys have to put up with. But Merman was great to me. She really helped me along."

Under the right circumstances, standing by or understudying can be a well-paying steady job in a profession where "well-paying" and "steady" are usually contradictions, and "job" is almost unheard of. The average unemployment rate in the Actors Equity Association is 98 percent.

Walter Willison understudied John Schneider in *Grand Hotel*. "I didn't want to do it in the beginning, but with John it was easy. He never misses performances, and if he left to go on vacation or do a TV show, you would know that in two weeks you were going to go on. I never had to worry about getting a phone call at 6:30 at night telling me I'd be going on that night."

In *Gantry*, Beth Fowler understudied the leading lady and went on when Rita Moreno developed vocal problems during previews. "I was literally thrown on. I did the show, and Helen Hayes was in the audience, and she came back afterwards to see me. Can you imagine what a thrill that was for me? Then she told her friend Anita Loos about me, and they were planning a musical based on Anne of Cleves from a play that Anita had written. Miss Hayes told Miss Loos that she had found the leading lady for her show, and Miss Loos came and loved me, and there were producers interested, and that lasted for awhile. But I thought, 'Here I go. I'm going to be a star.' That was how I got my agent."

After the ill-fated *Gantry*, Beth Fowler understudied Patricia Routledge, the leading lady in the ill-fated *1600 Pennsylvania Avenue*, a Lerner/Bernstein collaboration. The show didn't run long enough for her to go on, but she was called to step in during a rehearsal, which allowed her the chance to work with Bernstein. "Lenny was conducting, and I got to sing the entire score, including 'Duet for One.' Naturally, that was a thrilling experience for me." "Duet for One" is the tour de force solo for the leading lady, in which she portrays First Ladies Julia Grant and Lucy Hayes.

After her Broadway experience with *Bells Are Ringing*, Adrienne Angel was flown out as insurance to a summer stock production in Massachusetts, where the leading lady, Patricia Wilson, was in the first throes of laryngitis. Miss Angel recalls: "I was sitting in the audience watching the show, and after the first scene, a man came down the aisle and tapped me on the shoulder and said, 'Adrienne, you're on.' And I was. The stage manager made an announcement: 'Ladies and gentlemen, we're very sorry, but Miss Wilson is unable to finish the performance, but we are very fortunate that we have a young lady in the audience who was in the Broadway show who will now continue the show. I walked down the aisle and onto the set, never having met anyone in the company, and I finished the show. It was one of the most exciting evenings of my life. It got written up in the *New York Times*, and the *Daily News*, and they got a lot of publicity out of it."

There is a recurring dream people have about being called to go onstage unprepared, and the dream usually involves something like not having pants on. It almost happened to Patti Karr when she had to go on for the leading lady (Michelle Lee) in *Seesaw*. "I had no warning. I just happened to be at the theatre. I had no clothes—one pair of jeans I'd brought in myself. But they were so stiff, I couldn't sit down in them. I had to wear all her clothes—even her shoes. Then when I got onstage, I'd throw in stuff from different versions of the show. I'd say things like, 'What happened to the twenty-five thousand dollars a year?' and then say, 'Oh, we didn't talk about that earlier, did we . . .?' but we got through it. I never had so much fun in my life."

In *Something More*, it was hard for anybody to keep track of the changes in the show. Laurie Franks was understudying both Barbara Cook and Viveca Lindfors before Lindfors was fired out of town.

LAURIE FRANKS: "I was already Barbara's understudy, and when they fired Viveca, I'd only been looking at her part for a day or two—and it was never the same script. I went on that night."

Franks admits now that she didn't take as much advantage of the opportunity as she could have.

"I told them I couldn't do Viveca's song, because there wouldn't be any rehearsal. It was probably the biggest mistake I ever made. Viveca wasn't much of a singer, and I could have made a big splash. It was a great break for me, because I was getting double salary. But every night while I was going on, they were auditioning people to replace me."

It's not the most relaxing way to make a living. Liz Callaway was cast in *Merrily We Roll Along*. "I was covering twelve women. Then my agents got a call from the Public Theatre, where Richard Maltby was doing a show called *Gallery*. I had auditioned for it, and I was cast as one of the leads. So I gave my notice at *Merrily*. But Hal Prince told me that if I stayed, he would put me in the chorus, and I could understudy the lead. Against everyone's advice, I stayed."

Gallery never did open, but because of the experience, Maltby would cast her in *Baby*.

Occasionally, understudying gets to be a reverse fantasy: where the understudy is doing great as the star but is pushed off the stage by politics or circumstances. Patti Karr stood by for Carol Burnett in *Once Upon a Mattress*. "Jane White, who played the Queen, had an understudy who wasn't getting the part right, so they called me up in the middle of the night and asked if I could go into it for Jane, who I think had pneumonia, and would be out for quite a while. I was on for her about a week, then Carol was out—and they didn't know what to do. Well, Carol's old understudy was back in town from some show, so they put her on—and I was stuck playing the Queen! That wasn't the part I was there for, and I was livid. Well, the line 'You swam the moat' never had so much meaning. I wanted to push her back in there. It was a wonderful experience to play both parts; it's just unfortunate you can't do them both at the same time."

When *Cabaret* was revived, Laurie Franks was assigned to understudy the part originally created by Lotte Lenya, and now being played by Regina Resnik. "I went on a lot in the pre–Broadway tour. In Washington, Regina was out, and I think I was very good in the show, but they all wanted Regina back. Then Fran Weissler [the producer] came to town and told me that they were bringing in Peg Murray to stand by for Regina, and that I would just be the understudy. Peg would always go on if Regina was out. So I gave notice and yelled at everybody. Then Peg showed up and started to rehearse, and they were measuring her for costumes and everything. It wasn't that Peg and I weren't friends. We were, but I hadn't seen her in years, and I was mad at her, too."

Murray wasn't even particularly happy about doing the show. In the original production, she had won a Tony as a featured player.

PEG MURRAY: "I did the revival because they wanted me around, but it was a mistake. In the original production I'd stood by for Lotte Lenya, and I went on for her whenever she was on vacation or out sick. Here I'd look around me and see all these people in the same costumes, but they weren't the same people—and I missed the originals."

LAURIE FRANKS: "I was bound and determined not to stay. But I was talked into it. Then, when we got to New York and to the Minskoff, of course what happened was that Regina was out and Peg wasn't ready to go on. So Laurie went on! [Laurie sometimes refers to herself in the third person.] After that, whenever Regina was out, Peg went on. And that was that. Then at the last performance, Regina was out and Peg had already gone to the country. So Laurie went on!"

Everyone has a horror story. During *Cry for Us All*, Willi Burke was supposed to stand by for the leading lady, Joan Diener. "I wasn't allowed to watch rehearsals. I never had a chance to watch the show. I finally had to pay for my own rehearsal studio near the theatre. The stage manager would give me the music, and I would work on my own with a rehearsal pianist. I learned the role. And sure enough, it was about six o'clock, and I got to the theatre, and the director was there and said Joan was sick and she couldn't go on. Then he said to me, 'Of course, you're not ready to play this,' and I said, 'Oh, yes I will!' Now, it was two hours before curtain, and I found that Joan had left the theatre and locked her dressing room. And I just had a couple of schmattas to wear. Robert Weede was so sweet, he gave me his dressing room to use. I found out later Joan had been watching me from the back of the theatre."

Laurie Franks understudied one of the principal roles in *Applause*. "I went on for two weeks for Ann Williams out of town. She had pneumonia. But then I had pneumonia, too. The whole company had pneumonia. And there we were."

If you're paid to understudy, you go on.

After the experience with *Cry for Us All* in Boston, Willi Burke had her name taken off the program. Back in New York she ran into the show's composer, Mitch Leigh, one night. "He told me he was very surprised that I had done so well in Boston. He said what really happened was that originally they had wanted to use the girl who had stood by for Joan before, but she'd had another job, so they hired me. But then she became available, and they didn't rehearse me hoping that I would fail, so they would be able to fire me and hire her. That explains a lot."

When it opened in New York, the Richard Rodgers/Martin Charnin musical *I Remember Mama* had a lot of problems. So did Elizabeth Hubbard when she understudied its star, Liv Ullman. "When we came to New York, there was no understudy for Liv. I don't think she wanted one, or she felt that she was the only person anyone would come to see in the show. They probably just wanted to save money. But when we started previews, they asked me if I would stand by for the role. It was a wonderful role. Of course, I wanted to learn the role, but Liv didn't want me to. Now, come on! All I wanted to do was do the job they were paying me for. As it turned out, I had to watch the show and learn the role from the monitor at the stage manager's desk."

Understudying and standing by can be rewarding. It can also be humiliating. But it's a realistic way of surviving as a working actor.

16

The Present and the Future

AFTER *Hair* came in," says Susan Watson, "I was ready to retire. I thought, 'I can't play the guitar. That's it for me in show business. What's left for a soprano?'"

Watson didn't retire, but for working performers, 1968's *Hair* and the rock musical began the disintegration of the orderly, hierarchical business of the American musical theatre.

ADRIENNE ANGEL: "Everything changed in the late sixties. It was a change of attitude. They threw out romance and said, 'We have to be honest. We have to let it all hang out.' Letting it all hang out is the death of romance. The rock, the flower-child syndrome, and even women's lib changed it all."

Veteran Broadway performers began moving West to try and find work in film.

LOUISE TROY: "People like Karen Morrow should be working on Broadway all the time. Instead, people are sitting out in California, hoping they'll get to do a sitcom."

ANNE JEFFREYS: "I'd love to do one great Broadway show before I die, but I just don't see Andrew Lloyd Webber writing a show for me."

When a performer like Jo Sullivan started her career, there were revivals of classics like *Oklahoma!* and *Carousel* regularly staged at City Center, and they trained a new generation of performers in their craft. "City Center was a great place to work. You got the chance to do roles that were right for your voice. The composers were there, and were always interested in what was going on. Richard Rodgers auditioned us for *Carousel*. They did a season of Frank [Loesser]'s shows, and he was really involved. You learned as you performed."

Hair and the shows that followed, with their "let it all hang out" approach to the craft, broke those ties to ritual and tradition. But the shows were very popular. Broadway entered a schizophrenic period with the revival of *No, No, Nanette* in 1971. Traditional, original musicals were out. All that was being produced were nostalgia shows or rock spectacles.

Cashing in on the nostalgia craze, Jim Jacobs and Warren Casey came up with *Grease*. As *Nanette* appealed to the over-fifty crowd, so *Grease* was aimed at an audience who could get nostalgic about the fifties. Opening off-Broadway at the Eden Theatre in 1972, *Grease* moved to Broadway within six months and went on to become the third-longest running show in Broadway history.

Playing 1950s teenagers, two members of the original cast were Carole Demas, who played the virginal heroine, Sandy, and Kathi Moss, the Fiery Catholic School Girl, Cha-Cha.

CAROLE DEMAS: "Personally, the show was the high point of my Broadway career. High school was a terrible time for me. So it was great that I got to do it all over again with control, and got to get the boy and all that good stuff."

KATHI MOSS: "Audiences just adored the show and they would get up in the aisles and start dancing. People recognized themselves, or friends of theirs. *Grease* brought in people in their thirties and forties who had never been to a Broadway show before."

DEMAS: "I guess it was no secret that I was one of the oldest members of the cast, and some of the clothes that I wore at the Eden were actually mine. They had them copied when we moved uptown."

MOSS: "When we opened, we got mixed reviews. A lot of our families had come to the opening, and we had a party at Sardi's, and we had the TV on, and one review said that the cast was old and unattractive. Of course, our parents were appalled. They all thought, 'They're *supposed* to look like that—it's the fifties. Nobody looked good in the fifties.'"

DEMAS: "The basic reason that a piece like that could run as long as it did was because people just had a good time. And we did, too. There are a lot of experiences in the theatre where you feel like you're all a family while the show is on; and then it ends, and the relationships are over. *Grease* wasn't

The "David Merricks" Don't Live Here Anymore

Russ Thacker and Martin Vidnovic became important featured performers in the Broadway musical theatre in a time when there were still bankable stars and it was possible for a performer to go from show to show. Thacker, still an active performer, is also a record producer, and is responsible for many shows being saved on CD when they could have slipped into oblivion. Vidnovic temporarily dropped out of the business after working on the Cy Coleman/A. E. Hotchner *Welcome to the Club* in its out-of-town tryout. Now he has returned and is actively pursuing a career in musical- and straight theatre. Both he and Thacker realize that something important has changed.

"When I did the show in Florida," says Vidnovic, "there was a really negative feeling about the whole project. The whole thing was mean. It wasn't a good experience for me. Then they asked me to do it in New York. They had a new director and a new script; but when they sent it to me, all the bad feelings came back. You have to move forward, but at the same time think about the way you're moving!

"I'm a little more optimistic about the future of the American musical now because there seems to be a resurgence of interest in the form and in giving young writers and composers a chance to be heard. Unfortunately, money is still a big problem."

"It seems like a shame to me," says Thacker, "that you have to have a huge conglomerate behind you if you're going to succeed. To survive you have to have the critics; but we've given them their power, and if producers would stop printing the good reviews, then when they damn you whether they're right or wrong, it wouldn't be so important—or such a matter of life and death for a show.

"I liked it when there were stupid shows on Broadway. Not 'stupid'—but just shows that you could afford to go and see, like *Superman* and *Skyscraper* and *Bajour*. They may not have been great shows, but they were there, and they were fun. They still have shows like that in England and I go to see them all. They may be awful, but they are 'wonderful-awful'—and they're affordable. Here, if you're going to pay your $50 or $100, you'd better get your money's worth.

"I think maybe the day of the British musical is dead. It was purely a financial thing, and now they're having their problems, too. Maybe now we'll get back to shows that are about people."

like that. The women in the show all got together and supported each other. We still call ourselves the 'Pink Ladies.'"

Grease had no dance captain. It had a "dance queen" in Kathi Moss, who was with the show for about five years.

MOSS: "As dance queen, the producers gave me a tiara and a scepter. I took great pride in keeping the show as sharp as possible and as close to what had been originally intended."

As the traditional musical disappeared, the changing work ethic of young performers was reflected in shows like *Grease*.

MOSS: "I had been in the show for three years, and I would hear someone who had been there for six months say how bored they were; and I would say, 'Listen, I don't want to hear that. You have every right to have those feelings; it's normal, but leave them at home. There are a lot of people who want these jobs, and if you don't like it, then leave.'"

DEMAS: "Originally, the show worked so well because everybody got a chance to shine. Also, I wanted the audience to really like Sandy, and I think they did. I'm proud of that."

MOSS: "When we were doing *Grease*, somebody wrote that I was the oldest actress on Broadway. My God, Jessica Tandy was working then! 'Please, I'm not the oldest—the longest running, maybe!' But I did my job every night, and that's what it's all about."

Grease was a phenomenon, with one of the biggest repeat audiences of any show ever on Broadway. People who longed for the 1950s came back to see it again and again. The same creative team later came up with *Over Here*, which starred the Andrews Sisters, and tried to do for the 1940s what *Grease* had done for the 1950s. It didn't work.

Interspersed with the nostalgia and rock musicals of the 1970s were shows like A *Chorus Line*, *Chicago*, and *Ain't Misbehavin'*—all works that were unique and couldn't be fit into the traditional mold of the book musical.

Jesus Christ Superstar (1971) was also unique, and not just because it was successful; *Hair* and *Godspell* both had longer runs, yet *Jesus Christ Superstar* introduced a modus operandi that foreshadowed the way the blockbuster British imports would unalterably change the Broadway landscape a decade later. The Tim Rice/Andrew Lloyd Webber show brought something new to the business of show business: *Superstar* had been a bestselling record and had toured in a concert version—and only then was it turned into a Broadway show. It was the start of a trend that was the kiss of death for the American musical tradition.

Superstar also was the vehicle for Patrick Jude's Broadway debut: "Webber's best work came in the early years. But now, you go to the theatre, and forgive me, but what you see is a great makeup job; you have to listen to lip synching and prerecorded music. I resent that. The Phantom is onstage for twenty-one minutes—and a lot of that is prerecorded. That's not Broadway."

JO SULLIVAN: "When we did *Most Happy Fella*, of course we had no amplification. Robert Weede only did six shows a week—but that was to be expected. I did all eight shows a week. That's what I was being paid for."

ANNE JEFFREYS: "When Mary Martin and I were making $1,500 a week, we were considered the highest paid musical stars on Broadway. Now they make $20,000 a week, and they still don't do all eight shows."

PATTI KARR: "People aren't as disciplined as they used to be. Dancers are not trained in period styles. They don't even get ballet. They come out of the 'sidewalk' school of ballet, where they learn things like how to roll around on your navel. There's no technique to back it up."

MARIA KARNILOVA: "When I was in the chorus of the ballet and would watch a great ballerina onstage, I was always intimidated. I had admired all these ballerinas for so many years. Kids today don't understand the tradition, and they don't seem to care about the past. For them, Makarova is passé. We didn't just do steps. They don't understand; the movement is all there— but they don't understand what they're doing. The same is true in Broadway shows today. Everyone looks alike. All the men seem to act alike, and all the women are very beautiful, but they look alike."

ANITA GILLETTE: "It's more business now than it is show. All of that tradition is gone. Everyone just wants to know how much money they're going to make. That's why I decided I had to get out of musical comedy and just be an actor."

NANETTE FABRAY: "The Broadway musical will never die. But it's slowly bleeding to death."

In the 1980s, the invasion of British imports—multimillion dollar, long-running technical extravaganzas—monopolized the Broadway theatre: *Cats*, *Les Miserables*, and *Phantom of the Opera*, to name a few. Even as people stood in line for tickets to be awed by the falling chandelier of *Phantom* and the turntables of *Les Miserables*, for Broadway and the performers who inhabit it, the trend almost choked the theatre to death. The multimillion-dollar price tags of the Webber shows (and others), with their emphasis on technical wizardry, drove ticket prices up astronomically and bloated the American theatre, making it extremely difficult for less technically spectacular shows to compete or even survive. When a few shows entrench themselves for a long run, the casts tend to stay with them, and without the turnover, other performers don't get the opportunities to work. It becomes harder and harder for Broadway performers to work regularly. While the shows are recast after their move from London, the fact that they have originated overseas does affect American performers. Tony nominee Liz

Callaway could never get an audition for *Cats* or *Les Miserables*; she was considered "too American."

Naturally, this bothers some.

PENNY FULLER: "It's hard to talk about these British shows, because naturally, if someone said, 'Come and do one,' I'd be there. But what's happened is that they provide so much sturm und drang, there's no room for emotion. They leave no room for me and my imagination. They're trying to make films, and it takes away from the ritual of the theatre."

Cats took the Winter Garden Theatre, where Ethel Merman led the historic run-through of *Gypsy*, and had it decorated to look like an alley full of garbage.

BARNARD HUGHES: "I haven't seen *Cats*. I resent the fact that they have to tear the theatres apart for these shows. I wonder if the Winter Garden will ever be the same. I hope they have to return the theatre to pristine condition after it closes. If it ever closes."

As Andrew Lloyd Webber has said of himself, he is beyond critics. *Phantom of the Opera* gave us a falling chandelier, and the show transformed Broadway into a world where the scenery is the star. The recording, issued even before the show opened in London, helped ensure its success.

Bob Gunton played Juan Peron in the original Broadway cast of Webber's *Evita*. "Basically, I think Hal Prince was a little bored by the time he came to work with us; and he has a very low threshold for boredom [Prince had directed the show originally in London]. The creative environment wasn't very scintillating. But it was at the beginning of the Andrew Lloyd Webber phenomenon, and it was a presold hit. I remember coming into it knowing that it was going to run no matter what happened. We got mixed reviews— some quite poor. But it was already a hit. No one remembers that Walter Kerr didn't like the show."

A far cry from the hucksterism with which a Todd or Merrick used to sell a show, the Webber shows were pioneers in marketing techniques like issuing the hit record before the show opened. Because of this, the shows have a flop-proof element. *Aspects of Love* was Webber's one Broadway flop. It lost $8 million in its New York run. But in London it ran for 1,325 performances, making a profit that more than offset its Broadway losses. As with most Webber musicals, it followed up with a concert version, profitably touring the United States.

CAROL LAWRENCE: "It's diabolical. We gave birth to this medium. Musical comedy is an American art form—we perfected it. Then it got too expensive for us to produce, and they found they could produce these shows for one-third of the expense in England. So Andrew Lloyd Webber developed a repertory company of people who could sing his music, and then recorded the albums beforehand—so people could walk into the show knowing his songs."

The resentment in the Broadway community against these megashows is not isolated. *Forbidden Broadway*, the satirical revue, features a takeoff on *Les Miserables*:

> At the end of the play
> See the audience smolder
> Sitting flat on their butts for
>   three hours or more
> They can't wait to get back home
> And to read the libretto in bed
> To decipher whatever went on
> And what we said . . .
>
> I dreamed a show in days gone by
> When pathos wasn't overstated
> I didn't sing one song, then die
> I didn't act so constipated.

Writer/director/performer Gerard Alessandrini was not speaking just for the theatre community when he wrote these lyrics. A show like *Forbidden Broadway* doesn't run for as long as it has without a more general audience supporting it. The parody reveals the truth for the theatregoing public as well as for those in the profession: the parody is entertaining; the original is boring.

There is resentment about the success of some of the British shows, but it is not just sour grapes. As patrons stood in line for *Phantom* (ostensibly a good thing for Broadway), it was not even that one could go uptown to the Metropolitan Opera House and hear a similar melody in Puccini's *The Girl of the Golden West*. What really riles most is the havoc the 1980s shows wrought on the traditional values of the craft. A prerecorded score to which a performer lip-synchs before a theatregoer who paid $65 is an assault on the most basic integrity of the theatrical profession. If the audience has fun and enjoys the scenic effects, that's fine for the audience, in the short run. But it's a sad commentary on the state of performing, and on the performer–audience relationship, which is the sacred foundation of live theatre. The effects are far-reaching.

Amplification, for instance, has changed the way young performers learn their craft, and the way those who were trained to project have to perform. Leila Martin was featured in the cast of *Phantom*: "If you have an enormous voice, you'll get cut down because they try to equalize things. It's frustrating. I don't think we'll ever go back to the way things were. I don't think people are going to be trained to listen again. Kids who go to shows today now want that sound blasting out. It's sad, because you never really hear a voice anymore. I loved it at rehearsal when we all just sang, and you could hear your voice hitting the back wall, and could make any adjustments you wanted."

One hallmark of works like *Phantom*, *Les Miserables*, and *Miss Saigon* is the near-disappearance of dialogue in favor of sung-through, operatic-style scores. Liz Callaway was cast on Broadway in *Miss Saigon* after producer Cameron Macintosh saw her work in *Baby*. "The form of the show appeals to me because I'm more comfortable singing than acting. Sometimes, though, I miss talking. Why can't we just say what we have to say in a few lines, and not sing it and make it rhyme? It's limiting. But in this economy, any show that's a success is good for everyone. I'm thrilled to be in a hit. It's strange; it didn't matter whether we won the Tony for best musical or not. But with *Baby*, that nomination gave us at least another month's run."

CHITA RIVERA: "A lot of people don't like big musicals, but I love them. I adored *Saigon*, *Phantom*, *Les Miserables*; it was the Americans' time in England for so many years, now it's the English's turn. It's starting to turn around, though. The big sets and stuff are on the way out. We went through it, and we'll get to new stages. That's the survival element in me."

GEMZE DE LAPPE: "Everyone wants to see *Cats*. I knew very few people who really liked it, but people keep going to see it. I look at the Andrew Lloyd Webber stuff, and it's the emperor's new clothes. And *Les Miz*—you could predict every word that they were going to say. I was really offended by it. People accept things because of the scenery. That just isn't enough."

BARBARA COOK: "I wish we'd get back to more human values in musicals—caring about what happens to people. I think people want to get involved; they want to laugh, but they also want to cry. I guess it's not fashionable. I'm afraid audiences today don't accept the idea of characters bursting into song the way they used to."

Maria Karnilova and George S. Irving are seasoned theatre professionals. They also both tend to be chauvinistic and proud of it. Also, they both have very definite ideas on the British invasion of Broadway in the 1980s.

MARIA KARNILOVA: "I hate to go to the theatre anymore."

GEORGE S. IRVING: "I must confess, I have never seen an Andrew Lloyd Webber show. When *Cats* opened, Maria went to see it."

KARNILOVA: "How can that still be running? It's terrible. And the microphones. My God, people are miked all over—I can't believe it."

IRVING: "We're used to a different kind of theatre, when people spoke up and could be heard. And when there were big personalities out there. The American musical was built on using acting singers; the British musical seems more interested in technology."

As we move farther away from the 1980s, we can only speculate on how the shows that depend so heavily on scenic effects will live on. Susan Watson wonders how many productions of these musicals will be at Westbury, or Westport, or any of the other standard summer stock venues that keep our musical theatre heritage alive. Away from Broadway, what is their life going to be, except in concert form?

The average number of performances per year of *Oklahoma!*—in the United States alone—is 600. *South Pacific* is done approximately 500 times a year; the same goes for *The Sound of Music*. There are an average of 400 performances yearly of *The King and I*, 350 of *Carousel*, and 450 of *Annie Get Your Gun*. High schools could certainly do *Les Miserables* and *Phantom*—but will they be able to afford the revolving stage and the falling chandelier that seem vital to the success of those two shows?

During the British invasion, American producers occasionally tried to imitate the British imports. One expensive mistake was the 1981 *Marlowe*, which cast Patrick Jude in the title role.

PATRICK JUDE: "I was treated like a star. My name was above the title, and they did things like send me out to fencing classes. It fulfilled all the old Errol Flynn fantasies. But I didn't have any control; I wasn't allowed to have input on where the show was going."

The role of Emilia Bassano, the girl in love with both Christopher Marlowe and William Shakespeare and forced to disguise herself as a boy—a part that ten years earlier would have been given to Chita Rivera—was given to her daughter, Lisa Mordente: "There's so much hype now. Everything seems to be just for that moment. Everyone wants to work—but they don't want to work too hard. Mom used to come home from rehearsal with Fosse totally exhausted. They would work all day and then do some overtime. But they wanted to do it; they wanted it to be good. The reasons for doing things have changed, and I think that's very sad."

Broadway seems to have stopped producing theatre stars. If a "star" performer is needed, producers usually look to movies and television. Performers no longer go from show to show. Careers are no longer built in the theatre.

MARTIN VIDNOVIC: "Alfred Drake and Ethel Merman and Mary Martin were theatre stars, stars that Broadway made. But it was a different kind of theatre then. So how do you make a star? Now, Andrew Lloyd Webber's the star, or you have ensemble shows."

ADRIENNE ANGEL: "Where are the leading men today? Men who are electric and have a physical magnetism? It's very rare. And I miss the fact that we don't have songs like 'Some Enchanted Evening.' I want to stand up and cheer, and be really moved, and I'm not, anymore."

FARLEY GRANGER: "It's important to have stars in musical comedy. We need them. The scenery as the star is a bore. Mary Martin singing 'I'm in Love with a Wonderful Guy' was thrilling. When Rex Harrison did 'The Rain in Spain' you just wanted to jump out of your seat and yell. But we don't have that anymore."

Though the tide has definitely turned away from the British shows of the 1980s, the few successful new American musicals like *City of Angels* and *Grand Hotel* are "concept" shows that don't rely on star performances. The vehicle is the star. Kathi Moss went from a lead in Tommy Tune's *Nine* to a relatively minor role in *Grand Hotel*. Walter Willison was also in the cast: "The original intention, as far as we know, was that Tommy knew exactly what he wanted to do with the principals; but with some of us, like Kathi and myself, he was just going to wait and see what developed. Then we would have more to do. Because of all the plots, the secondary characters had to have their material reduced to make the whole show more accessible. That's the way it goes; but it's good to be in a hit."

KATHI MOSS: "A friend of mine once said that acting isn't hard. It's just talking and listening. I didn't have a lot to do in the show, so I had to change things a little to keep them fresh."

Theatre remains one of the few professions where just being employed is fulfilling in itself. While ingenues have never expected to stay ingenues forever, there used to be room in the musical theatre for performers to grow into other kinds of roles. But in today's economic climate, opportunities are scarce for veteran performers. Many who could be working have given up musical theatre for straight acting, or film and television work that brings a paycheck.

ANITA GILLETTE: "I decided to get out of musical comedy. I'm trying to grow up with the roles I'm playing now, without being like a freak or wearing a lot of makeup and trying to stay young. I enjoy playing character parts, or just women my own age."

MARIA KARNILOVA: "Life on Broadway is really tough. If you're an important member of the company, management is after you all the time: you can't get out of the contract. You can't get a day off. You can't get a rest. If you get sick, they're after you to come back because they're losing money. You're oppressed all the time. It's an oppressive, stressful way to live."

Goodbye Vinton Freedley, Hello TV

THROUGH good times and bum times, Benay Venuta's seen it all.

"In the old days—take a show like *Anything Goes*. Vinton Freedley produced the whole show for something like $2,000, or something ridiculous. He was a producer—and I don't think there are many people around now who do that: get the composers, get the stars, keep watch on the shows. I think now it's more about investing money and not about the shows themselves.

"Television has changed everything. Now you can see a wonderful movie on your VCR, so why go out? But people still want live theatre, if it's good.

"Chorus kids today do everything—sing, dance, act—I think they're much better trained today than we were. But when television came into our lives, taste seemed to change. The sad thing is that writers who could be working on Broadway are used up by television. The money is so good out there that a lot of guys who could be writing here are out there playing golf and driving their Mercedes. Who's going to struggle in the theatre when you can make that kind of money? All the talent that's wasted. . . ."

Gretchen Wyler is uncertain about her future in the business. "I loved my career. How many people got to stop a Cole Porter show? I don't love it now, though. I did one scene in the movie *Marrying Man* with Kim Basinger; I just did the 'Condo Circuit' in Florida with my cabaret act. But once you've played the Copacabana, it's hard to play the Condo Circuit. I want to walk away before I become bitter. It's very hard to be out here in California and see women that I've looked up to—big stars—who are now competing for small roles in small things. I don't want to do that. Besides, I've been in show business forty years, and I never did things for me. I never learned to cook. I never grew roses. I bought some land in Santa Fe, and I'd like to think that in a few years, I could just start riding horses and growing roses and cooking."

For some performers, though, life outside the theatre is unthinkable. "When I die, I'd like to be onstage," says Willi Burke.

PATTI KARR: "I figure in a few years I'll be a little old character actress, and everybody will be surprised when this little old gray-haired lady comes out and kicks up her heels. I did *The Rink* out in New Jersey, and I was dancing away. Friends came back and said, 'My God! Those legs still go up over your head!' But if you hang around long enough, you learn to make it *look* like they're going up in the air. I said, 'Illusion. It's all illusion.'"

Index of Musicals

Year following the title indicates the date of the original New York production.

General Index

Watkins, Maurine, 136
Watson, Susan, 18, 21, 31, 112, 113,
  129, 162, 178, 190, 206, 214
Watt, Douglas, 91, 109, 138, 167
Watts, Richard, Jr., 72, 87, 103, 159,
  165, 175
Waxman, A. P., 107
Wayne, David, 29, 94–96
Webber, Andrew Lloyd, 206, 209–11,
  213, 215
Weede, Robert, 96, 204, 210
Weeks, Allan, 3–5, 137, 191, 197
Weidman, Jerome, 149
Weill, Kurt, 18, 37, 79, 161
Weinstock, Jack, 61, 161
Weiss, George, 81
Weissler, Fran, 204
White, Jane, 203
White, Jerry, 186
White, Miles, 102
White, Onna, 61
Williams, Ann, 204
Williams, Emlyn, 32
Williams, Ralph, 57, 108, 110
Williams, Tennessee, 49, 53, 58
Williamson, Nicol, 80
Willis, John, 198
Willison, Walter, 118, 171, 172, 197,
  201, 215

Willson, Meredith, 7, 177, 184
Wilson, Dolores, 12, 19, 23, 45, 94–96,
  98
Wilson, Edwin, 109
Wilson, John, 20, 183, 189
Wilson, Julie, 71, 72, 183, 200, 201
Wilson, Mary Louise, 62, 64, 141, 143,
  145, 160, 161
Wilson, Patricia, 202
Wilson, Robin, 5
Winters, Shelley, 15, 36
Wisdom, Norman, 69
Wizard of Oz, The, 173
Wolfe, Thomas, 52, 94
Wolfington, Iggie, 2, 179, 180
Woodward, Edward, 129, 156
Wright, Martha, 3
Wright, Robert, 102, 111, 118, 148
Wulp, John, 114, 115
Wyler, Gretchen, 16, 17, 41, 143, 144,
  148, 173, 174, 181, 200, 216
Wyman, Jane, 95

Yamaguchi, Shirley, 64
Yearling, The, (novel), 94, 95

Ziegfeld, Florenz, 164